The Impact of the Professional Engineering Union

The IMPACT of the PROFESSIONAL ENGINEERING UNION

A Study of Collective Bargaining Among Engineers and Scientists and Its Significance for Management

RICHARD E. WALTON

Associate Professor of Industrial Management,
Purdue University
Formerly Research Assistant in Business Administration,
Harvard University

DIVISION OF RESEARCH
GRADUATE SCHOOL OF BUSINESS ADMINISTRATION
HARVARD UNIVERSITY · BOSTON · 1961

Library of Congress Catalog Card No. 61–9132

Published by Division of Research,
Graduate School of Business Administration,
Harvard University, Boston, Massachusetts

PRINTED AT
THE RIVERSIDE PRESS
CAMBRIDGE, MASSACHUSETTS, U.S.A.

Foreword

THE RAPID development of technological change in American industry has led to the prediction that the decade ending in 1965 will see a rate of growth among professional and technical workers which will be two and one-half times that of the entire labor force. It is generally agreed that one of the principal goals of the labor movement is to offset the decline among organized blue-collar workers by enrolling the growing complement of professional engineers and scientists into the ranks of organized labor. The prospects of such organization for collective bargaining purposes cannot now be appraised with accuracy. They depend largely upon the wisdom of management in dealing with the personnel problems of these professionals. This will determine their felt need for collective action. The prospects will also depend upon the capacity of unions to adapt their organizing techniques to and develop an understanding of the special, distinct concerns of these men.

Literature in the field to the present time has been devoted to an inquiry into the reasons for unionization among professional engineers. The issue of professionalism versus unionism has been given special attention. Little or no study has been given to the actual experience with collective bargaining between employers and unions representing professional engineers. Professor Walton's work is the first thorough and penetrating analysis of the impact of collective bargaining with professional engineering unions upon management.

It is an especially valuable addition to the literature for two reasons. First, it will assist managements in understanding the significance of collective bargaining for professional engineers in such matters as compensation, personnel administration, and the structure of the engineering and research departments. It provides necessary insight into the distinctions which must be made between the orthodox collective bargaining approaches toward production unions and those approaches required for professional personnel. Second, it serves notice to unions that the traditional collective bargaining goals and procedures cannot be applied effectively to the needs and interests of this unique employee group.

A careful reading of Professor Walton's study is likely to minimize unnecessary mistakes in the conduct of collective bargaining with this type of employee in the future. Eleven of the thirteen industrial companies whose professional engineers have certified bargaining units were included in this study. This book provides a rare opportunity for companies and unions, who may be on the threshold of a bargaining relationship, to benefit from the experiences of those who pioneered in this field and who did not have the wisdom of hindsight derived from Professor Walton's research.

The present study began as a thesis submitted by Professor Walton in partial fulfillment of the requirements for the degree of Doctor of Business Administration, which he was awarded in June 1959. Because of the significance of the subject and its recognized value to American management, the Division of Research of the Harvard Business School provided funds for the additional research and revision required for the publication of this manuscript. These funds came in part from the B. F. Goodrich Company Endowment for Research in memory of David M. Goodrich, and in part from the funds contributed by The Associates of the Harvard Business School.

JAMES J. HEALY
Professor of Industrial Relations
E. ROBERT LIVERNASH
Professor of Business Administration

Soldiers Field
Boston, Massachusetts
April 1961

Acknowledgments

A STUDY of this kind is usually a product of human and financial resources, only part of which are furnished by the author. Indeed even what the author himself brings to the study in question is very much a consequence of the intellectual forces which have acted upon him in the past. This study is no exception.

I feel particularly moved to express my gratitude to those persons who have provided for me the stimulus to scholarly pursuit. The early encouragement along these lines of Professors W. V. Owen and M. B. Ogle of Purdue University was a sustaining force even after I left Purdue to pursue further graduate work at Harvard University. Professors Benjamin M. Selekman and Stephen H. Fuller are responsible for the development of my interest at the Harvard Business School in the areas of labor and human relations. In particular, Professor Selekman's tremendous enthusiasm for investigating the problems of power, on the one hand, and systems of justice, on the other, was contagious; his remarkable insight into these problems was a constantly rising standard toward which to strive.

Many persons have contributed to the research and writing stages of this study. The companies and unions participating in the field research made an absolutely essential contribution. Representatives of these organizations gave significantly of their time, frequently in the face of pressing duties, but equally as often during evenings and weekends. Unfortunately neither the organizations nor the representatives can be acknowledged here by name because of the requirements of anonymity imposed on the total study.

I am grateful to several members of the Harvard faculty

who read the manuscript in its various stages. Professors Thomas Kennedy, Richard S. Meriam, and John T. Dunlop read and commented helpfully upon an earlier draft of the study as members of a doctoral thesis examining committee.

Professor E. Robert Livernash went over the manuscript very closely and made important suggestions for improving its organization and presentation. He was especially helpful in pointing out ideas which deserved further elaboration. Professor James J. Healy provided advice and encouragement at every stage of the study from its inception to its completion. Professor Healy was instrumental in obtaining the cooperation of the participating organizations, as well as in guiding my work throughout the research and manuscript phases of the study. His strong interest in the study and personal concern for the author's progress was itself as rewarding as any other aspect of the project.

I also wish to express my appreciation to the Division of Research, Harvard Graduate School of Business Administration, for making available the financial resources required by the study; and to Ruth Norton for her expert guidance of the manuscript into book form.

Finally, my deepest thanks go to my wife Sharon for crucial encouragement and assistance.

Nevertheless, I am solely responsible for the research findings and the conclusions which follow from them.

RICHARD E. WALTON

Lafayette, Indiana
April 1961

Contents

PART I. STATEMENT OF THE PROBLEM

PART II. IMPACT ON COMPENSATION

PART I

Statement of the Problem

CHAPTER I

Introduction

Background

Much of the organization of professional engineering unions occurred during World War II and in the immediate postwar years when the engineers in many companies took that action manifestly as a defense against inclusion in production and maintenance unions. The Taft-Hartley Act removed the necessity of such preventive measures in 1947, but the organized engineers continued to support unionization throughout the next decade, and a few additional units were organized in the years after the Act was passed. Accordingly, it would be a mistake to attribute the existence of these unions today to any single aspect of the historical circumstances under which they were born. In fact, probably conditions resulting from the growth and rationalization of the engineering function which have occurred in industrial enterprises over the past few decades are basically responsible for the appearance and continuance of collective bargaining among engineers. If so, one can well anticipate growth of engineering unionization in the future, halted or set back only during periods of general reaction to unionism such as that of the late 1950's.

The expansion of engineering and research activity is reflected in the employment figures for engineers and scientists. The U.S. Bureau of the Census, National Manpower Council, has reported that during the period from 1930 to 1956 the number of engineers and scientists in the United States nearly quadrupled, growing from 261,000 to 950,000. The number of engineers increased from 215,000 to about 700,000, and the number of scientists grew from 46,000 to approximately 250,000. An even more dramatic picture of this growth is presented if one considers that over the same period the labor force as a whole increased less than 50%, from 48.6 million in 1930 to 68.8 million in 1956. Thus, in 26 years the ratio of workers in the labor force per engineer and scientist had been reduced from 186 to 1, to 73 to 1.[1]

These trends in employment are expected to continue. Ewan Clague, Commissioner of Labor Statistics, has estimated that professional and technical workers will increase by 43% in the 1955–1965 decade—a rate of growth about two and one-half times that of the entire labor force.[2] The increase is the greatest projected by the Bureau of Labor Statistics for any group. The upward trend is also cited by a Princeton study, which attempts to identify the underlying reasons for this growth.[3]

The size and the growth of the engineering and technical segment of the work force give the student of industrial relations sufficient reason for studying the experiences of collective bargaining among these employees. Even greater significance may be attached to a study of the engineering group when one considers it as part of the white collar area (professional and technical workers, managers, officials and proprietors, clerical and sales workers) since that area now exceeds in number the blue collar area (craftsmen, operatives, and laborers).[4]

1 National Science Foundation, "Trends in the Employment and Training of Scientists and Engineers," Washington, May 1956, p. 5.

2 This estimate may well understate the increase for engineers and scientists because it applies to professionals in many fields including medicine and law, which in recent years have grown at a slower rate than engineers. See Ewan Clague, "The Shifting Industrial and Occupational Composition of the Work Force During the Next Ten Years," an address to AFL–CIO Conference on Changing Character of American Industry, Washington, January 16, 1958, p. 15.

3 Samuel E. Hill and Frederick Harbison, *Manpower and Innovation in American Industry*. Princeton: Industrial Relations Section, Princeton University, 1959.

4 Ewan Clague, op. cit., p. 14.

The reader may question whether we can learn much about collective bargaining among white collar workers generally through a study of engineering unionism inasmuch as the professional group is still only a fraction of the white collar area and possesses certain characteristics that differ from those of other white collar groups. Admittedly if one conceives of the groups of white collar employees as arranged on a spectrum according to a composite index of significant characteristics, such as the amount of formal education, the degree of responsibility and authority on the job, the opportunities for advancement into management, the size of salaries, and middle class background, one must place the professional employees on one end of the spectrum. This fact should make the study of greater, not lesser, significance, however. This conclusion is based on the premise that the end of the spectrum of white collar workers opposite the professional employees will merge into the blue collar groups. Thus, we can expect the experiences of other white collar unions to fall between those of the production and maintenance unions, with which we are already familiar, and those of the engineering unions, which we are presenting in this study. If engineering unionism is shown to be a form of unionism quite different from that of the industrial and trade unions, other white collar unions will probably be found to differ in that direction, albeit to a lesser degree.[5]

Certain developments in recent years have further indicated that a look at the experiences of collective bargaining among professional engineers during the past decade could be fruitful at this time. In 1957 and 1958, after seven years of scarcity of engineering and scientific talent, force reductions occurred in many of the unionized engineering departments, resulting in the largest, and in many cases the first, layoff of professionals under collective bargaining. Also in 1957 the

5 A review of the provisions of production agreements, office agreements, and engineering agreements tends to confirm the validity of the production–other white collar–professional spectrum.

most important instance of decertification in the history of the movement occurred shortly after the particular unit involved had voted to affiliate with the United Automobile Workers, AFL–CIO. Then the national federation of engineering unions, the Engineers and Scientists of America (ESA), dramatically split in two parts. The year 1958 contained yet another first: a purely professional unit resorted to strike action; equally noteworthy, it met with relative success! Finally, the years 1958 and 1959 were marked by repeated announcements by several industrial unions of the AFL–CIO about their intentions to increase their organizational efforts among engineering and scientific personnel.

Methods and Focus of the Study

In the production area, trade unions have proved themselves to be a force to be contended with, and have brought about certain changes in industrial management.[6] Does the unionization of professional scientific and engineering employees, whose training and work assignments differ markedly from those of the production workers, have the same kind of significance for industry as that of the unionization of production workers?

A review of the literature convinced the author that this question had not yet been adequately answered. Whenever the phenomenon of professional unionism has been dis-

[6] Several well-known studies have documented the effects of the trade union. See:

1. Neil W. Chamberlain, *The Union Challenge to Management Control.* New York: Harper and Brothers, 1948, 338 pp.
2. Sumner H. Slichter, *Union Policies and Industrial Management.* Washington: The Brookings Institute, 1941, 597 pp.
3. William Haber and Harold Levinson, *Labor Relations and Productivity in the Building Trades.* Ann Arbor: Bureau of Industrial Relations, University of Michigan 1956, 266 pp.
4. Sumner Slichter, James J. Healy, and E. Robert Livernash, *The Impact of Collective Bargaining on Management.* Washington: The Brookings Institute, 1960, 982 pp. The Brookings study, which was in its final stages when the current study was undertaken, actually served as an inspiration for the undertaking of this more pointed study into engineering union policies and engineering management.

cussed by the interested parties—businessmen, professional engineering societies, and unions—and by scholars, they have generally focused on one of the following aspects of unionization: (a) the reasons for unionization and the ways available to companies to avoid unionization, (b) the conflict between professionalism and unionism, (c) the need for unionization and the potential benefits to be obtained through unionism.

The available literature on the subject, especially that appearing in management publications, often led to the conclusion that professional engineering unions are essentially similar in nature to production unions, and tend to have impacts upon management policies and practices that are similar to those of production unions. Representatives of six nonunion companies who had had no direct experience with engineering unionism took this view in interviews conducted during a preliminary phase of the study. Specifically they expressed beliefs about what would happen if their engineers were organized, as follows:[7]

1. Salary adjustment. Pin-point rates with advancement based on seniority would be substituted for rate ranges with increases based on merit.
2. Engineering force. The union would "sanction minimum performance" preventing management from recognizing greater ability, thereby "breeding mediocrity" and increasing the quit rate of good men.
3. Professional competence. The union would "limit a full professional viewpoint," "control thinking and creativity as shop unions control productive effort."
4. Prerogatives. Under collective bargaining management would lose important rights such as those governing promotion, transfer, and work assignment.
5. Management recruiting. Unionization would cut off the engineering force as a source of future managers.

[7] These particular beliefs are also generally shared by unorganized professionals themselves. See, for example, John W. Riegel, *Collective Bargaining as Viewed by Unorganized Engineers and Scientists,* Report No. 10, Ann Arbor: Bureau of Industrial Relations, University of Michigan, 1959, 105 pp.

6. Allegiance. The union would divide engineers' loyalty.
7. Confidential status. After unionization management could no longer use the engineer in situations where he had access to vital company secrets.
8. Morale. The union would damage morale of engineers.

Thus, in effect, these engineering managers of nonunionized firms indicated that collective bargaining among engineers would have more dire consequences than shop unionism for management. Any attempt to compare or contrast the findings of the total study to these predictions systematically must be partially discounted inasmuch as the preliminary interviews cited above had two limitations: First, they were not exhaustive of the ideas of the interviewees; second, they were not intended to sample adequately the universe of nonunionized engineering employers. Nonetheless they were in agreement with most of the literature on the subject and accordingly constituted one referent for the study.

A pilot study at one unionized company indicated that contrary to the beliefs referred to above, there were important differences between the professional union and the production union.[8] Clearly, the subject of the impact of professional unionism required separate attention.[9]

[8] Of course it is a mistake to refer to the "production union" in this general way. The substantive rules, policies, and practices of industrial relations differ greatly among various industries, especially between dissimilar industries, such as automobile manufacturing and railroads. Accordingly, hereafter when contrasts or comparisons are made between collective bargaining involving engineering unions on the one hand and production or shop unions on the other, it is to be assumed that the production unions in mind are those in the same or similar American manufacturing industries.

[9] An appeal for research of the "impact" type was made by John R. Coleman of Carnegie Institute of Technology in a paper, "Research on Union Challenge and Management Response," *Proceedings of the Ninth Annual Meeting* (December 28 and 29, 1956), Industrial Relations Research Association, p. 306. He states: "Neither those inside nor those outside of industry have devoted close attention to this subject. [He noted as exceptions some of the authors cited in footnote 6 above.] As a consequence, we may in certain sectors of the economy be witnessing collective arrangements negotiated between labor and management which are designed to meet specific problems but which do so at costs above what a careful examination of alternatives might prove necessary."

Objectives of the Study

The preliminary interviews and the pilot study cited above were completed during the early months of 1958. The field research upon which this study is based was conducted during the latter half of 1958 and the first few months of 1959.

Three basic questions posed for research were:

1. What are managements' policies and practices in companies that have professional engineers' unions, and how have these policies and practices changed over the period of unionization? The policies and practices we have in mind are those pertaining to engineering personnel and covering salary administration, merit review, other incentives, employee recruitment and selection, training, promotion, transfer, work assignments, discipline, discharge, etc. We are also interested in certain organizational relationships within the company, such as those between the engineer and his supervisor, and between the engineering department and the personnel department.
2. What are the collective bargaining objectives of engineers' unions and what forms do the unions' actions take?
3. The third question relates the answers to questions 1 and 2. Which changes in managements' policies and practices actually result from the unions' presence and their actions?

Several purposes which underlay the study correspond to the above three questions. One reason for undertaking the study was to obtain a systematic description of the environment in which professional engineering unions develop and operate. This would be achieved by collecting and analyzing historical and current information about management's policies and practices. A second purpose was to gain insight into the framework of pressures within which management administers the engineering function in a unionized company—hence, our direct attention to the unions' objectives and actions. The third purpose of this study is already apparent to the reader: to draw certain conclusions regarding the impact of the objectives and actions of the professional unions on the policies and practices of management. This judgment would involve re-analysis of the information gathered for descriptive purposes. Finally, the findings would undoubtedly contain implications for managements and other parties to the relationships studied.

Methods of Analysis

It is one thing to analyze data in an effort to describe changes in policies and practices; it is another to determine causes for these changes. Similarly, it is one problem to describe union action; it is another to estimate the effects of this action. Sometimes it has been possible to "see" a probable cause and effect relationship. This became possible, for example, through a detailed description of negotiations because it is a relatively explicit, reasonably well-documented decision-making process. This point can be illustrated by outlining what a close look at negotiation records revealed in one instance.

> The company proposed a *flat across-the-board increase* of "X" dollars per month. During negotiations the company persistently argued the merits of a flat increase, despite the protestations of the union which was known to favor salary increases on a percentage basis. Finally, after prolonged negotiations the company acceded to a *percentage increase* involving a cost to the company comparable to that of its original offer.

The union's influence in this case was evident. Of course one must often make certain allowances for positions that the parties take early in negotiations for strategic purposes only.

In other situations it was impossible to establish a cause and effect relationship. For example, research in one company revealed that an unusually large number of former officers of the union were subsequently promoted to supervisor. Many explanations were offered: "It's simple—the engineers and management both seek the same qualities in their leaders." "The union office is one way to become known to higher levels of management." "It's purely a coincidence since management does not favor or disfavor a man for his union activity." There was a wide range of explanations, but no evidence available to corroborate any of them.

Most situations studied fell between these two extremes. Certain questions were applied in an attempt to determine whether a change of policies and practices described in the study actually resulted from union activity:

1. What was the sequence and proximity of the entrance or activity of the union and the given change?
2. Was the change both advocated by the union and opposed by the company before it occurred?
3. Did the union claim that its actions brought about the change?
4. Did management statements directly or indirectly attribute the change to the union?
5. Did the employees attribute the change to the presence or efforts of the union?
6. Was the change common to all unionized companies?
7. Had the change not taken place in nonunionized companies familiar to the author or had it taken place later?
8. Had similar changes already occurred with respect to other employees of the same company?
9. Were there alternate explanations for the change, such as special supply and demand conditions, changes in management personnel, historical accident, etc.?

Before we probe each of the many topics of this study asking "What has been the effect or influence of the union?", it is well that we familiarize ourselves with the basic position taken by a majority of the companies with regard to this line of inquiry.

One company that had a very active union and had been struck by this union insisted that the union did *not* influence the company's terms of employment. It was to be clearly understood that improvements camc only when they were introduced by management on its own, occasionally between contracts; gains were never a product of bargaining. According to the personnel manager, "Progress and change have always been posed as being effects that stem from good business operation." Moreover it was not true that management took the initiative merely to wrest it from the union. Management was never driven to do what it would not otherwise have done, especially since the engineers' union was without significant power.

The view taken by this management representative was extreme, but with two or three exceptions the others tended in that direction. A majority of the management representatives made the general statement that the union had not improved the terms of employment for their engineers, or otherwise affected engineering operations. Yet, comments made in subsequent discussions with the same individuals about specific instances not infrequently led to the conclusion that the union *had* been instrumental in bringing about certain changes in policies and practices.

The companies' official position on this question of impact is understandable. They do not want their respective unions to gain the reputation for being effective agents. Likewise, it soon became apparent that the unions' claims occasionally were also the product of wishful thinking, and for equally obvious reasons. For purposes of this study it was necessary to weight much heavier the statements by one party that are corroborated by the statements of the other, or by facts available to the author.

Scope of the Study

This study deals with large engineering and research departments in industrial companies where the engineers and scientists have organized certified bargaining units that remain predominantly professional[10] (hereafter "engineers" may

[10] Slightly less than one-half of the units studied are exclusively professional. The others include nonprofessional technicians in small percentages.

be taken to refer to both engineers and scientists), applying the definition of professional employee included in the Labor Management Relations Act of 1947:

Section 2(12)—Definition of Professional Employee.

The term 'professional employee' means—

"(a) any employee engaged in work (i) predominantly intellectual and varied in character as opposed to routine mental, mechanical, or physical work; (ii) involving the consistent exercise of discretion and judgment in its performance; (iii) of such a character that the output produced or the result accomplished cannot be standardized in relation to a given period of time; (iv) requiring knowledge of an advanced type in a field of science or learning customarily acquired by a prolonged course of specialized intellectual instruction and study in an institution of higher learning or a hospital, as distinguished from a general academic education or from an apprenticeship or from training in the performance of routine mental, manual, or physical processes; or

"(b) any employee, who (i) has completed the courses of specialized intellectual instruction and study described in clause (iv) of paragraph (a), and (ii) is performing related work under the supervision of a professional person to qualify himself to become a professional employee as defined in paragraph (a)."

At the time of the study, about thirteen companies employing over 35,000 unionized professional engineers fell within this universe. Four were aircraft companies, three were scientific instrument firms, two were petroleum companies, and the other four were electronic and electrical equipment companies.[11] The great majority of these engineers and scientists

[11] The aircraft, the electrical equipment, and the petroleum industries happen to be among the dominant employers of engineers and scientists in the United States. According to the National Science Foundation ("Scientists and Engineers in American Industry—January, 1957," *Scientific Manpower Bulletin*, No. 10, Washington: December 1958, p. 2), in January 1957 these three industries employed respectively 84,900, 92,900, and 50,700. Two other dominant employing industries which have not been affected by unionization are machinery (74,100) and chemicals and allied products (72,200).

were engaged in research and development activities.[12] Excluded from the scope of this study were another 6,000 unionized professional engineers employed in eight nonindustrial organizations including utilities and public works departments;[13] and several thousand professional engineers who were scattered among over a hundred industrial companies and represented by unions in which other types of employees predominate.

The large engineering and research departments containing over 500 professional engineers were selected for study because this is increasingly the pattern of employment of engineers.[14] Since the professional engineers outnumbered any other employees in these units, the researcher could be reasonably certain that he was observing collective bargaining patterned by engineers. This would not have been true had the study dealt with engineers included in relatively small numbers in production and maintenance and other nonprofessional bargaining units.

Eleven of the thirteen companies constituting the universe of the study were actually researched. Field trips to seven of these companies involved visits with both management and union officials. Field research was conducted in three additional companies with the representatives of one party only; in two companies these were management personnel, and in one they were union officials. The eleventh company was researched in the field in only a minor way.

12 According to National Science Foundation, op. cit., p. 1, less than one-third of the engineers and scientists in the United States were then engaged in research and development. Thus research and development activities have been more affected by unionization than other engineering activities.

13 A complete listing of engineering unions as compiled and published by the National Society for Professional Engineers is included in Appendix A.

14 See *Scientific Research and Development in American Industry—A Study in Manpower and Costs,* Washington: Department of Labor Bulletin No. 1148, 1953, p. 106. The 1953 study reports (page 7) that of the companies surveyed those with professional research staffs of 500 or more employed approximately 48% of all research engineers and scientists in the survey. Because of the growth in research and development departments generally since 1953, the proportion of employed professionals on staffs of 500 or more has increased substantially.

The field research consisted of interviews with the participants—various levels of management, union leaders, and engineers—drawing upon their memories for facts and soliciting their opinions. The early interviews in each company were unstructured and exploratory. Later specific questions were asked in areas previously undiscussed, using a mental check list of management, supervisory and personnel functions, and relationships. Additional data were obtained from published materials—speeches, union and management publications, and collective bargaining agreements—and from unpublished materials of the companies and unions including written statements of policy, organization charts, minutes and transcripts of negotiations and grievance meetings, personnel records, reports, and memoranda.

Limitations of the Findings

The scope of the study, in terms of the number of companies studied—eleven out of a universe of thirteen companies—must be regarded as adequate for generalized answers to the questions posed for the study, despite the qualification that, as it happened, not every aspect of the union's influence was explored in every company studied. It must be acknowledged here that further research of the experiences of comparable companies that have nonunionized engineering departments would have provided the basis for firmer conclusions with respect to impact. Unfortunately such a comparative study would have required a sample of case studies in excess of those possible within the time and financial resources available for the study.

Plan of the Book

Chapter II presents a historical perspective to collective bargaining among professional engineering unions in which special attention is paid to the causes of unionization, the various patterns of union-management relationships existing in the companies studied, and the characteristics of professional unionism.

The core of this study—Parts II, III, and IV—begins with Chapter III and consists of a separate look at each of about a dozen areas of management policies and practices. Occasionally companies have been designated as "Company A," "Company B," and so on. These designations apply only within discussion of the same subject, not throughout the entire study; that is, "Company A" will not necessarily refer to the same actual company in Chapter IV as it does in Chapter IX. The requirements of disguise have imposed certain other limitations affecting the manner in which the material is presented: in a few places the text is deliberately vague about precisely who or which party furnished the information used; often in such instances the information was actually corroborated by observations made by representatives of both parties. Also in the interest of disguise the engineering organizations have been referred to in certain instances as "unions" where their own preference is to be called "associations." Numbers and names have been changed in a few instances to prevent identification of participating organizations.

Whereas in most of the study an effort has been made to indicate approximately the degree of prevalency of a given practice and the amount of generalization that can be made about associated effects, in the summaries and conclusion this effort has not always been continued except to the extent that we have labeled, on the one hand, those findings that seemed to be universally applicable, and, on the other hand, those that seemed to be based on isolated occurrences. Other practices and effects may be assumed to have been found in a "significant number of cases." Above all, it should be borne firmly in mind that all of these findings do not apply to every company; rather, that some findings apply to some companies, some apply to other companies. This would have been eminently clearer if the data were presented in case form, or if a company's experiences in one policy area were related to its experiences in another area, thereby identifying the various configurations of company experiences; however, the requirements of disguise precluded either alternative.

Some readers will complain that illustrative material is not abundant enough; others may find the amount and detail of illustrative material excessive. The author has tried to err on the side of greater rather than lesser illustrative detail, without in any instance using redundant material, primarily because this is the first time the descriptive and illustrative material of this kind on the collective bargaining of professional engineers has been published—recall that two of the three purposes of the study were largely descriptive. Thus the author has attempted to meet the need underlined by John R. Coleman:

> The nature of the union's challenge is seldom examined in any detail. In most instances, union contractual demands are taken at face value without probing into their underlying roots. . . . On the employer's side, the picture is all too sketchy when it comes to setting out with clarity managerial perceptions of the union as a challenger and of alternative impacts likely to flow from union policies. As a result, we do not get from these studies enough feeling for either why or how a company moves in a given direction in its union relationships.[15]

The concluding chapters, contained in Part V, are used primarily to treat the significance of the changes resulting from unionization, and suggest further the implications of the findings.

[15] John R. Coleman, "Research on Union Challenge and Management Response," p. 307.

CHAPTER II

A Historical Perspective

Impetus and Causes for Unionization

The image of the engineer as an independent entrepreneur providing professional services to a client in return for a fee is outmoded. Only a few consultant-type engineers practice the profession today in a way that fits this image. A substantial majority—about two-thirds—of the approximately one million practicing engineers and scientists in 1957 were employed by industry.[1] Even recognizing this, one may be inclined to think of the employed engineer as a privileged, semi-independent, quasi-manager—a status obtained by the first engineers who entered industry and still held by a few engineers employed by industry today. For the majority of the engineers in industry, however, conditions have changed drastically over the last few decades.

Engineering activity mushroomed during the emergency of the Second World War. New engineering organizations cropped up. Employment in established engineering departments grew from dozens to hundreds, and from hundreds to thousands, providing new opportunities for rationalization of the engineering function. The work could be broken down and assigned in new ways. The urgency of engineering projects undertaken during this period was an additional impetus for management to subdivide the tasks. Management and supervision of the enlarged undertakings had to be rationalized also. Companies adopted formal control tech-

1 National Science Foundation "Scientists and Engineers in American Industry—January 1957," *Scientific Manpower Bulletin No. 10,* Washington: December 1958, p. 1.

niques, many of which had been developed in the shop and were not believed by engineers to be appropriate for engineers. Probably the most "notorious" of the techniques borrowed from the shop was the time clock; it was despised by professional engineers.

As the engineering organization grew, the engineer lost some of the privileges he had enjoyed. As the work was fragmented, the engineer began to doubt that his broader engineering training and abilities were being properly utilized. Other conditions were changing. The wage differential between the engineers and the shop employees was being narrowed, perhaps partly as a result of unionization in the shop.[2] Moreover, the engineers shared the general uncertainty of workers about employment in the postwar years.

All these factors created unrest among engineers, making them more amenable to organization. Still in most cases conditions were not sufficiently unfavorable to cause engineers to seek out organization on their own. Rather, it was an interest in them manifested by the industrial trade unions that prompted engineers to decide in favor of organization, but organization on their own, and for defensive purposes. The engineers recognized that organization by professionals provided them with the best protection from being submerged by the shop union inasmuch as the National Labor Relations Board under the Wagner Act had demonstrated a willingness to sometimes place professionals against their wishes in bargaining units composed predominately of nonprofessional employees.[3] Thus, the majority of the unions

2 For more detailed discussion of salary differentials and other conditions existing during the early period of unionization, see the historical sections of the following publications: National Society of Professional Engineers, *A Professional Look at the Engineer in Industry,* Washington, 1955; Herbert Northrup, *Unionization of Professional Engineers and Chemists.* New York: Industrial Relations Counsellors, 1946; M. E. McIver, H. A. Wagner, and M. P. McGirr, *Technologists' Stake in the Wagner Act.* Chicago: American Association of Engineers, 1944.

3 National Society of Professional Engineers, *A Professional Look at the Engineer in Industry,* pp. 3–7.

within the scope of this study cropped up between 1945 and 1947 under the encouragement of some of the professional societies which had become alarmed that the unions might make serious inroads into the engineering profession.[4] Surprisingly little relation existed between the organization of engineers in one company and that of another; sometimes one group was not even aware of the existence of the other.

The great majority of engineering unions not only remained separate from the industrial unions which represented shop employees but they also stayed independent of the over-all labor movement in the United States, as represented by the AFL and CIO organizations. The last section in this chapter will briefly set forth the relationship that existed between the engineering unions and the AFL-CIO in 1959.

The explanation of the impetus to the formation of engineering unions as defensive in nature does not apply so fully to a minority of the organizations. A couple were organized before the war or during its early years and grew out of company unions or employee representation plans. Two major engineering unions were not organized until much later, one in the late 1940's and the other in 1951, after the Taft-Hartley Act of 1947 effectively eliminated the possibility of engulfment in industrial unions.[5]

[4] See *Manual on Collective Bargaining for Professional Employees* published in 1947 by National Society of Professional Engineers, Washington. There were six cooperating engineering societies: American Society of Civil Engineers, American Institute of Mining and Metallurgical Engineers, American Society of Mechanical Engineers, American Institute of Electrical Engineers, American Institute of Chemical Engineers, National Society of Professional Engineers.

Also see M. E. McIver, H. A. Wagner, and M. P. McGirr, *Technologists' Stake in the Wagner Act,* Appendix A, which details the experience of the ASCE in the promotion of professional engineering unions for defensive purposes.

[5] Section 9b of the Labor Management Relations Act, 1947, as amended provides: ". . . the Board shall not . . . decide that any unit is appropriate for such purposes if such unit includes both professional employees and employees who are not professional employees unless a majority of such professional employees vote for inclusion in such unit. . . ."

The above account of the timing of the organization of the units studied raises the question of the rate of growth of the engineering union movement. None of the basic units studied was organized after 1951, and there have been very few new bargaining units of the smaller variety not included in this study. The growth in the absolute numbers of engineers represented by professional unions over the last decade is attributable almost wholly to the growth in the size of the units that were certified during the 1940's. There are no reliable comparative statistics available to indicate whether the absolute increases represent a growth or decline in the proportion of eligible engineers who are organized. On this question, however, the phenomenal expansion of the unionized electronic and aircraft firms is probably more than offset by the tremendous growth in the numbers of large engineering and research organizations where unionization has not occurred.

The continuing causes of dissatisfaction among engineers, which were generally believed to underlie their interest in collective bargaining, received wide attention during the 1950's. The following list, which resulted from a two-year study sponsored by the Engineers Joint Council,[6] is typical:

PROFESSIONAL STATUS AND EMPLOYMENT CONDITIONS

Professional treatment

1. A feeling among engineers that they were not identified with management.
2. Inadequate channels of communication between top management and nonsupervisory engineers.
3. Inadequate recognition of the engineer as a professional employee.
4. Assignment of engineers to subprofessional work.
5. Undue retention of engineers in specialized and narrowly compartmentalized assignments.
6. Lack of appropriate means for resolving individual problems.

[6] Engineers Joint Council, *Professional Standards and Employment Conditions,* Report 101, New York: May 1956, p. 1.

Personal treatment

1. Inadequate recognition and treatment of the engineer as an individual.
2. Lack of broad classifications and appropriate titles by which the engineer could measure his progress.
3. Inadequate or nonexistent plans for training and job rotation.
4. Inadequate understanding of promotional policies and belief that progress and promotions were not commensurate with ability and performance.
5. A feeling of insecurity of employment.
6. Management human relations knowledge and skills have not kept pace with the expanded utilization of engineers.

Financial treatment

1. Engineering salaries not commensurate with fundamental contribution.
2. Too small a differential between the pay of engineers and members of the skilled trades.
3. Salaries of experienced engineers not sufficiently increased, in comparison with present starting salaries.
4. Wide variation in salaries paid to engineers doing comparable work in different organizations.
5. Dissatisfaction with merit review systems and inadequate understanding of salary administration.

Composition of Bargaining Units

Despite the similarity of origin among the units born immediately after the war, they varied considerably in the way in which they were constituted. Some included technicians and draftsmen, to the point where these employees made up 30% of the unit. Many included only professionals, but varied in the type of engineer placed in the bargaining unit; in some units the semisupervisory engineer, commonly called Group Leader, was placed in the bargaining unit; in others, he was excluded. One group of engineers sought to encompass within the bargaining unit all engineers, supervisory and nonsupervisory alike, up to and including the level below the Chief Engineer. Naturally, the NLRB did not grant a unit of this scope. Over the years the composition of the unit has been raised as an issue in many companies with certain modifications resulting; basically, however, those units that were founded as purely professional are professional still, and those that were certified as heterogeneous continue as such.

One professional unit was induced by one company studied to take in the tool engineers, who were considered to be nonprofessionals by those already in the bargaining unit. By this single maneuver the company removed the tool engineers from the grasp of the production and maintenance union, enhanced the tool engineers' status, and at the same time rendered them impotent within the organization of professionals. The engineers' union, which had elected to assume a very professional posture, later regarded the tool engineering group as a liability to be sloughed at the first opportunity.

Another professional union with the same attitude toward the nonprofessional employees—in this instance, technicians, engineering aides, draftsmen, and so on—has placed the latter employees in a separate bargaining unit but continues to service their contract and provide leadership for their negotiations. The professional union would like to be rid of the technicians entirely because they are thought to be a handicap to recruiting professionals into the union.

Contrariwise, a few of the heterogeneous unions have tried to expand the scope of the unit to include other types of nonprofessional technical employees, only to be met with the opposition of the particular companies involved, primarily because in each case the engineering union had already demonstrated tendencies of militancy, and because there was no other organizational threat affecting these employees. For instance, one union sought on several occasions to represent one or more of several technical groups including Engineering Aides, Parts Catalogue Writers, Plant Layout

Draftsmen, Architectural Designers, and Process Layout Engineers; and it was successful with regard to certain classifications.

The composition of these units has proved important to collective bargaining in certain other ways. The mixed units, compared with the purely professional units, are more likely to present contract proposals and employ bargaining techniques that approach those of the traditional trade unions. The employers, for their part, seem to be strictly opportunistic about the question of scope of unit. Prior to a certification election an employer's preference seems to be governed by his judgment regarding which make-up of voters is most likely to defeat the union. When no question of general certification exists, however, the employer is more interested in achieving a unit that optimizes resistance to militant tendencies on the part of all the employees under consideration, including non-professionals.

Metamorphosis of Engineering Unionism

Early Relationships

Consistent with the purpose for which these engineering "associations," as they preferred to be called, were founded, were the parties' approaches to collective bargaining once a union was certified. The first concern of the associations seemed to be to convey the impression that the engineers by their unionization did not mean any harm to management. Individual leaders were cautious in carrying out their duties lest management misinterpret their actions and reflect unfavorably upon them as individuals. The companies that generally favored the separate organization of their engineers expected and encouraged the organization to be inactive. The above attitudes are reflected in the fact that it took the parties in many companies the best part of the first year to negotiate an agreement, meeting only occasionally when the management personnel representing the company could find time.

The agreements themselves included many secondary clauses from the shop agreement, some having almost no relevance to the engineering department. But shop clauses that would have seriously impaired engineering management, such as pin-point rates and seniority applied to layoff and promotion, were omitted (with few exceptions) since neither the professionals nor management believed they were appropriate. In these areas, and many others, management merely agreed to state in very broad terms the existing company policies.

Certain professional items, such as patent payments and professional society dues, were important to the engineering associations, and did engage the parties in considerable discussion during negotiations for the first contract. Salaries were a factor, too, because the engineers believed that they were overdue for larger increases than the companies had in mind. In the final analysis, the contracts were settled basically on the terms of the respective companies.

Despite their own admissions that the first negotiations were not completed successfully, the associations' leaders were neither discouraged nor shaken in their faith in the approach to collective bargaining that they had used during this period. Essentially the approach can be paraphrased, "We have certain needs, and these are reasonable needs; therefore, all we have to do is educate management regarding our problems; being comprised of reasonable men management will set about to solve the problems."

Disillusionment

When subsequent annual negotiations resulted in only minor changes in the agreement, or none at all, disillusionment spread among many of the association leaders. Some dropped out and were replaced by others who had confidence in the same approach characterized above, but who thought they could do a better job. The engineers themselves continued to adhere to this approach and blamed the leaders for not going about implementing it correctly. Some new leaders who appeared on the scene during this period and a few who stayed on from the previous period, however, adopted a tougher line.

In any event, the unions continued to function despite the fact that the primary impetus to organization had been largely removed by the Taft-Hartley Act. It can be assumed that individual leaders struggled to preserve the institution partly because of their own vested interest, but it is also apparent that the rank and file engineers themselves thought that the organization served some useful purpose, or promised to do so in the future. Conclusive evidence on the latter point was presented by the experience in one company in 1949. This company played a leading role in forcing a decertification election because less than one-third of the unit belonged to the association. The engineers, who failed to support the union by joining, were not willing to have the organization and representation junked—they voted 83% to keep the union, with 86% voting in the election.

National Affiliation

Both approaches to collective bargaining utilized by the various associations—the "educate-management" approach and the "get-tough" policy—were handicapped somewhat by the isolation of each of the independent unions from the others. The education approach was in part dependent upon salary and job evaluation data and other comparative information on a national scope. Similarly the get-tough policy, particularly the threat of economic sanctions, could be more effective if the individual union could count on financial support and advice from a national organization.

There were several unsuccessful attempts to establish federations of engineering unions or other coordinating organizations, many of them on a regional basis.[7] In 1952 the representatives of 17 separate engineering unions, including many not within the scope of this study, met in Chicago and founded a national federation of engineering unions called Engineers and Scientists of America (ESA).

Being a federation, the ESA had no individual members, but only the groups themselves, called Member Units. The ESA handled matters of national scope, and did not concern itself with the internal operation of the Member Units or with the negotiation of their individual agreements, although it did stand ready to give such assistance at the local level as might be requested and as was practicable. The ESA Constitution and By-Laws listed the purposes of federation:

> It shall be the purpose of ESA to promote the economic, professional, and social welfare of engineering and scientific employees by:
>
> a. Gathering and disseminating to the Member Units, engineering students, and other interested parties, information concerning salaries and working conditions, living costs, bargaining procedures, legislation, and other pertinent information;
>
> b. Assisting in the establishment of collective bargaining units of professional employees, and assisting such units upon their request in bargaining negotiations with employers, and in proceedings under the National Labor Relations Laws;
>
> c. Rendering assistance in the organization of other similar homogeneous groups of professional employees;
>
> d. Acting as spokesman for all engineering and scientific employees before governmental bodies;
>
> e. Seeking improvement in the quality of engineering and scientific education and promoting, in educational institutions, a better understanding of industrial employment.

Tests of Strength

The mere fact of national affiliation did not prove to be

[7] For an account of these attempts see Council of Western Electric Technical Employees, *Council Compass,* Newark: January 1953.

of much assistance. To be sure, the member units were able to formulate and present their bargaining demands on the basis of more extensive information, and were therefore somewhat more persuasive in negotiations. But the leaders, who began increasingly to question the effectiveness of good arguments alone, looked around for means of backing up these demands.

A three-day strike occurred in one company in 1950. The engineers gave the strike action reasonably good support, but when the production and maintenance workers started crossing the picket line on the second or third day, the action was called off. Although this strike had not proved effective in improving the terms of the contract settlement, it had "broken the ice," so to speak, opening up for organized engineers the whole area of economic sanctions.

With increasing frequency the unions started entering negotiations with a strike authorization from the membership. Moreover, each of the three years, 1953, 1954, and 1955, saw major engineering union strike action. It should be noted that each of these strikes involved heterogeneous units. One strike in 1953 and one in 1955 resulted from one company's determination to change the terms of the contract to the disadvantage of the union. The union was largely successful in preserving its contract. Two other strikes, waged by unions for offensive purposes, ended without the unions obtaining any further concessions.

Most of the other unions that did not actually go on strike during this period nevertheless were either on the verge of striking or of invoking other economic sanctions. Let us listen to an association leader describe this period at his company, picking it up with the period of disillusionment:

> Negotiations were a frustrating affair. We would spend months deciding what we wanted and why, and yet when we met with the company it would be obvious that the company hadn't given the proposals any consideration. We would sit

down to a bargaining session, to have the company team ask, "Now, where were we last time?" Then they would simply say "no," often without trying to convince us of their position.

The interested members were looking around for a way to increase the organization's effectiveness when in the last part of 1951 a couple of engineers decided to build a representative system to distribute literature. They had a home brew outfit; fellows started dropping over there and talking, mostly the philosophy of the thing at first, but before long there was a sizable group of guys who had begun to talk action; they called themselves the "Hungry Hundred." Their spirit was infectious and considerable opinion developed in favor of rejecting the company's offer in 1951; many were disappointed when we didn't. Membership surged the following year, and engineers had high hopes for their proposals, especially a 30% salary increase that was required to achieve parity with what Engineers Joint Council statistics showed the situation required. Although the negotiation team didn't think they could get the 30%, they expected to break loose from the shop pattern for the first time in history. Negotiations were scarred by frequent blowups. The top people who were on the company's committee from engineering were replaced by their subordinates; then, rubbing salt in open wounds, the vice president of labor relations shunned the sessions.

Meanwhile our action committee had developed what they thought was an effective club; they would schedule a Manpower Availability Conference in this city inviting over a hundred companies to participate by recruiting our members, reasoning that if the company's statements that it was paying competing salaries were correct it had nothing to fear from the recruiting conference, but that if the company's salaries were not up to snuff, the conference would be devastating. Before the plan was implemented, the guy principally involved in arranging the conference was fired. That was it! Some wanted to walk out right then. Some were gutless and lost any spirit they had. I think the association could have carried off a strike but chose to go the legal route instead, with the result that the trend of events reversed direction.

The development of the Manpower Availability Conference was being watched closely by other bargaining units. One was preparing to spring a similar conference on its company until the plan was abandoned at the first company. Engineers in other companies, who could not bring themselves to strike, supported their demands by staging demonstrations or by boycotting overtime periods.

Some other ideas generated during that period have never been tried: refusal to submit engineering reports, refusal to do engineering work directly affecting production. Some officials thought that these ideas deserved attention. A few thought that they were unethical. Others discounted the ideas as unenforceable, alleging that the typical engineer cannot resist the temptation to improve his standing with his supervisor even at the expense of his fellow engineers. A further drawback to the refusal to do engineering work affecting production is that the burden would fall on a few individuals.

During the period when the unions were experimenting with sanctions, roughly 1950 to 1955, the range of other union activities was increasing, and the size of the bargaining unit and total union membership were expanding rapidly; these two factors combined to make it necessary and financially possible to provide for full-time union officials. These officials were generally recruited from the ranks of the professional engineers, although they were also selected from a great variety of backgrounds, including previous employment as a Fur and Leather Union business agent, a Teamster organizer, a lobbyist, a university economics instructor, and a labor relations director for management. The full-time officials, especially those brought in from the outside, tended to strengthen the organizations' ambitions to become effective bargaining agents.

Emerging Relationships

The results of the major engineering strikes definitely played an important part in structuring the relationships between the parties in the subsequent years. In one company where the union lost its strike, union membership dropped from 70% of the bargaining unit to less than 50% within a period of a few months. The union leader responsible for the strike "fiasco" soon resigned; and the union adopted a relatively soft sell approach for the next several years. Subsequently, however, it returned to a militant position. In the company where the engineers withstood management's challenge to their organization throughout two long strikes, relationships subsequently improved; management discontinued its threats to the engineers' union, and the union leadership responded in kind. In the other company where a major strike occurred, the action did not result in a winner or a loser, and deliberately so: the strike was called for a definite duration without any expectation that management would revise its offer. It was intended to be a strong demonstration of dissatisfaction against the company's "inflexible, intransigent attitude" toward the union. The result of the action was to reinforce the pre-existing tendencies of the parties. Their relationship had been tense; it became hostile, ending in decertification several years later.

The periods of crisis in other companies have altered union-management relationships. The association leader quoted in the preceding section continued his description of the post-crisis period:

> . . . events reversed direction.
>
> Many engineers had disapproved of the union's behavior; others were simply weary of the whole affair. The "stabilizers" grabbed the ball; they hired a hall for a rump meeting, and later elected a whole new slate of officers, and accepted the company's package.
>
> From then on we've had improved relationships with the

> company. The association had tested its own limits to action; and while the company hadn't been hit with a strike, they had suffered plenty in terms of engineering output during the 11 months when matters were at their worst. They're trying harder now.

The experience just cited was typical of relationships in three companies.

In one company the major crisis came as late as 1958 when the unit struck—the first of the wholly professional units to take that action. Thereafter, the relationship continued on a much more serious plane. A second strike occurred in 1960. Whereas in 1958 the professional union did not ask any of the other company employees to respect their token picket line, in 1960 they asked for and received such support from all other unions representing employees of the company.

Patterns of Relationships—A Recapitulation

The purpose of this chapter is not to develop the history of the engineering union movement, nor to record the sequence of events in all, or any, of the companies studied. It is merely to develop an appreciation that the character of the unions has been transformed over the years, accompanied by changing union-management relationship patterns. A way of identifying and expressing the complex changes in union-management relationships has been set forth by Professor B. M. Selekman and subsequently used by many other students of labor relations.[8]

Four of the types of institutional relationship patterns distinguished by Professor Selekman are of particular interest here: (1) conflict, (2) containment-aggression, (3) accommodation, (4) cooperation. The first two periods identified below do not fit neatly into any of these patterns, but the subsequent periods can be enlightened by utilizing these concepts.

[8] Benjamin M. Selekman, Sylvia K. Selekman, and Stephen H. Fuller, *Problems in Labor Relations,* New York: McGraw-Hill Book Company, Inc., Second Edition, 1958, pp. 1–11.

1945–1947. Out of fear and hostility toward production unions the engineers and the company had collaborated to conceive and establish the engineers' association in order to exclude other bargaining agents, which often countered with specific charges of company domination.

1947–1949. The incipient unions stressed those engineers' goals that appeared to be in complete harmony with company objectives; they perceived their job as one of education; their approach was one of problem solving. For managements' part, they paid little attention to the ineffectual behavior of the associations. Hence the pattern of relationship was one of mere one-way cooperation.

1949–1953. The engineers began to realize that the interests of the parties were not always identical; some interests were in harmony but others were in conflict. At this point the engineers became interested in exercising their franchise—to bargain collectively. They endeavored to expand the scope of bargaining beyond salaries and professional fringes. But managements could not accept collective bargaining with their professional engineers and all that it entailed. Besides, when managements analyzed the situation they discovered that a very decisive element in collective bargaining—power—was largely absent on the associations' side. Because of the manner in which engineering work is scheduled and performed, a temporary delay in engineering activity is seldom serious for a company. For that reason the unions could not strike with any effectiveness; for psychological reasons the professionals probably would not strike at all. It happened that among the engineers in any given company there was usually a group who were also aware of these factors. They set out to redress the imbalance of power by (a) reorienting the engineer psychologically, so that he could strike without seriously violating any self-concept; and (in some cases) (b) forming a bond with the production union which possessed power. Several unions succeeded in the former of the objectives (one union also succeeded in the latter), applying economic sanctions in an attempt to enlarge their scope of activity and influence.

Managements, for their part, sharpened up their own tactics. The written remarks of one union president on the subject are paraphrased and condensed here:

> There are many devices that the company uses to fight, the foremost of which is *secrecy*. Knowledge is power and we are kept ignorant of every aspect of company policy. It makes Association leaders appear inferior and subordinate, on the one hand, and our negotiators to fritter away their energies on peripheral issues, on the other hand.
>
> We are kept ignorant of fringe benefits, the gross cost of insurance programs, pension plans. We've made inquiries about sick time—how much we're actually getting under the Exempt employees' sick provisions which were paraded for years. And the merit review—it's a citadel. There's an absolute value placed on keeping us ignorant that's got nothing to do with the subject under discussion.
>
> Another device is to *undermine the union leadership*. There's the constant misrepresentation of union policies. Two classic examples were the stories peddled during negotiations. They brutally distorted our seniority demands and claimed we were trying to control the merit rating system. We were simply trying to find out what goes on.
>
> Finally, there is *controlled irresponsibility*. The personnel officers are puppets who are only authorized to receive concessions, not to make any. There is a federation of departments instead of one company, as far as the union is concerned. When we deal at the top level, the supervisor's authority is represented as complete and practically untouchable. When the members and Reps try to obtain concessions at the department level, they find, naturally, that the supervisor has negligible influence.

Now under more pressure from the unions than before, however, the companies bargained grudgingly, giving way as gradually as possible. The pattern that resulted was one of *containment-aggression*.

1953–1958. A few managements, regarding the union as inimical to good engineer-management relations, embarked upon campaigns to rid themselves of the "intruders" entirely. Among other measures, they denied the unions and their leaders any of the courtesies or the protocol that were commonplace in other relationships. Denied a status of legitimacy, these unions in turn reflected little concern for the welfare of the company. Perhaps cause and effect operated in the reverse direction; that is, the unions' lack of deference to the interests of the companies may have fashioned the managements' attitude toward the unions. Either way, the parties had entered a structure of *conflict*—a pattern of no-holds-barred that was dominant in industrial relations before 1940. The national score on these engineering struggles is even—the union won one and is now recognized by management as a legitimate force; the company won another, succeeding in decertification; the outcome of another battle in which the parties have been engaged for several years had not been determined by 1959.[9]

Five or six of the eleven situations studied continue in the *containment-aggression* pattern. Aside from such situations, and one marked by continuing conflict, the others have entered a pattern of accommodation, wherein the parties:

> . . . concentrate practice and procedure upon establishing wages, hours, and conditions of employment and then upon administering the jointly established standards. Although not unduly alarmist about the potential of every demand for encroaching upon managerial prerogatives or of every counter-demand for affecting shop rights, the parties to accommodative bargaining do maintain alert watchfulness upon these ramparts of principle, these orbits of respective equities and privileges.
>
> But within these bounds the leaders, the ranks, and the

9 This battle over certification was decided in 1960, when the union was defeated. A responsible company official said, however, that management could take no satisfaction from the outcome of the vote since the majority margin was "far too small."

organizations linked by relationships of accommodation interact within comfortably "customary" familiar patterns of behavior. They have evolved their routines of recognizing functions and settling differences. They have learned how to adjust one to another in daily affairs, to accept the reduction of conflict as an accomplishment without demanding its total elimination. They have proved themselves willing to compromise whenever possible, to conciliate whenever necessary, and to tolerate at all times.[10]

Two of these relationships show signs of entering the *cooperation* structure. The tenor of the union publications in these companies is one of helpfulness to management, lecturing on the evils and costs of absenteeism, stressing the need for maintaining maximum production, urging the engineers to accept transfers for the company's convenience willingly in the interest of an urgent project, and so on. An excellent illustration is the recommendation of the president of one of these unions issued *during a lay-off situation* in 1957:

> The present circumstances present an unusual opportunity for [Association] engineers to make suggestions which will improve [the company's] efficiency. Do you know of any specific situations in which changes in procedures can get work done better, quicker, or cheaper? *Write* them out in full detail and mail them—don't phone them—to the [Association] office. Would you like to serve on a committee to develop these suggestions? Volunteers are solicited. The Company has repeatedly invited [The Association] to forward any and all suggestions for improving engineering efficiency. Top management should be especially receptive to good, practical suggestions right now.

Management in these two relationships in turn consults the union representatives on matters not covered by the agreement, and recognizes the union's institutional needs for security.

[10] Benjamin M. Selekman, Sylvia K. Selekman, Stephen H. Fuller, *Problems in Labor Relations,* p. 6.

Characteristics of Engineering Unionism

The foregoing discussion has sketched the ways in which the character of unions has changed during their short history. The discussion has not, however, sufficiently stressed certain persistent profile features which actually characterize professional unionism and which operate to distinguish the phenomenon from other types of unionism.

As a whole, professional engineers demonstrate little aptitude for collective bargaining as it is practiced by other unions. The educate-management approach of the engineering unions was mentioned previously; and while its relative importance has declined somewhat over the years, it still is the unions' chief strategy. By his nature and in accordance with his training, the engineer firmly believes in the power of facts and logic. Often these logics conflict with the realities of economic life, and when they do the engineer cannot give way; he holds to the logics. Thus the engineering unions tend to substitute debate for give-and-take negotiations.

Related to the above characteristic is the engineer's lack of appreciation for the need for off-the-record discussions between negotiators in advance of contract negotiations. These informal conversations can often assist both parties (a) in preparing their own principals for the other party's proposals and (b) in formulating their own proposals in such a way as to permit whatever compromise might be necessary with a minimum of embarrassment or disappointment. The following comment is typical of those made by several company negotiators.

> Another thing the leaders failed to do was to notify the Labor Relations people by some means or another what the union will have to insist upon, so that Labor Relations can go to their principals to see what can be worked out. The company did not know that the union would be so insistent upon a [certain proposal], that it would be a strike issue. Furthermore, the merit system and layoff procedure pro-

> posals required months of study before they could be agreed to by the company. Yet they did not advance these proposals until late in the negotiation procedure. A more mature and competent leadership would not have made these mistakes, which resulted in bitterness and misunderstanding, damaged relationships, and affected morale. It would also have achieved more of its objectives, as company study would have revealed ways in which these could be accommodated.

Those leaders who have seen this need, however, have come in for severe criticism from other engineers on the bargaining committee who do not think such talks are ethical.

The union leaders who negotiate for the engineers are seldom in a position to speak authoritatively for the union. As a rule, the engineers are meticulous in their attention to democratic form. A negotiating or executive committee makes few decisions independent of the membership. Even minor proposals will be taken back to the membership for approval prior to giving the company a decision. Moreover, there is no telling whether union committeemen who leave the bargaining table will sell a proposal that they seem to have agreed to. Often they will have become convinced that the company's offer is about as good as they can expect, but the membership will vote against the offer and send the negotiating team back to the bargaining table. As a further ensurance that decisions are arrived at democratically, several unions make extensive use of the mail ballot.

Still another characteristic of the professional union is the rapid turnover of leadership. The trend toward full-time officials cited earlier has provided more continuity in leadership, but the problem persists in several forms. First, the mortality rate of full-time officials runs high. Second, where an individual does remain in the full-time position for several years, he must contend with newly elected officials in the other offices annually. Third, a few unions do not have any full-time officials. In part, the turnover can be attributed to the engineer's unwillingness to become too closely associated with the union in his supervisor's thinking. The union leaders themselves stress the sacrifice entailed, in terms of their own professional development. They cannot afford to lose more than a year to union duties. Many emphasize that they run for office only out of a "sense of public duty"; indeed, it often is a draft candidate situation. One unit made the following provision for distributing these "public duties":

> Every engineer in the unit must serve his turn on the grievance committee and as grievance chairman. Men will be committeemen for two years, and chairman the third year. These rotating assignments are made according to a complete roster of unit membership.

This system also yielded somewhat more continuity than normally found.

A question related to the preceding one is: what type of engineer assumes the leadership positions in these unions? The nonunionized engineering employers believed that the membership and leadership for the unions would come from among the below-average engineers. Some managers of unionized companies also "felt" this to be the case but admitted there was no systematic evidence that supported that notion. The total exposure in the companies researched left the author with the impression that there was no correlation between the quality of an engineer and his activity or membership in a professional union. Some paradoxes may exist to prevent such correlation. For example, some less competent engineers who might like to support the union because of the protection it affords them are also too insecure to risk management's disapproval—so they don't join. Also, because of the value placed by engineers on technical ability, the more competent engineers who are active naturally are supported for leadership spots.

Are there any useful distinctions that can be made about

the types of engineers who become members and leaders in the union? Although presented here tentatively and with some misgivings, the following characteristic types seemed to emerge:

The middle-class-conscious engineer. He would be extremely management oriented and would see the union as an obstacle to this orientation and to attaining or preserving his class status.

The traditional-professional. He would view the profession in its traditional context. To him, the union is a negation of individualism, which he closely associates with professionalism.

The socially aware. He would have a general interest in social problems; e.g., he might be an engineer who is also likely to participate in interracial living experiments, or he might have been raised in a family active in social welfare. To him the union is a means of expression, of self-help; it is a means of influencing his environment.

The leader aspirant. He would enjoy positions of authority in organizations—business and political. To him, the union provides a means for exercising organizational and leadership skills and a means for attaining recognition.

Naturally, leadership and membership in the professional union come chiefly from the third and fourth types.

Unfortunately for the union, the latter types are often a minority or only a small majority of the bargaining unit. This brings us to another characteristic of the engineering union—the great proportion of its energies are diverted to recruiting new members. At the head of the lists of "current objectives" and "current activities" of these unions were membership drives. Only one engineering union had a union shop. While the leaders of many of the others unions would have liked a union or agency shop, the memberships of these unions were far from united in support of compulsory unionism.

Another interesting aspect of professional unionism is the reluctance of its members to process grievances. Considerable effort is expended by the union officials in encouraging members to use the grievance machinery when they have complaints. One grievance chairman used the following arguments to persuade individuals to file grievances in their own behalf:

1. If you don't grieve, there will be no change.
2. The grievance relates to a policy higher than the supervisor, and this is the only device for taking the matter up. You should not think of this as criticism of your supervisor.

Engineers want conditions which are the subject of their complaints to be attended to by management, but they do not want to become involved personally. Timidity on the part of engineers will even occasionally cause them to change their minds after the grievance machinery has started.

Union leaders ascribed the engineers' cautiousness to "the company-dominated merit review system," not to any inherent docility. "They have to be pretty mad before they will jeopardize their chances for increases." On this point of supervisory retaliation through the merit system, however, the unions are understandably ambiguous. On the one hand, a union official will imply that supervisors are not above such things. On the other hand, that official risks confirming the engineers' fear that they *will* be retaliated against if they file a grievance, thereby discouraging the engineers from using the grievance procedure.

The reluctance of engineers to file grievances places two limitations on the union's effectiveness in collective bargaining. First, it substantially reduces the importance of one way in which a union can normally demonstrate its value to its members. Second, it handicaps the union in negotiations when the union cannot cite instances in which present practices and policies have proved inadequate.

Relationship to the Labor Movement

The ESA remained aloof from the rest of the labor movement, its executive council having never seriously considered affiliation with the AFL-CIO. This attitude of the majority of the member units is expressed by one engineering union in a statement containing the unit's founding aims:

> It is the belief of the founders of this organization that these objectives can best be obtained within an association which *avoids entangling alliances with dissimilar groups* . . . (emphasis added).

If the above position of avoiding entangling alliances seems to be based on strategic considerations, the position of one union leader alludes to more basic philosophical differences between the engineering union and the labor movement:

> We are organized to make use of those features of the national labor laws which are useful to us [but] we are not part of the labor movement nor have we any particular kinship with those who are.[11]

Nevertheless, in 1956 the ESA lost one of its member units to the International Union of Electrical, Radio and Machine Workers (IUE), AFL-CIO. The engineering unit went over to the IUE shortly after the engineers had engaged in a long strike, an experience which had demonstrated the benefits of close cooperation between the production and engineering employees in imposing economic sanctions. The following year, one of the larger and more active engineering unions quit the ESA and voted to affiliate with the United Automobile Workers, AFL-CIO, only to lose completely in a decertification election a few months later. Still later, in 1957, the ESA split into two parts, ostensively over the issue

[11] "Engineers' Stand on 'Right to Work'," *Business Week,* October 25, 1958, p. 139.

of whether the member units should be purely professional or should be allowed to include nonprofessional technical employees.[12] The split also grew out of differences in the approach to collective bargaining, with the mixed units advocating greater priority to organizational efforts than to lobbying and publicity.

The following statement[13] summarizes the reasons for the eventual division as they were perceived by the group that split off:

> From the earliest days of ESA, it was apparent that there was a divergence of opinion as to the role ESA should play on the national scene. One faction, firmly convinced that a national organization should devote a large measure of its efforts toward the improvement of the economic status of engineering employees, has advocated measures which would encourage and improve the effectiveness of collective bargaining. In order to accomplish this, it has vigorously supported the organization of additional units, compiling salary statistics, unit officer leadership training, and creation of an emergency fund.
>
> Other factions in ESA proposed that the national organization pattern itself after the technical societies with the emphasis on prestige and public relations. Collective bargaining was advocated, but the effort in this direction was to be merely nominal.
>
> During the formative years, ESA avoided conflicts over viewpoint by concentrating on the creation and development of its administrative machinery. At the third national Convention, it became apparent that these differences were slowly emerging, but a number of compromises were effected and the organization was tenuously held together.

12 The "purely professional" faction retained the name ESA. The other faction adopted the name Engineers and Scientists Guild (ESG), but subsequently abandoned the idea of forming a rival organization. Early in 1961, after a key professional unit withdrew its support, it appeared as if the ESA itself might not recover.

13 This statement appeared in the *E.S.G. Outlook,* Vol. 1, No. 1, July 1957, a publication of the heterogeneous groups that planned to establish the rival organization named the Engineers and Scientists Guild.

Meanwhile the IUE, which already had two locals that were predominantly professional units, and the UAW, and the USW had each begun to lay plans for a concerted organizational drive among white collar workers, including engineers. Faced with growing automation of manufacturing processes, these unions and others foresaw declines in membership unless the growing numbers of professional technicals could be brought into their organizations. In January 1959 the Industrial Union Department of the AFL-CIO held a conference titled "Meeting the Needs of Scientific and Professional Workers," attended by leaders representing some of the ESA and former ESA member units. The independent units and the international industrial unions talked of closer cooperation, with at least one independent engineering union showing keen interest in joining the IUE, which already represented the production workers in the company's plants.[14] One condition imposed by this engineering union for joining was that a council of engineering and technical units within the IUD be established giving these units considerable autonomy apart from their international union affiliation.

It is not clear just how interested those engineering union leaders who express an interest in affiliating with the shop union international really are. The threat to cooperate or affiliate with the shop union constitutes one of the most effective threats the engineers have to strengthen their own bargaining efforts. In effect they confront management with the following reasoning: A failure of the company to meet the needs of the members will convince these members of the necessity for stronger affiliations. In order to reduce the future effectiveness of this stratagem, one company obtained the following provision from the union during negotiation in 1958:

[14] This particular engineering union *did* vote to affiliate with the IUE in May 1960.

> The Association for itself and its members agree that affiliation with any labor organization which is composed of or represents directly or through an affiliated, subsidiary, or constituent organization, employees engaged in maintenance or production work or in any other work not recognized as professional or scientific, shall not be effective unless first approved by a majority of all employees within the bargaining unit represented by the Association by a closed ballot vote to be conducted by the American Arbitration Association which shall certify the results thereof to the [Association] and to [the company].

Before the above provision became effective, all that was required in order to affiliate with any organization was a majority vote of members present at each of two successive membership meetings 30 days apart.[15]

The American Federation of Technical Engineers, another AFL-CIO affiliate, chartered originally by the AFL in 1918 under a different name, has an interest in the engineers included within the scope of this study; however, this craft-type international is even less attractive to the engineers in the units studied than are the international industrial unions. Its organizational successes have been mostly among technicians, draftsmen, and other subprofessional employees.

[15] Interestingly, this engineering union proceeded to affiliate with a production and maintenance international—it is the unit cited in the preceding footnote, which joined the IUE in 1960. In doing so the engineering union ignored the restrictive contract provision requiring a majority vote of the entire bargaining unit. It merely obtained a 60% majority in two successive membership meetings attended by a fraction of the bargaining unit. There were further developments in this story. According to a union official, the company applied for an injunction to avoid "effective representation" by the IUE. Later, a group of engineers obtained a decertification election which resulted in a vote of approximately 1,700 against the union to 1,500 for the union. When this book went to press, however, the union had protested the election before the NLRB on the basis of alleged irregularities in the decertification petition and election, and it appeared to be confident that its representation status would eventually be confirmed.

PART II

Impact on Compensation

CHAPTER III

Salary Levels

CHAPTERS III through VII are concerned with compensation. Chapters III and IV will deal with the unions' policies and influences on general salary increases, premium pay, and fringe benefits—items which determine the level and composition of the compensation scheme. Chapter V will examine the unions' impact on the companies' base salary structures. The two succeeding chapters will analyze the role of the engineering unions in the areas of the merit budget and the individual salary review.

The first section of this chapter will set forth briefly the manpower market context within which salary negotiations have occurred. The second section will examine the standards used in salary negotiations; namely, separate treatment, competitive rates, cost of living and productivity, moral concepts, and trends in the hiring rate. The next section will consider the unions' efforts to obtain the salary data upon which many of their other activities in the compensation area depend. The final section will discuss the limited evidence on impact available for this study.

MANPOWER MARKET

The decade beginning in the late 1940's, the period under consideration, was generally one of high demand for engineers. The general boom in defense and industry was accompanied by ever greater amounts of research and development.[1] Although record numbers were being graduated from

[1] For example, between 1953 and 1956 industrial research and development performance in the United States increased by 76%. The aircraft industry,

engineering and science college programs, the supply never caught up with the demand;[2] the adjustment in the supply of professional engineers was delayed several years because of the time needed to acquire the necessary training; and it was delayed even further because many of the trained engineers were taken into the military service upon graduation. The lag between demand and supply, as measured by the number of engineers quoted by industrial firms as required and the number they obtained, increased for several years during the early 1950's and then began to decline. While 1957 was not a year of surplus of engineers for industry as a whole, specific companies, particularly those in the aircraft industry, did reduce their employment by cutting recruitment activities and by releasing some engineers.

Under generally favorable conditions, engineering salaries, especially starting rates, climbed more rapidly than wages and other salaries. The statistical data were not available to make a comparative analysis of engineering salaries in the unionized firms with those of similar nonunionized firms, or with those of industry in general. Even if such an analysis was made, one would be cautioned as to how he could interpret any differentials that appeared, since there are many factors, apart from collective bargaining, that could have an effect on the salaries a firm pays its engineers, such as the rate of growth of the engineering department, the proportions of

---

which figures importantly in the present study, experienced a threefold increase during this same period. See National Science Foundation, "Research and Development Costs in American Industry, 1956," *Reviews of Data on Research and Development,* No. 10, May 1958, p. 3.

2 This condition has been profusely described and documented elsewhere. Of special interest here is a study reported by the National Science Foundation, "Shortages of Scientists and Engineers in Industrial Research," *Scientific Manpower Bulletin,* No. 6, August 1, 1955, pp. 1–5. The study states that at least half of 200 companies surveyed (which together employ well over half of all scientists and engineers in industrial research and development) reported that they were unable to meet their needs, and one out of every three said that they had major or substantial shortages of such personnel. Moreover, it states that the proportion of companies reporting shortages of research and development scientists and engineers was largest in *aircraft, electrical equipment, petroleum,* and three other industries.

commercial and defense work, and the particular product market of the commercial work—to mention but a few.

Most of the companies studied were heavily committed to work on military contracts, under which engineering salaries were directly reimbursable. Such defense contractors have been accused by other employers of paying excessive salaries to engineers. Some companies performing research and development on both commercial and defense projects complained of the difficulty of paying as high a salary scale on commercial projects as on defense projects. The compulsion to do so was greater, incidentally, because of the presence of the union, which according to one manager otherwise "thrives on the appearance of inequities."

Can we infer that the unionized companies, because their engineers were employed on defense work, became a relatively easy touch for a salary increase? That is difficult to say, but there were instances where pay and benefit provisions demanded by the union were made contingent upon the government's decision to reimburse. In these cases, the unions that were affected, recognizing the important role of the government in these decisions, brought pressure to bear on the government's procurement administrator in Washington. Beyond the mention of a few instances of that nature, managements were notably reticent on the subject of the role the government's policy of reimbursement played in determining salaries. They did insist, however, "We need to keep salaries down in order to be able to bid on future contracts."

Standards for Salary Determination

The Basic Policy of Separate Treatment

In almost every company the union has tried to induce management to negotiate engineering salary increases as a matter separate from the company's production and maintenance wage negotiations. Naturally, the unions are after a larger increase, but they also view separate treatment as a matter of prestige; they are annoyed at "being the tail wagged by shop negotiations." The companies preserve the tandem relationship between the two negotiations, first to avoid granting the engineers anything extra for which the engineering union might claim credit, and second to avoid the repercussions that would come from the shop union if the engineers' union were granted a larger package. If there are compelling business reasons for the company to raise the engineers' salaries more than by the amount granted in the engineering and shop negotiations, which has frequently been the case in the past ten years, the company can step up engineering merit increases, although by so doing it may encounter difficulty with the union, as we shall see later.

Thus, typically the companies time their negotiations so that they settle with the shop employees first, and with the engineers shortly thereafter. With few exceptions the engineering unions have not been able to change this pattern. One engineering union had to wait from January 1, 1958, the expiration date of its own agreement, until May 1958, after the company had signed with its production and maintenance unions, before it received any economic offer from the company. After several years of protesting such treatment, the union in each of a few companies gave up trying to "set its own mark" in compensation.

If the majority of the engineering unions do not accept the package of the production and maintenance union as the measure of what they should get, what do they advocate? We shall take up several union approaches to salary negotiations in what has been a futile search for "objective" standards.

Competitive Rates

One of the most frequently used bench marks is "What competition pays." This is usually the company's defensive gambit; at times it is also the union's offensive pitch. In the companies studied management invariably explained that its engineering salaries were "equal to or better than competition."

How do the parties know what competition pays? Some companies obtain "a pretty good idea" through recruiting, hiring, and turnover. They "know" when they are "in line." Others may receive salary surveys conducted by other organizations; they may conduct their own. Because the salary survey is anything but an exact science, however, the unions find it necessary to conduct their own. Indeed, one of the primary purposes of the Engineers and Scientists of America is to provide the affiliate unions with salary data on all the unionized companies. Frequently, then, negotiations take the form of a debate as to which survey is appropriate. This type of debate can become quite heated. Take the case of negotiations in one company.

Both parties made their own salary survey. When significant differences appeared in the results of the two surveys, both parties agreed to go over the surveys to see if they could iron out the discrepancies. Management wanted to avoid disclosing the specific company data in the survey, because it would put the company in an "impossible position" with those companies that had provided the information on a confidential basis. The company's apprehensions on this matter were well founded because later, when it appeared that the company had confided in the union, several of the surveyed companies refused to furnish salary data to the subject company for a number of years thereafter. Furthermore, management believed that one of the discrepancies was the result of the way in which the union had tried to determine comparable skill levels at various companies, a step essential to providing meaningful salary comparison. Management doubted that discussions with the union in this area could prove anything in the negotiations. The union's view was that the company's own determination of which grades represented comparable skill levels could not be defended in open discussion or the company would have been willing to discuss them.

The union disclosed the sources of its survey data. Management discounted the survey results because (1) the data had been gathered primarily from individual contacts (frequently by mail), and thus did not contain all salaries in each category, nor were the salaries subject to factual payroll verification, (2) the grade slotting of individuals through interviews was subject to bias from both the respondent and the surveyor, and (3) it was limited to companies whose engineering departments were unionized— "A small sample, loaded with traditionally high-salary companies from traditionally higher paying industries and currently tight labor market areas." Management took the company's story to the engineers. A letter cited the differences in results of the surveys "without questioning the sincerity of the union's efforts, which were based on interviewing employees in other companies." Before negotiations were concluded they had become very tense around the survey question and the union had talked about strike action.

Similar disagreements were experienced in most of the other companies studied. While such debates are by no means unique to collective bargaining among engineers, these discussions do assume unusual importance in negotiations with engineers because of the amount of faith placed by the professionals on rational persuasion.

Cost of Living and Productivity

Although many unions have cited rising living costs and increased productivity to support their requests for salary increases, only a few have proposed contracts that incorporate automatic general increases based on these factors. Companies normally insist that they can agree to a cost-of-living clause, if at all, only in a long-term contract, a condition which usually makes the option unacceptable to engineering unions. Two companies, however, have granted both of these provisions in two or more contracts of several years' duration.

One company established the pattern of granting a 2.5% general increase annually and a cost-of-living adjustment automatically if they can be negotiated in a long-term contract; but cost-of-living adjustments are granted periodically and are not fully retroactive if the contracts negotiated are short term.

Salarywise, provision for automatic increases can work to only the engineering employers' disadvantage. There are three possibilities. First, if the general level of engineering salaries rises by an amount corresponding to the guaranteed increases, there is nothing lost and nothing gained for either party. Second, if engineering salaries generally rise by less than the amount of automatic increases provided by the company's agreement, we shall assume that the company is paying its engineers more than it otherwise would. Third, if competition's salaries rise by an amount in excess of the automatic increases, the company's salaries will fall below competition—an intolerable condition. The company, not wanting to cramp its recruiting efforts or increase its loss rate, will voluntarily offer to institute a general salary increase, or will proceed to increase salaries generously through the merit system. Only the first and third possibilities have occurred in practice: increases in the competitive salary level have equaled or exceeded the automatic increases guaranteed by the contract. Therefore, historically, the provisions probably have not resulted in any net cost to the companies, but this is no guarantee that they will not do so in the future.

The two-year contract has become more common in recent years. In 1958 a typical two-year contract called for a 6% general increase the first year and 3% the second year. This lower increase for the second year was a hedge against the second possibility resulting from automatic or guaranteed increases described above.

"Moral" Concepts

Trade unions have sought "a fair day's pay for a fair day's work," "a living wage," and so on. The engineers' unions also advance certain payment standards "on moral grounds," namely (a) the historical salary ratio between the engineers and skilled labor or production employees, and (b) the engineers' "true worth."

The National Industrial Conference Board reports that between 1929 and 1955 average wages of production employees trebled. During approximately the same period—1929 to 1954—median annual salaries for professional engineers with about ten years' experience doubled.[3] In 1956, for example, one union argued:

> The position of technical employees relative to production workers has deteriorated over the last 25 years by about one-third. No one expects a 33% general salary increase based on inequity with respect to production workers but. . . .

The criterion of "true worth" combines the cost of engineering training and the engineers' economic contribution. An editorial in one of the union's publications, reprinted in other engineering union publications throughout the country, summarizes these ideas:

> What is the worth, to society, of men on whom the technological progress of mankind is entirely dependent?
>
> What is the value, to the entrepreneur and corporate structure, of the work that maintains and increases the industrialization of our economy?
>
> What is the value, to a nation at war or in defense preparation, of the men whose minds develop the most modern military measures and countermeasures; of minds that find new ways of obtaining power and utilizing low grade resources efficiently when high grade resources are rapidly diminishing?

[3] National Industrial Conference Board, Inc., *Unionization Among American Engineers.* Studies in Personnel Policy, No. 155, New York 1956, p. 5.

What is the value, to humankind, of the men who produce the ideas and methods that make life easier, more comfortable, and longer for all the species?

Unquestionably, without the engineer and scientist, Malthus' theory (that the human race will diminish in size and deteriorate economically to bare subsistence) would be gradually proven. Our entire social and economic structure is dependent upon the work and abilities of the technical mind. The hope of an eventual day of economic plenty for the entire world devolves upon the engineer and scientist.

This is your intrinsic worth as a scientist.

What are the costs involved in becoming a scientist?

Consider spending about $2,000 per year for living and education during the period of specialized training. Add to this the loss of potential earnings, say $2,500 per year, as an untrained worker during this time.

What is the price of marriage and family postponed until education is complete? Add to these the less tangible costs of a period of intense training and study.

The question that arises is one of whether or not your *income* is based upon your *intrinsic* economic worth.

* * * * *

It is impossible to state how much employers are influenced by the engineers' moral arguments. Often they are persuaded that the unions "have a point," but hasten to add, "everyone believes he is worth more than he is paid."

Trends in Hiring Rates

Another consideration in negotiating salary increases is the movement of the hiring rate from one year to the next. This is similar to the salary survey approach described earlier in that it is based upon measures of the general competitive conditions of supply and demand. It is dissimilar, however, in other respects, as will be seen.

The experiences in one company (call it Company A), where the union has placed great weight on changes in the hiring rate, is of interest here, and will provide a vehicle for exploring the many facets of this salary criterion. This union has been more interested in salaries than any other issue or aspect of employment, and seemed to be relatively more interested in salaries than any other engineering union.

The union's sequential efforts in the area of general salary levels are designed, first, to divorce general salary increases for engineers from those of the production worker and, second, to relate through general increases the general salary levels of Company A's engineers to the changes in the *hiring rate* of graduating engineers, even if this latter action also divorces the company's over-all salary levels from those of the rest of industry. By urging hiring rates as the criterion for general salary increases, the union ties the question of salary level to the question of salary structure, but let us defer the latter question temporarily.[4] With narrow vision we can look directly at the influence or potential influence of the hiring rate criterion in determining general salary increases.

The union in Company A claims some success in its application of the hiring rate standard. Until 1957 the general percentage increases granted to the engineers were identical with those negotiated by the production union. For the first seven years of collective bargaining these general increases happened to approximate the movement in beginning salaries for engineers. Then between 1953 and 1956 hiring rates increased 26% while blanket increases totaled only 10%, leaving a "deficiency" of 16%. When in 1957 the company broke tradition and granted the engineers a slightly higher increase than it granted the shop union (4% vs. 3.5%), the union took this to mean that the company partially accepted the principle of the union's proposal which linked the general increase to the percentage the salaries of beginning engineers in 1957 exceeded those of 1956. The real significance of the 4% figure is difficult to assess inasmuch as it coincided

4 Salary structure is the subject of Chapter V. The reader should also be advised that another issue related to this discussion—that of flat versus percentage increases—will be deferred to Chapter VI.

with an amount granted by a close competitor earlier that year.

During negotiations the company had indicated that it did not take the union's arguments too seriously; that it regarded the idea as somewhat of a "gimmick." The company negotiators believed that the membership would only support this formula in those years when it would result in a large increase.

The situation in 1958 tested this notion. As the parties approached negotiations, it was expected that beginning salaries would be higher than those of the previous year by a percentage that would be lower than the shop union would receive. After this situation was explained to the membership, a questionnaire assaying the members' interest in the union's negotiation proposals showed that 70% of those responding still favored this approach to salary negotiations.

The company offered a general increase of 4.5% which came within a few tenths of a percentage point of being the figure generated by the statistics on the 1957 and 1958 starting salaries. Significantly, it was not the exact figure produced by the formula, which was 4.36%; and this fact chagrined the union. The company went beyond the union's demands in another respect, by including in the economic package an extra 1.5% to be distributed on a selective basis, apparently aiming at the 6.0% figure that was the amount negotiated with the production union, and also the amount granted engineers in other closely competing companies. The union, however, regarded the 1.5% as a close approximation of the special request it made for 1.41% to make up for the smaller than usual merit review in 1957. Thus, the issue of whether the company had complied with the union's formula approach was thoroughly confused, and either party could claim whichever was its pleasure.

The hiring rate approach to general increases contains several desirable features for the union: (1) it effectively separates the engineers' employment conditions and negotiations from those of the shop union; (2) it tends to prevent salary differentials from being narrowed; (3) it is also peculiarly suitable for "professional" type bargaining. The union president at Company A, writing in a union publication, focused on the last point:

> . . . it is necessary to start this explanation with basic policies. . . . [Trade] union salary negotiations are based on the union's economic power through strike or threat of a strike. . . . [Our bargaining organization], on the other hand, seeks to attain its objectives through a combination of persuasion and patience. The one item which lends itself most poorly to persuasion is a blanket salary increase. Such an increase is obviously self-serving in that it is virtually impossible to convince a company of an increase being justified by some mutually acceptable principle.
>
> In seeking to justify a salary increase on rational grounds, it is common to resort to comparisons. However, company negotiators quickly become cynical about these comparisons as they see one group tendered as the comparator one year and another group tendered the next.
>
> * * * * *
>
> The hiring rate approach [does], by its rational and reasonable basis, greatly increase our persuasiveness in bargaining.

The hiring rate formula had a fourth advantage for the union; (4) it would free the time of the negotiating teams for other matters. The union official stated:

> It would, by settling the blanket increase question for as long as we continued this approach, free our negotiations for the consideration of other important items. Since we have found that we can only secure adequate attention for a limited number of major items each year, it has been necessary to defer consideration of several others. This situation would be eased considerably because the blanket increase discussions always consume the major portion of our attention.

Each of the four advantages to the union just described present some corresponding drawback for the company. First, for the company to separate the negotiations with its engineers from those of the shop union may be to make itself vulnerable to whipsawing tactics. Second, for the company to be committed to a program of raising the entire salary structure annually by the amount of increases in hiring rates greatly reduces its flexibility. In practice the company may not object to a moderate narrowing of differentials in some years, particularly if it is occurring in other companies also. Third, the more persuasive the union's arguments are, the more difficult it is for the company to say "no," because to deny really persuasive arguments is to risk the disapproval of the engineering force, including the sometimes neutral engineering supervisors. Fourth, the company is not interested in freeing the union negotiators' time to consider other union objectives.

A spokesman for Company A expressed other misgivings. In his opinion this formula could not be binding on future negotiating teams. The union admitted that it would abandon the method if the long-term outlook for engineering salaries was unfavorable. Also, no cut was possible under the union's proposal; the minimum increase would be zero. However, it was not completely a one-way-street proposal. It provided for a carry-over to credit one year's decrease in starting rates against the next year's increase.

Although the formula had been "in the ball park" the last few years, the company might not be able to use hiring rates as a standard in the future. Circumstances of several types would make the formula inappropriate. To cite one such circumstance, the company might require more selective hiring one year than it had the previous year, with the result that the company's average hiring rate would be higher that year; but this is quite unrelated to general conditions of supply and demand, conditions which the formula is intended to measure; therefore the hiring rate approach should be discounted. Incidentally, it is considered very likely that the trend in aircraft companies will be in the direction of more selective hiring due to the qualitative requirements of missile engineering and development.

The unions in other companies have not proposed that changes in hiring rate should be the sole, or even predominant, determinant but they have used hiring rate data to supplement other arguments in salary negotiations from time to time.

Quite apart from whether or not hiring rate data are referred to in negotiations, the unions recognize that general salary levels will be affected to some degree by the prevailing hiring rates. They acknowledge that engineering salaries are largely determined by supply and demand in the manpower market, but since only new graduates and engineers changing jobs actually enter into the market, only the hire-in rates are actually set there; other engineering rates are adjusted by employers by extrapolation.

If this be true, the unions' reasoning continues, it is all important to affect hiring rates themselves. How can this be accomplished? The engineering manpower market is, essentially, made up of a relatively few large employers and thousands of individual engineers. The companies generally have more information on which to judge an engineer's value to the company than does the engineer, giving the company an advantage in bargaining for employment. The unions can give the employable engineer some bench marks to apply in looking for a job, making him less easy "prey" for "dollar-minded" recruiters. Accordingly, the ESA issued a series of special reports aimed at the engineering graduate and designed to equip him for choosing a job.

The ESA's primary objective here was to affect starting salaries, which would thereby put pressure on other engineering salaries. The special reports are persuasive in offering (other than the obvious) reasons why the engineer-applicant should be concerned with his starting salary. One of the reports, entitled "Minimum Starting Salaries" reads in part:

> . . . it is possible for an engineer to underestimate the importance of his starting salary on his future professional and economic development. However, we also recognize that few engineers have sufficient statistical data available with which to evaluate an employer's offer. To fill this need, the Engineers and Scientists of America have analyzed the salary data which we have available. From this we have developed a chart of minimum starting salaries which we believe represents the engineering salary practices which will be in effect during most of 1958. [This chart was presented along with directions for its use.]

The combination of two factors—(1) large spread in salaries between various "quality" levels and (2) inability to determine absolute values of "worth"—causes an engineer's starting salary to have an unexpectedly large influence on his professional career. This happens in two ways.

Salary Influences Assignment

Most salary administration practices seek to maintain consistent relationships between an engineer's salary and his work contribution. Thus an engineer whose starting salary is higher is more likely to be assigned a somewhat more responsible job. This assignment in turn results in a higher rate of development of the engineer's professional competence. This in turn results in his earning a larger merit raise. And so on. The compounding effect of even small differences can become very significant over an engineer's whole career.

Reverse Evaluation

An employer's task of properly evaluating an engineer-applicant is quite difficult. In these cases, it is common to (unconsciously, perhaps) reverse the usual procedure and actually "evaluate" the engineer's "worth," at least to a considerable extent, by his present salary. (It is common practice to offer an engineer more than he is presently making, but usually only a limited amount more.) Thus if an engineer is working for an employer whose salaries are uniformly low, he is likely to be in trouble if he decides to change employers. Even though his present salary will be low, his prospective employer will not be inclined to offer him more than the "normal" increase over his present salary. Thus he will fit into his new employer's salary structure as if he were a lower "quality" engineer than he really is. This "reverse evaluation" will often influence both his salary and his work assignments for many years to come.[5]

Once the engineer-applicant realizes how influential his starting salary will be with respect to both his future salary advancement and the nature of his job assignments, he will be inclined to drive a harder bargain before accepting employment, thereby contributing to higher starting rates and engineering salaries generally. We cannot say in practice whether any applicants who were advised by the unions of these facts-of-life thereby became tougher bargainers. Logically, however, it is possible.

SALARY DATA

To be effective at all, each of the above arguments regarding salary standards must be accompanied by the appropriate salary data. Whether the company shall furnish the union with salary and other personnel data has been a troublesome issue in collective bargaining with engineering unions generally, assuming much more importance than in collective bargaining in the shop.

In the early years of their existence the engineering unions relied upon their own devices for obtaining salary and personnel statistics. Much effort was required to survey and sample members and nonmembers in an effort to gain some idea about the actual level and distribution of salaries and the rates of the salary progress. Later they became more aware that they were entitled to certain salary information by law, and on this basis experienced some success in obtaining data from the companies.

5 "Minimum Starting Salaries," *Special Report,* Washington: Engineers and Scientists of America, 1957.

The form of the data furnished the engineering unions by their respective companies varies. In several companies the data furnished are detailed, but on an anonymous basis; that is, data are provided on each man, but not by name. One union that was furnished individual data, but denied these data by name, contested the company's action in arbitration in 1951. The union claimed the right to individual data by name under the law, and specifically under the contract. The contract negotiated in December 1950 had contained a new clause:

> The employer agrees to furnish the association with complete up-to-date data on employees' salaries, salary increases, classifications, ages and date of hire, and detailed figures on the operation of the merit review, on June 1 and December 1 of each year during which this agreement shall be in effect.

The company's position was that this clause did not require the company to furnish names of employees along with other salary information. Nor did the company believe that it should divulge such information without the consent of the individual employees because this would constitute an invasion of their privacy. The results of a union poll prior to the negotiation of that contract clause were cited by the company as evidence of employee opposition to the practice advocated by the union. The poll was taken in June 1950, with 63% of the employees in the bargaining unit who voted registering their opposition to the publication of salaries by name. In another union poll some time later, however, 57% of those who voted then favored having the company provide the union with salary data by name. It is not clear whether the results of this poll were available at the time of the arbitration in question. In any event, the arbitrator ruled against the company; the "complete up-to-date data" and "detailed figures" required by the agreement must include the names of individuals.

One union continued until 1957 to rely upon its own surveys of professionals for the salary data published for its members and used in preparing for negotiations. It had signed a memorandum of agreement in 1947 renouncing its legal right to ask for salary data. In December 1956, in preparation for 1957 negotiations, it asked the company to supply this information. The company hesitated at first, but later decided to meet the union's request. Shortly thereafter the company began to furnish directly to the engineers charts and curves based on this information.

Throughout the history of the same company an individual's classification as well as his salary have been kept well guarded secrets between the man and the company. In 1955 a referendum was conducted by the union to determine whether the members approved or opposed publishing individuals' classifications. It was argued, on the one hand, that this would violate the "sanctity of private affairs"; that it would only be a "short step" from knowledge of individual classification to information on individual salary; that the morale of those embarrassed with their classifications would suffer; finally, that this issue risked splitting the union organization. On the other hand, publishing individuals' classifications would provide a means of recognition of advancement, would let an individual know where he stood in relation to his fellow employees, and might contribute to the fairness of merit review administration. A majority of the union members voted against the idea. In a similar referendum in 1957, the membership partially reversed itself, voting to have the company publish the names of all engineers along with their classifications, excepting the lower classifications. Management complied with the membership's desires since "it was a matter of indifference to the company."

Why has the furnishing of salary statistics and personnel data customarily been such an important issue between the engineering unions and companies? Obviously much of this information is essential to the union for intelligent collective bargaining. It can be used by the union for many purposes, including policing the salary provisions of the contract and influencing the distribution of merit monies. In negotiations, complete and accurate data are particularly important to the professional union which relies heavily on persuasion. From the companies' point of view it has been thought better not to voluntarily furnish information that would then make the unions' demands more difficult to deny. Still, the conflict of interest here may not be so sharp as these statements imply. In some cases the data have given the unions a basis for making their demands less ambitious and more realistic, since the union negotiating committee no longer needed to add a margin of safety to allow for what it did not know, but what it believed might be so. Furthermore, in at least one case the company's data provided the union with the basis for completely reversing an antagonistic position it previously held.

The issue is important for reasons other than those revolving around contract negotiations discussed above. The data probably have a more important function in the individual bargaining context, a subject which will be treated again in Chapter VII, Merit Review Systems. Through these data the individual can know how he stands within the company. When these data are combined with those obtained from other companies, he can learn how his employer's salaries compare with those of other employers. Making these bench marks for appraising individual salary performance generally available has given managers trouble. One manager said:

> A man will go to his supervisor with the union chart wanting to know why he isn't where he "belongs." If a man is below the curve, he will believe he is underpaid compared with others in the company. If he is above the curve, he will think that the company's professionals as a whole are underpaid.

Other managers complained that the age or experience versus salary curves provide the engineers with "a handle" in bargaining for individual merit increases. Some objected to the treatment the salary data receives. For example, they deplored the age versus salary curve as having a downward bias because it did not contain data from those who had been promoted into supervision. Such a curve could not provide an appropriate basis for a young man to predict his own future salary position. Still other managers thought that the curves produced from the data focused too much attention on salaries, distracting the professional from the work itself.

In some companies the union's data are used not only by the engineers but also by their supervisors. Several companies inform their supervisors only of an engineer's salary, the date and amount of his last merit and reclassification increase, and the number of years of engineering experience. It is the union's contention that additional information is required to make salary recommendations. Since evaluations are relative and salaries are relative, the supervisor also needs overall data, termed "ball park information" by one union. Thus, the union believes that by supplying the years of experience versus salary curves in quartiles or deciles it is contributing to more consistent and uniform salary treatment.

Perhaps the greatest disadvantage to the company in the salary data arrangements are their influence on the engineers' orientation. The engineers now rely upon the union for this much desired information, reducing their dependence upon their supervisors and weakening their orientation toward management. Recognition of this effect has led some companies to start furnishing the data directly to the engineering staff, but not without creating new problems. Whatever is gained temporarily in employee relations is more than offset by deteriorating union relations, which in turn probably adversely affect employee relations.

One other aspect of the salary data issue deserves attention: some unions do not treat the individual salary data confidentially. In the fall of 1958 the management of one firm was very much disturbed by a recently adopted union practice of distributing salary data to departmental representatives. Previously the union had kept individual salary data "locked up in its office," using them for compiling charts and for analysis. When the new practice was announced, it was opposed by a substantial number of members and led to an internal union dispute. The controversy was resolved on a department-by-department basis, with most departments voting to make the data available to a member upon request. The representatives were free to pass on to the union members certain information about their fellow workers.

The dissemination of individuals' salaries had a disruptive influence on the engineering work, but the company was at a loss as to how to respond. It could only hope that the practice would backfire for the union. The expressed purpose of making individual salary data available to members was to put the supervisors' merit review "on show," to give a member being reviewed equal data from which to argue or discuss his increase with his supervisor. The practice had been in effect for only one review period at the time this company was studied. The actual demand for information had been very light during that time.

In two other companies information about individuals' salaries had for several years been made available by the union to members upon request. Spokesmen for both companies testified that they had anticipated more trouble at first than they had actually experienced. But one manager did concede that distributing such information had had a salutary effect, "the company does a more careful job of auditing salaries." As an example of how it can have more specific impact, one engineer whose salary was way out of line on the high side was fired to avoid the trouble that would be caused if the other engineers learned of his salary.

Evidence of Impact on Salary Levels

In two companies not mentioned previously, management indicated that the general level of its engineering salaries had been raised by the union. One company which recruited chiefly from the New York City metropolitan area had been paying substantially below the national averages. Unionization resulted in an increase of about 25% which brought the company in line with competition throughout the country. The other company had allowed the union to push the company's engineering salaries "to a higher place with regard to competition." According to the director of labor relations the union had "won very substantial increases." The union president was given credit for having done "an excellent job in preparing for negotiations." He had "mustered his forces and timed his negotiations and the use of economic force such that a strike of the engineering force would have been effective." These were exceptional cases.

None of the other employers was 25% below competition; nor were any disposed to speak in glowing terms of either their union's negotiating ability or its economic strength. In fact, almost every comment made by other managements was to the contrary. One manager said, "These engineers will make unrealistic demands, and what's worse they stick to them." Another remarked, "They prepare for negotiations by computing historical ratios between the pay of skilled trades and engineers, which demonstrates how little they know about how their salaries are determined." Several managers cited instances in which the union had in their opinion cost the engineers some money through a delay in an adjustment. Such instances occur when negotiations do not result in agreement on a general increase by contract termination date; the engineering unions will often continue to negotiate beyond that date—rejecting the increase offered by the company, but without striking. The union may merely want to demonstrate its disappointment in the size of the offer, or it may hope to induce the company to increase its offer by causing management embarrassment. Whatever the reason, the tactic seldom results in a further increase; since the company refuses retroactivity in such cases, the engineer loses money in the amount of the increase times the length of the delay. Whether the embarrassment suffered by the company, if any, makes it liberalize its offers in the future is another question.

SUMMARY AND CONCLUSION

Engineering salaries in virtually all companies, unionized and nonunionized alike, advanced rapidly during the period under consideration, mainly because of the tight engineering manpower market in this country.

The evidence of actual net effect of the engineering union on the level of salaries, if any, during this period is skimpy and inconclusive. An examination of the factors discussed by the parties in salary negotiations does at least reveal some of the potential influences of engineering unionism in this area.

The "going rates" as indicated by salary surveys are the first and most obvious referents for discussions of salary levels. Since each party conducts its own survey, the results of surveys can be used to support opposing conclusions; and the surveys probably yield no net advantage to either party. The unions' "moral" arguments—that the greater historical ratio of engineering pay rates to the crafts' pay rates was "deserved" and should be restored and that the engineer's contribution to social walfare exceeds his monetary rewards—these arguments may be partly conceded by management representatives, but without any effect on salaries. Certain other arguments common to shop negotiations, such as ability-to-pay, seldom enter into engineering negotiations.

The cost-of-living clause and the annual improvement factor, because in practice they place a floor, but no ceiling, on salary increases, seem to offer the union a reasonably good opportunity to influence salaries. With a few exceptions engineering unions have tended to ignore these features, for at least two reasons. First, the clauses are contained in the shop agreements and to embrace the same features would bring them into closer relationship with the shop negotiations.

Second, the features go with a long-term contract, which the engineering unions will not accept, partly because they want to discuss noneconomic items no less than every year or two.

The starting salary argument can be used persuasively by the unions, and may well be used to a greater extent in the future. It appears to be a double-edged weapon that can work to the unions' disadvantage in certain years. It probably would not work that way, however, for reasons similar to those applying to automatic cost-of-living and productivity increases: if the hiring rate formula produces an increase figure below that of competition, the company will be compelled to grant supplementary increases in the amount of the differences.

The unions have become increasingly successful in obtaining the data necessary to prepare and support their various salary arguments, despite the opposition of the majority of the companies. According to many managers, the unions' presentation of the data sometimes leads to misconceptions. On the other hand, some managers agree with the unions' assertion that the unions' analysis and publication of data have led to more consistent and uniform salary treatment. In any event, the data have provided the basis for dissatisfactions among the engineers and for individual grievances. Also, the fact that the engineers rely upon the unions, not their supervisors, for this information has weakened their orientation toward management.

CHAPTER IV

Premium Pay and Fringe Benefits

THE engineering unions' main thrust has been for higher salaries but they have also exhibited a moderate degree of interest in related compensation areas, some of the more important of which are overtime issues, out-of-plant service payments, fringes, patent rights and allowances, professional recognition benefits, and working conditions. Of course, as we shall note later in this chapter, the unions do not consider these items as merely forms of compensation; likewise for the company more is involved in granting them than their cost. A final item which is included in this chapter, not because it is necessarily a fringe benefit, but rather because it is a direct cost item, is the time allowed for union activity.

OVERTIME ISSUES

Overtime Pay

Union Objectives. Overtime compensation has been a stubborn issue in engineering union-management bargaining, particularly during the early years of the relationship. The issue is essentially two-fold: Should engineers be paid for work performed in excess of the normal work week? If so, should they be paid at premium rates? The engineers answer affirmatively to both questions; the companies disagree, since the engineers are exempt as professional employees from the overtime provisions of the Fair Labor Standards Act and the Walsh-Healey Public Contracts Act.[1]

[1] The Fair Labor Standards Act of June 25, 1938, as amended by Public Law 393, January 25, 1950, requires employers engaged in interstate com-

After World War II the companies cut back the regular work week of their engineering departments from 48 hours to 40 hours, but continued to require extra hours from the engineers on a less regular basis. The engineers, who had already witnessed a narrowing of the differential between their own base rates and those of organized employee groups, now received *no extra pay* for occasional extra hours, while the organized employees earned *premium* rates for extra work, with the result that the differential in earnings became narrower still and was not infrequently eliminated completely. This was an "injustice" that even the most "professionally" oriented of the engineers' unions wanted to rectify. Pay for overtime work became one of the top bargaining objectives for the newly organized engineering units. One union set forth its arguments in its monthly publication:

> . . . it is not a matter of "right." It is simply the stand of the employee who says that beyond a reasonable number of hours, time spent on the job conflicts with responsibilities to home, health, and recreation. And if these conflicts persist because of directed overtime, that this excess time be paid for by employer and customer at premium rates. . . .
>
> But doesn't a professional man have a duty to see his job done regardless of the time or effort it may take? Isn't this one almost a definition of professionalism? Note however that the overtime pay demand concerns *directed overtime only*. Thus when arrangements between company and customer are such that the employer elects to *impose or direct* overtime, then these conditions can not be held to define a duty on the part of the . . . (exempt) employee to serve under a reimbursement policy inferior to the one applied to other employees.

Interestingly in this one area engineers advocate treatment

merce to pay premium rates of not less than one and one-half time for hours in excess of 40 hours per week, but exempts professional employees from its overtime provision. Most engineers and scientists are also exempt from the Walsh-Healey Public Contracts Act, Public Law No. 846, which requires employers with government contracts amounting to more than $10,000 to pay premium rates for hours in excess of 8 hours per day.

similar to, not different from, the treatment accorded shop employees.

The unions have unmistakably made progress in obtaining pay for overtime. Typically, they first gained some extra compensation for an extended work week, establishing the principle that overtime work should be compensated. Only the lower salaried employees were paid for overtime at more than straight time rates. Those exempt engineers who were within the pay ranges of nonexempt employees were paid at time and one-half, but in succeeding negotiations the unions were able to push upward the cutoff point for premium rates, and the somewhat higher limit on total earnings that could result from overtime pay. Since 1955 companies have agreed to very few further concessions on overtime.

A typical overtime provision incorporated in a 1958 contract provided time and one-half for employees whose base monthly salaries were $570 per month or less; time and one-half declining to straight time for employees whose salaries fell between $570 and $1,106, respectively; additional compensation on a descending scale basis for salaries between $1,107 and $1,400, to zero additional dollars at $1,400.

The above rates in this particular company applied only when the overtime work was scheduled as a part of an extended work week. In practice management would require overtime on a regular basis for as much as six weeks without paying extra compensation before they determined that an extended work week should be "scheduled." A variation of this qualifying clause in another agreement required that unless more than four extra hours per week were scheduled the engineer would not be compensated for any extra hours.

Company Position. The general policy position taken by companies on the overtime pay issue is that all employees should be compensated "fairly with due consideration to their over-all contribution to the company and the level of work to which they are assigned." These considerations should determine the basic salary of the professional engineer; and it follows that the engineer's basic salary is compensation not only for regular hours but also for normal amounts of overtime. Company policies allowing the engineer occasional time off for personal reasons without loss of pay are cited as evidence that the companies genuinely subscribe to the philosophy that salaried engineers are paid for performing specific functions or assignments rather than for actual hours worked. Certain statements made by representatives of the companies studied indicated, however, that they are not really committed to the principle underlying such a policy of compensation; that they are actually apprehensive about the practical difficulties of the alternative presented by overtime payment. Companies simply do not want to get into the position of paying overtime to employees whose work cannot be measured, and who can, to a large extent, determine the amount of overtime they work.

One director of labor relations puts his company's position bluntly:

> There is a little bit of larceny in every man's heart. If you provide premium pay, some engineers are going to manufacture reasons for working a pot full of overtime. No one is looking over the engineer's shoulder to see whether he is really working the first eight hours on the job. After all, the engineer who has his feet on his desk or who is staring out of the window may be having his most productive moments. There is no way to check abuses.

Another manager described how engineers would even unconsciously pace their work to a six-day week when an extended work week was being considered, if overtime pay was involved. Because of the difficulty of measuring output, even at the level of the total engineering task, an engineering group can easily get "locked into" an extended work schedule. On the other hand, it is sometimes an advantage to provide adequate incentives to work overtime. The manager added:

If a guy finally gets a fix on a solution on Friday, it definitely is in the company's interest for him to work straight through Saturday and Sunday if he likes. It's certainly worth more to the company than the premium incurred. And if there were no premium involved, he might wait until Monday.

Company Abuse of "Casual Overtime" Clause. Engineering contracts make a more basic distinction between overtime which is scheduled by supervision and that which is casual or volunteered by the engineer. One contract reads:

> (Exempt) employees are expected to work additional time over and above the Regular Work Day or Work Week at their own discretion and of their own choice, without their being directed to do so by the Employer. Such work shall be termed "nondirected overtime" [also called "volunteered" and "casual" overtime] and the employee shall not be compensated therefor, nor receive credit toward the 40 hours which must be worked before an employee becomes eligible for overtime payments.
>
> * * * * *
>
> When the Employer directs (exempt) employees to work overtime in excess of the Regular Work Day or Regular Work Week, employees so directed are expected to work such overtime, hereinafter termed "directed overtime," [also called "scheduled" overtime] and shall be paid for such directed overtime. . . .

The unions concede that it is appropriate for an engineer to put in a few extra hours on his own if he wishes, *and if the overtime is not "expected" by supervision.* This gives rise to a difficult administrative question; namely, whether given hours of overtime worked are casual, that is, are being volunteered, or whether this work is in response to workload requirements scheduled by supervision. The distinction between casual and scheduled overtime is not clear cut.

One instance can be cited that is suggestive of the amount of discretion involved in administering this aspect of the overtime provision. In January 1950 the union charged the company with violating the overtime provision, because a group of engineers in one department had been required to work overtime without pay for a period of two months, overtime varying from 12 to 117 hours per man. The company refused overtime pay on two grounds. First, it was management's opinion that these men were capable of judging the need for their talents, and since these engineers had accepted supper money (an allowance customarily provided for engineers who *volunteer* overtime), they indicated that in their judgment they were working voluntary overtime. Second, the company contended that the job involved had taken longer than the ten months originally scheduled to complete the job (it took 20 months) because of "poor engineering," presumably the fault of the engineers. The latter argument appeared to be weakened, however, by the company's admission that supervision had not advised the engineers of their poor work at the time of the performance review. In settling a grievance on this dispute the company granted the engineers up to five days off their regular work schedule. Other grievances of this type have resulted in reversals in departmental practices and in retroactive pay.

Proceedings during a similar dispute in another company revealed that supervision was maintaining records of voluntary overtime. Management claimed that this practice was proper since casual overtime is an indication of merit for purposes of individual salary adjustment. The union objected vigorously to this management claim, saying, "The keeping of records for merit purposes is a device to stimulate the engineers' willingness to undertake voluntarily the overtime required to meet unrealistic scheduling commitments. In so doing management is circumventing the contract." To prevent similar situations from developing in the department which it represented, one union requested a blanket guarantee that overtime which is in any way indicated, implied, suggested, or indirectly requested be treated as "scheduled" overtime and thereby subject to the overtime pay provision.

Employee Abuse of "Scheduled Overtime" Clause. Many managers express a belief that overtime pay has adversely affected the engineer's attitude toward his work and the company. This matter of attitude is important in itself and will be treated in Chapter XIV. One consequence of the change in attitude, however, is believed by management to be a decreased inclination on the part of the engineer to work casual overtime;[2] and since this is clearly a cost item it is of importance to our present discussion.

We have indicated that the organized engineer generally may be less apt to volunteer for overtime. It is more accurate to state that he is less inclined to volunteer for *uncompensated* overtime. According to the latter view, the engineers are just as willing to pursue the task outside of the regular work week on their own initiative, but are, in practice, able to secure overtime pay for this time by requesting it from the supervisor; supervisors are reported to be increasingly lenient in allowing compensation for voluntary overtime.

Here, obviously, practice diverges from the contractual provisions and from company policy. The distinction between casual and required overtime breaks down, this time in favor of the engineer, as contrasted with the other instances cited above in which the unions filed grievances on management's abuse of the casual overtime clause. In those instances the company was requiring uncompensated overtime. Now, the engineer is in effect volunteering "scheduled" overtime for which he is compensated. The two practices ap-

2 Apparently this disinclination to work casual overtime applies less to the more creative groups, such as the preliminary design and advanced electronics sections in the aircraft companies. Here the engineer (often a scientist) has his own project with which he becomes identified; he sees immediately the consequences of not continuing to work overtime on his particular problem or project when it becomes necessary.

pear to be casually related: the practice cited here results in part from the engineers' formal and informal pressure to have the supervisors reverse earlier interpretations of scheduled vs. casual overtime. A typical statement by management was, "We assumed that time off for personal reasons and casual overtime would wash out. Now we have a feeling that supervisors schedule such occasions for overtime to a greater extent than had been anticipated." A union officer at the above company agreed, "Now the company pays even casual overtime."

Controlling Amount of Overtime Scheduled. A few companies report that overtime payment practices handicap a company's manpower control. During periods of expanding need and limited supply of engineering talent, supervisors have a tendency to hoard engineers. If a few groups are working overtime on actual pressing problems, the supervisors of other groups may believe it would look better if they were working their groups overtime, too. An individual supervisor who wants to support his requisition for more engineers, or who wants to justify his present staff, will be even more apt to work his staff overtime. Inject overtime pay, particularly premium pay, and this practice becomes expensive. Furthermore the pay itself eliminates one check on the practice: "You can't count on the engineers to squawk about make-work or nonessential overtime, as you could if they were not being paid extra."

Related Pay Practices for Supervisory Personnel. Overtime pay for exempt engineers also complicates pay practices as applied to engineering supervision. The engineer-supervisor situation is comparable to that which existed several years ago between nonexempt employees and exempt engineers: slight pay differentials are narrowed still further by differential overtime payments. In other words, the problem has been merely shifted upward on the salary scale. Companies applying overtime pay on a regressive sliding scale have minimized the problem of inequities at both ends of the scale. Still, a few companies have felt compelled to pay supervisors overtime on the bargaining unit formula whenever their salaries fall within the affected ranges. Other companies have developed overtime formulas especially for supervision through department heads. Of course, the many difficulties encountered in paying engineers overtime cited above apply with even more force to the administration of supervisory overtime.

Compensating Time Off Policy. As a single contrast to the other unionized companies one company has been able to hold the line on overtime pay in negotiations, but perhaps not without "cost" in terms of union-management and employee relations. The union agreement contains no provision for premium pay for exempt engineers. Instead, overtime hours performed at the request or with the approval of the employee's supervisor are designated "C time" and are compensated by an equivalent number of hours off at a time acceptable to management.

The company's policies and practices have been the subject of controversy since the union's inception in 1943. Early in its history the engineers' union obtained a decision from an outside agency requiring the company to pay the engineers retroactively time and one half for hours worked in excess of 40 hours per week during the war period 1942–1945. The policy of C time, compensating time off, was then written into the contract at the company's request. While the union agreed that casual overtime would be taken care of adequately by C time, it insisted that scheduled overtime deserved premium pay.

A dispute that occurred in the fall of 1955 will illustrate the difficulties encountered by the company in administering this policy under collective bargaining.

> Beginning in August the company embarked upon an urgent engineering program requiring an extended work

week and involving over 100 exempt engineers. How was the company to compensate the men for the abnormal amount of overtime required during this period? Too many overtime hours were involved to be covered by C time without affecting the company's ability to handle normal work loads later in the year. The company, therefore, wanted to apply some other compensation arrangement for this period. The union saw in the situation an opportunity to establish the principle of premium pay.

Offers and counter offers were made. The company offered to pay straight time for overtime hours, but this offer was rejected as an even less desirable one than C time, because the latter compensates inconvenience with convenience, whereas straight time does not compensate for inconvenience. The company's next offer to give each employee his choice of straight time pay or C time was also unacceptable to the union.

The union then charged the company with unilaterally extending the work week and requested arbitration on this matter since it had no contractual case on the overtime pay issue. The company clarified its position: management had not extended the work week; the engineers were working the extra hours on a voluntary basis. Thereupon the membership complicated the position of the company by giving the union leaders authority to call upon the members to refrain from volunteering to work overtime. No member would be expected to refuse to work if specifically requested to work by the company in writing.

Some dissension developed among the ranks of the engineers. A few thought that the threatened action was conceived in confused and emotional thinking, that it was unprofessional, and that it was unfair to take advantage of the company during an emergency. Another minority favored a company proposal that the engineers accept straight time pay for the hours worked while they continued to negotiate for the additional half time despite the leaders' objection based on strategic grounds, that such a temporary settlement would compromise the union's position seriously.

Then the union surveyed its exempt members to determine

if any had performed nonexempt work during this period. Such work would automatically require the payment of time and one-half if the work exceeded the minimum amounts established for professional employees by the Fair Labor Standards Act. When the individuals refused to have their cases cited, the union was forced to abandon this tactic. A company announcement that it intended to approach individual employees on the unresolved matter was matched by a union threat to file an unfair labor practice with the NLRB if the company carried out its intentions. Later the union decided it could do no better than to accept the company's offer of individual C time or straight time.

Notwithstanding the success of the company's bargaining efforts, one management person commented, "To say the least, the affair created a great deal of animosity." In a final effort to harass the company and make its point the union urged every one of its members to choose C time.

This company would like to get away from even the C time policy. It would extend salary *ranges* 6% to 10% and eliminate any extra pay or time off for overtime. Management thought that it would be tough to accomplish this change under collective bargaining. "We don't have anything we want to give them in exchange." Management did not believe that the union would place any significant value on the extension of the ranges without specific adjustment of actual salaries paid.

Scheduling and Obtaining Overtime

Is overtime compulsory or voluntary for the engineer? In all but a very few agreements, overtime would appear to be compulsory, although this was not stated in so many words. Only one firm had a voluntary provision in the contract. The agreement states: "Except in emergencies, an employee may not be required to work more than 40 hours in any 'regular week,' or on recognized holidays, or on 'scheduled days off.'" This clause, which has been in the collective agreement for several years, apparently does not satisfy the union officers, who reported in an interview that despite the language of the contract men have been pressed to work overtime; and that when engineers have failed to work overtime at their supervisor's request, they have been called uncooperative and unpatriotic, and informed that their attitudes would affect their merit increase. A spokesman for the company, who thought that the overtime option presented no material bar to scheduling overtime, stated that "engineers should not throw the contract back at the company but rather should meet their responsibilities."

During negotiations in 1958 the union sought to substitute the following language for the clause quoted above:

> An employee may, without prejudice, decline to work more than 40 hours in any "regular work week," or on recognized holidays, or on "scheduled days off." It is understood, however, that when an emergency arises in connection with a project, the obligations of an engineer's professional relationship with the company will, as a matter of course, cause him to carefully consider the company's needs before refusing to comply with an overtime request.

The clause "played a big part in negotiations." The union merely wanted to clarify the engineer's obligation to work overtime to make it clear that he could *in practice* decline his supervisor's request for overtime, and that he could do so without prejudice. When a spokesman from engineering management said he thought that management could agree that overtime was not compulsory, he was questioned by a union official whether he thought in fact that the supervisor's rating of the man for merit purposes would not be influenced by the man's decision to decline overtime. The spokesman replied that since supervisors were human, naturally the supervisor's appraisal of the man would be affected. To the union the engineering manager's reply illustrated the futility of trying to secure other job rights for the individual engineer as long as the merit review was based on the subjective feelings of the supervisor rather than upon objective criteria of performance. The union assured management that as professionals, the engineers on their own would act responsibly in meeting legitimate overtime requirements. Members of the union elaborated the point along the following lines:

> The company has not really lost anything by making overtime voluntary. Sure, there are occasional refusals. There are basically two kinds of reasons. First, the engineer may feel the request for overtime is ridiculous, for example, when a supervisor feels it looks better to have a lot of men on the job. In this instance the supervisor will normally not make a show if a man refuses; he just drops it there. Second, an engineer may see the need for overtime, but have good personal reasons for refusing. This guy will work all the harder during regular hours. The engineer feels responsible for his work. The point is the engineer doesn't refuse without good reason. He doesn't want to antagonize the supervisor. About 95% will go along.

There was no significant change in the 1958 contract.

While the voluntary overtime provision is clearly the exception to the rule (and is itself not completely effective in practice), union officials in several companies firmly believe that the presence of the union tends to prevent supervision from placing unreasonable overtime demands on the engineers.

Generally the engineering unions have not been concerned with the question of distributing overtime, primarily because men are on assignments with durations from two weeks to over one year. If overtime is called for, it is required on specific projects and therefore required of the engineers assigned to those projects, and there is usually no question about *who* should work overtime. Nevertheless, one union has taken the precaution to secure a clause from the company agreeing that overtime will not be used as a method of discrimination either for or against an employee.

Out-of-Plant Service Payments

By the very nature of engineering work, engineering departments must frequently engage in field service, sometimes at far-flung field stations. This is particularly true of the engineering departments engaged in military work. The location of these field stations many times inflict unusual hardships and inconveniences upon the engineers who are assigned to these departments, giving many unions a reason for negotiating detailed provisions on bonus pay and expenses for field service. Other unions have sought such provisions but have not given them priority among bargaining demands. These out-of-plant provisions have figured importantly in union-management relations in one company, Company A.

In negotiating its first contract in 1951, the union obtained a 10% bonus for all employees on out-of-plant assignments, regardless of work station. A few engineers were located at remote field test stations, but many were assigned to liaison work in the plant of a West Coast aircraft company, an assignment which normally would not require any bonus pay. After 1954 the company received mounting pressure from the Air Force to bring its costs back into line with competitors. According to a company spokesman, an Air Force policy change announced in December 1954 made any out-of-plant bonus negotiated after that date nonrecuperable.

In December 1955, after a three-month strike, the company eliminated the flat 10% bonus, substituting a provision whereby if either the company or the union wished to establish, revise, or discontinue an out-of-plant pay allowance the matter would be subject to negotiation. If no agreement was reached, the company could take action, and the union could grieve and arbitrate. Shortly thereafter the union submitted a list of active out-of-plant sites and proposed an allowance for each, but management rejected all but the Alaska site. The union selected the dispute over one site, China Lake, California, to process through the grievance procedure. Management held to its position of zero allowance and the issue reached arbitration December 1956. The arbitrator did not award an allowance, but in a compromise move the company agreed to increase the per diem rate applied to China Lake.

By negotiating a removal of all reference to a bonus in 1958, Company A was able to make another gain and to place itself in a position to base its bonus policy on (a) what competition at the field service base pays, and (b) what incentive is required to get the company's engineers to accept the field assignment.

Until recently, another costly feature of Company A's out-of-plant service was the requirement that the company reimburse employees for all reasonable expenses they incurred while out-of-plant. With this arrangement the company's costs consistently exceeded those of other companies and those normally allowed by the military contractors. Under pressure from the government the company repeatedly sought to change over to a per diem basis. In 1956, anticipating rulings by the government that would deny allowance for excessive expenses on current field service work, the company unilaterally adopted a uniform expense policy, which provided for per diem of $14 for the first 90 days, a practice that clearly differed materially from the contractual requirement to pay for reasonable expenses. An arbitrator ruled this policy illegal.

By 1957 when the Air Force told the company that no future contracts would cover the liberal provisions of the union agreement, the relationship between the union and management had improved materially. The company was able to sit down with the union and explain the implications of the tightened Air Force policy on reimbursement for field service, on the one hand, and the company's need to negotiate new large-scale services contracts, on the other. The company stated that it would not consider incurring the losses which would result under the union agreement; and that it would have to make arrangements to subcontract the field work, despite its preference not to build up a competitor's competence in that work.

Appreciating fully the company's competitive position, the union opened the contract to negotiate a generally less liberal field service provision; for example, per diem would be set unilaterally by management but would have to be stated in the job posting and be applied impartially to anyone filling the job.

In other companies, where the contract does not cover out-of-plant pay and expenses, the union may influence the administration of company practices in this area by inducing the company to detail and publicize its practices, and by processing individual grievances. Finally, the union's very existence at the home plant may be an influencing factor. According to one manager, the company gave the engineers transferred to out-of-plant sites much better packages of insurance, overtime compensation, expenses, and bonuses because of the "silent threat of organization" at the sites.

Fringes

Fringes that engineering unions have attempted to negotiate include additional holidays, extended vacation benefits, pension improvement, additional sick leave, and insurance improvements. Their efforts have met with limited success pursuant to four primary objectives:

1. Separate and differential treatment. Plans tailored to engineers' needs.
2. Getting the most benefit for the cost.
3. Increasing the benefit programs.
4. Incorporating the benefit plans into the union contract.

Certain negotiation requests are related only to one or another of the above goals, but frequently, of course, these objectives merge in one proposal. Let us look at two illustrative experiences.

Several engineers' unions have successfully sponsored the

idea of major medical or catastrophe insurance as more suitable to the engineers' needs than the regular medical plans covering shop employees. A manager in one company testified, "The engineers accelerated study of the extended medical plans, finally inducing the company to put it into effect." The labor relations director for another company commented, "Without a separate voice this type of medical scheme would not have been considered." This union was able to achieve a measure of success in each of its four objectives listed above.

One other instance, involving pensions, deserves special attention. After several unsuccessful attempts to negotiate the pension plan included among the union's bargaining objectives each year, the union made a pension plan the *only* proposal one year. This stratagem did not produce immediate results, but representatives of both parties were in agreement that it had hastened the preparation and introduction of a pension plan subsequently adopted.

In general terms, the key to the unions' successes in the area of benefits are their efforts at systematic determination of the engineers' needs, independent investigation of plans available, and thorough comparative analysis of the available plans. Because any plan they negotiate will almost always be extended to other salaried groups, the engineers often receive crucial support in these efforts from individuals in management who serve as their "lawyers inside the house."

At the same time, the companies exercise more initiative with fringe benefits than in other areas of employee compensation. The "negotiation" of benefits in one company described below is a pattern that is also followed in others.

A company introduced an Educational Assistance Program, effective January 1, 1957. On January 25 the union informed the company by letter that it regarded the program as desirable but that it was perturbed by the failure of the company to follow proper and estabished procedures in the promulgation of the plan; that is, by the company's failure to negotiate. The union also suggested that the company's course of action constituted an unfair labor practice. The company had the initiative, however, and intended to keep it; if anyone was obstructing progress, it was the union! The company answered:

> We regret that you object to our promulgation of the program for . . . [the union] represented employees. In our opinion, the program is not a subject for mandatory bargaining, and since the association had not, at the time the program was made effective, introduced a proposal relating to educational assistance into the bargaining process, we do not agree that the company committed an unfair labor practice. . . .
>
> Prior to receipt of your letter, the company received 23 applications. . . . The company considers itself committed to these individuals involved. . . .
>
> In regard to future application of the program to . . . [the union] represented employees, the company representatives will be pleased to discuss the subject with the association at your earliest convenience. In the meantime, all applications received from . . . [union] represented people since receipt of your letter will be held in abeyance, and the employees concerned will be advised to that effect.

The union immediately proposed inclusion of the program in the contract, and the company agreed.

Patent Rights and Allowances

Patent payments were an important objective for the engineers' unions during their early history when most of the provisions covering patent payments were negotiated. In certain cases the company seemed to have no objection to patent allowances and sometimes even favored them. In other cases the union was granted the allowance provision only after several bargaining attempts.

One condition of employment for engineers in most industrial plants, irrespective of their unionized status, is the signing of a patent agreement in which the engineer guarantees to sign and execute all documents necessary to assign the employer the right to benefit from his invention. Provisions covering the signing of individual patent agreements are contained in the majority of the union agreements studied. One engineering union contract differentiates between inventions "directly applicable to the employer's business" and those that are not. The latter remain the property of the inventor, provided that the employer has licensing rights at "a royalty no greater than that paid any other licensee under the same patent." Other contracts differentiate between inventions resulting from research on a private basis and work done for the company.

About half of the unions have obtained provisions for payment of fixed allowances for an invention, amounts to individual inventors ranging from $25 to $100. They seek the patent allowance for the following reasons listed by one union:

1. Improves employee-company relations.
2. Improves engineer morale. Holds good engineers.
3. Stimulates new and better ideas.
4. Produces more disclosures and inventions.
5. Improves disclosures.
6. Pays for the extracurricular work of preparing disclosures and checking drafts.
7. Aids patent attorney in asking for prompt approval.

Those companies that oppose the patent bonus give many reasons for their position, although it is not clear whether the apprehensions expressed are borne out by practice in those companies with the bonuses. They believe the patent bonus destroys team effort, encourages an individual to keep his ideas to himself, brings forth a large number of ideas which cannot be used, can be a source of friction, and so forth.

Generally the disagreements arising out of the patent provisions are not processed through the normal grievance machinery. There are apparently very few disputes of this type. One contract specifically prohibits the use of the grievance procedure to settle patent disputes. Another authorizes the use of the grievance machinery except that such disputes cannot be arbitrated. The subject of patent rights and bonuses has received much less attention in recent years.

Professional Benefits and Recognition

Professional Benefits

Professional fringe demands, such as payment of professional society dues by the company, paid time off to attend meetings of professional societies, and tuition refunds, stem directly from the engineers' professional consciousness. Regarding dues, the practices in this area range from payment of full dues to the payment of no dues. Pay while attending meetings of the societies is provided by a few contracts but is not common. Companies prefer to retain the right to select individuals to send to such meetings, expenses paid, as a reward and incentive for superior performance. Tuition refund to employees taking courses related to their work outside working hours is commonly a term of the engineering contract. These fringes are sought by the engineering unions as a method of securing employer recognition of their professional status, more than for their money value. Nor has the money value of these provisions been significant to the company, with one exception which will be discussed shortly. Most companies believe that these professional fringes serve the company's interests as well, but in many cases they were prompted by the union to see these interests and establish the professional fringes.

At least one instance can be cited where a concession on a professional fringe turned out to be "a mistake" for the company. This company had liberalized the tuition refund provision repeatedly at the union's request. In 1956 the company agreed to grant full refund of tuition, fees, and essential materials, eliminating any limit on the total amount per person per year. With this incentive, many more engineers took advantage of the plan (and each took more advantage!) than the company had anticipated. There were some abuses—men taking courses unrelated to their jobs—and the total cost ran to $600,000 per year, against the $150,000 to $200,000 budgeted by the company. After a period during which the plan was loosely administered, the company tightened up and refunded only for those courses of direct benefit on the job or those required toward a specific engineering degree. As a result several grievances, including a few successful ones, were filed by individuals who believed they were entitled to refunds that had been denied. Thus, this plan turned out to be costly, difficult to administer, and a source of friction in employee relations. Finally in negotiations in 1958 the company set a limit of $150 per semester, an action which constituted "taking something away" from the engineers and consequently was an irritant to union relations.

Although the unions have often been the initiating party regarding professional fringes, this area has not been the subject of significant controversy. In fact, many companies have responded favorably to requests for a number of these special fringes.

Professional Recognition

Much of an engineer's reward for work is recognition; and his most valued asset is his professional reputation. One union requested that engineers receive recognition for their reports which were circulated outside the company. Specifically the union asked that the names of the engineers involved be attached to the report, a practice which was prevalent in other companies at that time. The company argued that reports are company property and are normally a product of the work of too many people to assign responsibility correctly. The company also contended that the recognition of the drafters of a report would invite customers and other interested parties to contact the engineers directly, and thereby facilitate pirating.

The issue was finally resolved to the union's satisfaction in the 1956 negotiations by a verbal agreement which the union labeled "a notable accomplishment." According to the agreement, if up to five names of engineers are involved the names will be published. A union official estimates that the policy affects 30% of the company's engineers—those in basic research and development and new product preliminary investigation. In research and development each individual contributes to about 10 to 12 reports a year that would qualify him for having his name published. In the new product field an individual will share responsibility for three to four reports per year.

Working Conditions

The unions use publicity and persuasion to bring about improvements in working conditions. There are innumerable instances that could be cited where the unions have complained about working conditions, with varying degrees of success. They include:

a. an overheated and stuffy department
b. extreme conditions of noise, dirt, and crowding of a section located centrally in a machining area
c. an overcrowded work area
d. an environmental and vibration test machine in the middle of an engineer office area
e. rubber seat cushions that need cleaning
f. engineering work area adjacent to a large door that had to be opened every 25 minutes letting in the cold wind
g. the odor, appearance, and atmosphere of a cafeteria at an engineering plant

Engineering management, especially, is willing to grant that the union has a legitimate interest in matters of working conditions. In fact, engineering management often uses the union as a bargaining tool to get conditions improved in their section. Before the union entered, many a supervisor would like to have been able to alleviate certain annoying conditions but was not able to obtain action. Now he joins in with his men in encouraging the union to approach management.

Time Off for Union Activity

Most of the agreements allow certain representatives of the union to investigate and process grievances without loss of pay. One contract qualified this privilege by stating, "except in the event that the time so spent becomes excessive." Under another contract the union representative can absent himself from his work unless the absence would be "impracticable from the standpoint of performance of the group of which the representative is a part."

A limit may be placed on the amount of union time spent by the union on investigating and processing grievances; for example, one agreement allows five hours per week each for 27 section representatives or a total of 135 hours per week and also allows seven grievance committeemen a pool of a maximum of 140 hours per week. The full allowance of hours is equivalent to almost six and a half full time employees, a little less than 1% of the payroll.

A few companies give the union representatives broader license to handle union matters during working hours. One agreement permits representatives (one for every 50 employees) to use "a reasonable amount of time during working hours in the performance of their duties required in the administration of this agreement. . . ." The representatives must inform supervision whenever it becomes necessary for them to leave their work area. Other agreements require permission to leave the work area. In one company management decided that a supervisor who complained about a representative leaving his desk was "cutting it too thin," so they agreed that the requirement that "supervision must be informed" applied to leaving the building.

The broadest statement of union activity permissible on company time was contained in the following clause:

> A representative may devote time (without loss of pay) during his normal working hours to do such association work as may be necessary or proper, provided, that should the amount of time spent or character of work be unreasonable or unwarranted, this privilege may be revoked by the company.

There were, however, several indications that the practices in the above companies bear little relationship to these provisions. At one extreme, a contract prohibits any union work or activities other than grievance processing to be conducted on company time, though in practice many purely internal union matters are performed by men who check out on grievance activities. At the other extreme, in a company where the union has the broadest contractual license to engage in union work on company time, the union uses very little time even for grievances. In still another company, the president of the engineers' union complained about the trouble he had in getting representatives to spend any time on union activities.

Negotiations represent another area where the companies may be paying for time lost from engineering work. Several companies make it a practice to pay for the time spent in negotiating sessions held during the regular work day. A few pay only half of the union representatives' normal rate of pay. Others do not make any provision for compensation during negotiating sessions.

How much total time lost at the companies' expense is actually involved in these negotiation and grievance activities? Few companies were willing to quote an amount. An executive in one company with 2,000 in the engineering bargaining unit thought that the total time spent by the union in one year cost the company about $10,000 to $15,000. We cannot quote any other amounts, but we can cite a few relevant factors. Negotiations tend to be long-drawn-out affairs, perhaps a dozen or more meetings over three months. Grievances tend to be few and far between, but the occasional grievance may be relatively time consuming. An engineer's time has a high price tag on it, but basically he is reluctant to take time away from his work. On one occasion, in the middle of a tense negotiating session, one of the union negotiators excused himself because he had a hot project back at his desk.

Managements and supervisors have from time to time objected to the amount of time consumed on grievance and union activity. A few grievances have been filed by union representatives who have been denied the time off or who have been penalized because of their recent activity. In one situation the company filed a grievance under the past practices clause, alleging that the number of grievances being submitted was abnormally large, exceeding any past practices. The company undoubtedly had an eye on the amount of time spent in grievance work.

Other related issues have arisen. Many of the unions that were permitted in their early years to distribute their publications and other literature on company premises and during working hours have since been denied that privilege, thereby forcing the unions to rely completely upon the U.S. mail. Management has in each case argued that too much company time was consumed by the distribution and reading of the literature.

Where the parties have agreed that literature can be distributed on company premises, they may nevertheless disagree over what facilities should be made available for union use. In 1953 one union reported an attempt on the part of the company to deny them the use of a platform bicycle for distributing union literature throughout the plant. The use of the bicycle speeded up the dissemination of flyers and other material which at that time happened to be strongly anti-company. The company wanted to withdraw the use of the bicycle on the grounds that the CIO shop union did not have the use of one. After an investigation revealed that the CIO had the use of fork trucks and an in-plant office, the company dropped its objection to the bicycle. At another time the company protested the union's use of the company mail system.

Summary and Conclusion

The engineering unions have shown less interest than other unions in obtaining improvements in the areas of premium pay and fringe benefits. In order to permit the point to be made efficiently, consider a conclusion of a Brookings study: "Unions have *spearheaded* the liberalization of *major* benefits, particularly vacations, paid holidays, and overtime and premium pay. They are working increasingly for liberalization of sickness, medical, and pension plans. . . ."[3] [emphasis added.] This statement, except in its reference to overtime pay would not hold for the engineering unions.[4] Where the latter have shown an interest in employee benefits, their greater influence has been to improve the use of funds applied to employee benefits rather than to raise the over-all level of the benefits. As we have seen, however, the unions have made serious attempts to establish the principle of premium pay for overtime. Moreover, certain *minor* fringe issues have entered into the collective bargaining relationships studied.

All the overtime issues discussed—distinguishing between casual and scheduled overtime; preventing inequities from developing between engineers and supervisors; using voluntary overtime as a factor for merit purposes; determining when overtime is actually required by the workload and not merely generated by the engineer in one situation or by su-

[3] Slichter, Healy, and Livernash, *The Impact of Collective Bargaining on Management*, p. 443.

[4] It has been suggested to me that this may be merely a matter of priorities. In the case of industrial unions interest in fringes began somewhat late; and engineering unions might well become more interested when their more immediate objectives have been met.

pervision in another—all these issues, and others, emphasize the administrative difficulties of overtime payment. That the engineering unions are largely responsible for the overtime payment policies is generally conceded by management. Although several large engineering employers who do not have engineering unions are known to have policies of extending overtime pay under certain circumstances, the sequence and pattern of adoption of such policies suggest that the engineering unions through the companies they have organized have been influential here, too. No manager will venture an estimate as to just how much direct cost the overtime pay practices cause. All seem to agree, however, with the statement of one person who said, "Premium pay is no longer a penalty to the company, it's a gravy item. If the amount of overtime work is cut back, the engineers and the union squawk." Only one unhappy union had none of the gravy, merely compensating time off.

The issue of compulsory versus voluntary overtime has been given little attention by the parties, as a rule. Where the union has obtained some option in the contract, supervisors are still able to obtain necessary or "legitimate" overtime hours: first, because the merit review indirectly places pressure on the engineer to do what is expected of him; second, because the engineer has a genuine interest in meeting project deadlines. Whenever the business need for overtime is questionable, however (the supervisor may only be trying to *look* busy), the engineers are more apt to refuse such overtime under collective bargaining whether they have an option clause or not.

The amount of out-of-plant service payments, bonuses, and per diem, and the conditions under which they are paid, were crucial issues in one company whose costs in this respect remained out of line for six years. The company then came under serious pressure from the Air Force. Fortunately the company had made progress in developing an accommodative relationship with the union, and so was able to negotiate tighter payment policies with very little discontent or bitterness. In the majority of companies field service payments provisions have not been negotiated with the unions, but the unions encourage the companies to publish their practices. They also may process individual grievances.

In the area of such fringe benefits as holidays, vacations, pensions, sick leave, and insurance, the companies continue to initiate most of the improvements. Moreover, a separate study is not required to note that these changes in unionized companies merely correspond to those improvements being made in the larger population of nonunionized engineering employers. The unions are not without suggestions in this area, but their ideas usually sell on their merits, and whatever changes result from their activity probably are regarded favorably by management. Sometimes the parties have disagreed about whether a plan should be incorporated in the union agreement, but these instances have not been serious.

In two other areas—patent rights and allowances and professional benefits—the union has shared responsibility for improvement affecting the engineers. In their early histories the unions demonstrated great interest in these issues, but this interest has declined in recent years. One management was persuaded to add the names of the authors to reports circulated outside the company, a form of recognition which had already been practiced voluntarily by many other companies. Collective bargaining has resulted in a multitude of minor improvements in working conditions, primarily it would seem because it gives lower levels of management some leverage in expediting these improvements.

Some engineering time is lost to collective bargaining, to be sure, but reportedly it is a negligible amount in most cases. Managers did not volunteer this as an effect of unionization; it was referred to as an "overhead item." Managements may be reticent on this point because it is an item they would not want their military contractors to dwell upon when considering their bids against the bids of nonunionized companies.

CHAPTER V

Salary Structure

IN THEIR MOST simplified form the schedules of salaries for engineers consist of a series of overlapping salary ranges corresponding to a small number of hierarchical classifications, such as those in the following series: Assistant Engineer, Associate Engineer, Engineer, and Senior Engineer.[1] Within these classifications engineers are frequently given designations associated with their functional activities, such as chemist, materials testing, metallurgist, standards, design, quality control, systems, environmental, and so on. A particular functional activity may or may not contain positions at all the classification levels. If it does, the promotional lines are clear to even the casual observer. More often the titles of jobs in a promotional sequence bear no apparent resemblance one to the other, except to those conversant with the engineering activities themselves. The approximate monthly rate ranges in a typical salary structure with four classification levels in 1957 were: first level, $400 to $520; second level, $470 to $720; third level, $600 to $970; fourth level, $736 to $1,136. The maximum of each range approximated the mid-point of the next higher range.

In this chapter we shall focus on several aspects of salary structure: rationalization of the salary structure; administration of the salary structure, including promotions; and ex-

1 The reader interested in the general subject of salary administrative practices in engineering and research organizations may refer to John W. Riegel, *Administration of Salaries for Engineers and Scientists,* Report No. 8, Ann Arbor, Michigan: Bureau of Industrial Relations, University of Michigan. Riegel reports the findings of a study of ten nonunionized companies conducted mainly by interviews of executives, supervisors, and nonsupervisory employees.

panding the salary structure. A section will be devoted to each topic. Procedures for moving individuals through a given salary range will be deferred until a later chapter.

Rationalization of Salary Structure

There was no formal salary structure and no systematic salary administration before unionization in most of the companies studied. Engineers were paid "what they were worth." Once unionized, the companies were induced to rationalize and formalize their practices in this area. That the salary matters had become subject to collective bargaining was sufficient reason for an overhaul in this area, but the unions placed even more direct pressure for change. High on their bargaining agendas were requests for the development and publication of position descriptions, the completion of position evaluation studies, and the development of definite salary ranges for all engineering positions.[2]

Companies generally complied with the unions' demands, although some did so only with great reluctance. One company waited for an arbitration ruling to the effect that the matter was bargainable before it would disclose its position descriptions. Position evaluation was sometimes performed by a joint union-management committee; more often, however, it was completed by management and then submitted to the union. The unions, which did not as a rule have much influence over the specific results of these studies or the salary schedules developed from them, were nevertheless satisfied with having established a more explicit framework for engineering salaries.

The union claims several advantages for the engineers under a formal salary classification system, some of which may be construed as disadvantages for the companies: the lines of

2 "Position description" and "position evaluation" (rather than "job description" and "job evaluation") are the terms frequently used in engineering salary administration since "position" more aptly connotes a level of responsibility whereas "job" would be used if it were intended to represent a set of specific tasks.

nonsupervisory advancement are well defined for the individual; the range of rates available to the engineer on a merit basis without promotions is stated explicitly; the duties and responsibilities for different levels are spelled out, better enabling the individual to determine for himself whether he is being correctly paid and classified for the work he is doing.

Administration of the Salary Structure

Promotion Practices

Before we turn to a discussion of some of the above mentioned difficulties in administration caused by formalizing the salary classification scheme, we should familiarize ourselves with how men typically move through the salary structure. In the following account by one manager, note particularly the level of work associated with each classification and the importance of length of engineering experience in promotions.

> A man is hired and taken from the training course as an Assistant Engineer. As such he is helping others design something. His salary will be increased periodically until he hits the maximum in that range. Theoretically we review the man's performance to see whether he is capable of doing Associate Engineers' work; it would normally require about two years to reach that level. Practically a man will go to Associate Engineer in about one year; right now it is averaging one year and three months.
>
> An Associate Engineer can take an assignment from a more senior engineer and complete it without close supervision. Usually a man will spend about four years as an Associate Engineer. More consideration is given to the promotion to an Engineer classification than to an Associate Engineer. Management will say no to 1% or 2%. An Engineer is capable of designing a major part of a system or a complete small unit by himself, although this does not hold for an Engineer who is a specialist in one area.
>
> From an Engineer classification a man may progress a little

> further up the technical ladder, or he may go into supervisory ranks. A man who continued to advance technically may be promoted to Senior Engineer after five to seven years as an Engineer. He would be, on the other hand, the more studious engineer, interested in equipment. After an engineer hits the middle of the Engineer bracket, he may be moved across into the supervisory category, if he possesses the qualifications—if he thinks the way the people in the group think and is well liked—and if he is interested.

Thus, the theory and the practice of the salary structure differ. Theoretically, a different level of duties and responsibilities is associated with each classification in a promotional ladder. In practice, the engineer is given more complex assignments and greater responsibility as he demonstrates the required capabilities; and meanwhile, his salary is also being advanced, but not necessarily at exactly the pace at which the level of work performed is rising. There would be, at best, a constant lag between changes in duties and adjustments in salary. More likely, the *rate* of salary advancement is materially faster or slower than that anticipated by the formal classification system. Whether the rate is faster or is slower depends upon the salary practices required of the company in order to recruit, maintain, and motivate the engineering force. An engineer becomes eligible for promotion to the next higher classification and title after his salary has passed the mid-point in his current classification rate range, his eligibility increasing progressively as he approaches the maximum in his classification. Often, it is more correct to think (a) that an engineer's classification is determined by his salary than it is to assume (b) that his salary results from his placement in a given classification, such placement being determined by the level of work he performs.

In effect, the movement from one classification to another is barely distinguishable from the upward movement within the salary range; that is, the classification promotion is no more likely to coincide with a change in duties or responsibilities than is the merit raise. Nor are the considerations entering into the supervisor's decision to promote and his decision to give a merit raise substantially different. The movement from one classification to another does, however, involve a new position title. Therefore, it can provide, if management desires, a discrete control point, an opportunity for more rigorous scrutiny of the individual's present capabilities and his potential for development. Accordingly most companies *attempt* to treat merit raises and promotions somewhat differently in the sense that they require of the supervisor a little more evidence to support his promotion recommendations. But the point is that the difference, if any, is one of degree, not kind. For this reason and inasmuch as salary adjustment is involved in both cases, the discussion of the merit review system in Chapter VII can also be assumed to apply to promotions.

Two further aspects of the promotion procedures should be mentioned here. First, unions have occasionally sought formal posting and bidding procedures for filling vacancies. Second, they have tried to obtain preferential treatment for current employees over outsiders. However, the few provisions covering these matters should be placed in perspective. They apply to only a small proportion of the promotions that occur within the bargaining unit—those where specific positions are declared vacant, and then filled. In the engineering departments, a position is an elusive concept, because in a sense it exists only when it is filled. For example, a promotion to the rank of Senior Engineer normally does not depend upon the existence of a vacancy, but rather on having a man who should be promoted. At the same time the man who is hired from the outside as a Senior Engineer is hired because of a general need for this quality of engineer, not because any vacancy exists. In view of these factors it can readily be seen why these particular provisions covering promotion have been of little significance to management.

Classification Grievances

The definition of duties and responsibilities for different levels of engineering can cause a company difficulty. The publication of job descriptions and the incorporation of these into the collective agreement give occasion for individuals to disagree with their classification—sometimes on the grounds that they meet or surpass the minimum qualifications for a higher classification; at other times that the work they are currently performing is that of a higher classification. There have been innumerable such disagreements, often on a friendly basis, that have occurred between engineers and their supervisors without being filed as grievances. In recent years disagreements over classification in a few companies have been processed through the formal grievance machinery. An account of one of these grievances will illustrate the difficulties that can be encountered under collective bargaining in administering a promotion system based on published classifications. The grievance discussed below occurred in a heterogeneous unit and involved a subprofessional claiming he was entitled to the classification of the first level engineer.

A Sample Grievance. The grievance was one of several grievances over job assignments and promotions contained in the files of one engineering union for 1958. It involved an individual, whom we shall call Davis, in an Engineering Aide classification (subprofessional). He demanded that he be promoted to Assistant Engineer (professional) immediately, on the grounds that he was doing work of the higher classification. Davis, who had two years of college and had completed additional courses on subjects such as transformers and servo mechanisms, was hired as an Engineering Aide in May 1957. From June 1957 to February 1958 he was assigned work on capacitators and components clearly within the Engineering Aide classification. Beginning in March 1958 he was assigned a different job, designing amplifiers. Other men who reported to the same supervisor and who were doing the same type of work were Assistant Engineers.

Management's answer to the grievance was that the work he was performing was "not of such scope as to warrant an engineering classification" and that he did not have sufficient background. In later proceedings the company elaborated the two points. After acknowledging that "Employees who show ability are given more extensive and higher duties in the course of time [and] when the extent of the duties reaches the next higher classification, they may be given promotions. . . ." the company spokesman stated:

> All of the work which an Engineer Aide does is work which is within the duties of an Engineer. However, what the Engineer Aide does are the simpler duties of the Engineer or duties which do not involve the broad range of knowledge on all fields which the Engineer must have. Other than routine work of an Engineering Aide, of the lower levels of skill exercised in the Engineering Aide classification—Davis has designed and built a feed back amplifier. This is work, however, which is also done by Senior Lab Technicians. The latter classification consists of technicians in the salary bargaining unit represented by [the production and maintenance union]. That classification clearly is below that of Engineer and does not even qualify for a professional status. The designing of a feed back amplifier is only one part of the field of circuit design which in turn is only a part of the area with which an electrical engineer must be familiar. Thus, Mr. Davis has come nowhere near demonstrating the broad scope of knowledge which an Assistant Engineer must have.
>
> Moreover, an Assistant Engineer must have knowledge or training equivalent to that of a B.S. which he does not have. Nor does he have the equivalent.
>
> The job description of the Assistant Engineer provides: "Solves a variety of well-defined engineering problems for which the solution is straightforward, involving one area within a field of engineering or applied science.

"Performs engineering work which requires a knowledge and understanding of one broad field of science equivalent to that usually associated with a bachelor's degree in engineering or applied science from an accredited college."

The job description for an Engineering Aide has the following educational requirements:

"Requires the knowledge and understanding usually associated with the first three years of college mathematics."

It happens that in this instance the grievance was not decided on its merits. The company was able to obtain a court stay of arbitration on the grounds that the promotion being questioned was actually a form of merit increase, which was excluded from the arbitration machinery by the collective agreement. Management is not always that fortunate.

The Union's Position. The unions do not support such promotion grievances with only the specific case under review in mind. They believe it is necessary to stand vigil over the entire classification system which could be "rendered meaningless" if the companies' use of employees out of classification were permitted to continue unrestrained. The practice could be particularly troublesome if a reversal in manpower supply and demand conditions caused a downward pressure on engineering salaries. Unionized companies probably would not be able to cut the salary structure, but they could reduce the volume of merit increases, and make fewer promotions. Gradually, the work in the higher classifications could fall to employees who were not being upgraded from lower classifications, unless the union had established a precedent for stricter observance of classifications.

The Company's Interest. Managements have become concerned about the increasing tendency for engineering bargaining unit employees to file classification grievances. The upgrading grievance can raise havoc in an engineering department because of the limits on management flexibility implicit in such a grievance. Flexibility to administer a constantly changing engineering program is dependent upon management's ability to assign individuals over a period of time a variety of tasks, at differing levels of complexity. Equally important is the flexibility required to develop technical personnel. Such development likewise depends upon management's ability to broaden the individual's experience through assignment to a variety of tasks, and to increase his skill through occasional assignment to more complex tasks. It would be extremely difficult to write job descriptions that allow the flexibilities required. One cannot anticipate in the description the many tasks that any given individual will be expected to perform during a future period of time. Moreover, even if one could anticipate an individual's future assignments, the job description drawn up around those assignments would not be applicable to other employees. Few people would suggest that completely individualized job descriptions are appropriate for salary classification purposes.

It should be noted that the engineering employees do not take a strict view toward assignments that fall outside their occupational classification, inasmuch as they recognize how important this experience is to professional development and future promotions. Likewise, they normally do not complain about assignment to higher classified work within their occupation since this usually presages a promotion. But occasionally a man becomes impatient waiting for the promotion or actually believes he is being exploited. He grieves, not to be relieved of the higher rated duties, but rather for promotion.

Effects of Classification Grievances. What are the effects of these grievances? Even if the company has a record of winning these grievances, management is inclined to place limitations on it own flexibility—assigning fewer Engineering Aides to Assistant Engineer duties, for example; and to promote after a shorter "demonstration period"—upgrading the Engineering Aide to Assistant Engineer sooner, for example.

Another way of avoiding grievances that can be used at the lower level of jobs in the engineering organization is to sever the lines of promotions between classifications. In our example this would mean denying Engineering Aides access to Assistant Engineer positions. The last step has the important disadvantage of removing one incentive to do outstanding work at the Engineering Aide level.

There is one other problem. The fact that job evaluation and classification is subject to collective bargaining also encourages union demands for reclassification of specific jobs. Some of the requests are granted, perhaps compromising the company's best interest in a minor way. But equally important for the company are the demands which are not granted and which result in dissatisfaction among the employees affected.

Expansion of the Salary Structure[3]

The compression of engineering salaries which resulted from flat across-the-board cents-per-hour increases during and after World War II gave the newly organized engineering unions one of their principal reasons for existence: to reverse the trend of narrowing salary differentials. They have adopted four lines of attack.

(1) At first they merely rejected the management offers of flat increases and insisted upon percentage increases.

(2) Later, they proposed unleveling increases, which favored the higher salary levels with larger percentage increases.

(3) In a less significant way they have tried to minimize the leveling tendency in merit distribution, by scolding the companies and supervision for not giving "equitable treat-

[3] The phrase "expansion of the salary structure" is commonly used by engineering unions to refer to the restoration of salary differentials which had been decreased. "Unleveling salaries" is another phrase peculiar to the industry which is used in the same sense.

ment" to the higher salary brackets. (There has been a tendency for supervisors to distribute proportionally more of the merit monies among the younger engineers in the lower salary brackets.)

(4) Finally, they have pressured for more generous salary treatment for engineering supervision, since supervisory salaries more or less place a ceiling on their own top brackets.

A review of the relevant histories of a few companies will illustrate the first two of the above efforts. The other two approaches, which have been less significant, will not be illustrated.

Percentage and Unleveling Increases

In the first case history we shall review, negotiations in 1945 and 1947 resulted in increases. The company urged flat across-the-board increases, but finally granted percentage increases of 10% (with a minimum of $30) in 1945, and 2.9% in 1947, as concessions to the union. In November 1947 the company negotiated a flat increase, arguing the fairness of this type of increase to meet the cost of living. The union had favored a percentage increase. When a union salary survey, completed in 1948, gave a clear indication of a narrowing differential between starting and over-ten-year experience salaries, the engineers stepped up their campaign for the percentage type of general increase. Despite the union's growing opposition, the company again negotiated a flat increase (the equivalent of five cents per hour) in the fall of 1948, this time on the grounds that such a small increase on a percentage basis (1.78%) would have led to "administrative difficulties and inequities." An increase in May 1949 was also flat—three and one-half cents per hour.

The first percentage increase to be negotiated after 1947 came in December 1950. The company offered the union five cents per hour, the amount the shop union had won. The union sought an unleveling sliding scale, the percentage increasing 2% for each $800 per year over the starting rate. The compromise—a straight 5%. Another percentage increase was granted by the company in September 1951.

The union in 1952 obtained its first salary expansion increase, over and above a 2.6% general increase. The expansion was based on the years of engineering experience—0.75% for engineers with one to two years up to 8.25% for 25 years.[4] The following year the union proposed a very pronounced sliding scale, from 12.5% for Senior Engineers to 0.0% for Assistant Engineers in addition to a 7.7% general increase. The company at first opposed any expansion, and then settled for a less dramatic increase of 3.1% for Senior Engineers to 0.0% for Assistant Engineers over and above the general increase. The overwhelming support the union received from the membership during these negotiations was demonstrated in a membership meeting during working hours. Significantly, the support derived from an almost unanimous interest in two issues:[5] (1) the salary expansion, although only 15% would receive the extra 3.1% and the majority less than 0.7%, and (2) whether the union had to take what the other unions had negotiated. The settlement in this company more than restored the differential eliminated by the three across-the-board increases between 1947 and 1950.

Another expansion increase of 1.25% for Senior Engineers to 0.0% for Assistant Engineers was gained in 1954. Between

[4] It should be emphasized that the important factor stressed in engineering salary evaluations is an engineer's total number of years of engineering experience, not his length of service with a particular company.

[5] This unanimity among the engineers from the bottom to the top of the salary structure contrasts sharply with the attitudes of production employees on the same issue when it has affected them. The clash between skilled and unskilled over differentials has threatened many production and maintenance unions. Probably the explanation for the differences in the two types of unionism lies in the fact that the junior engineers identify much more closely with the senior engineers with whom they have a common professional bond than do the unskilled with the skilled; also, there is more consistent upward mobility through the engineering classifications than from unskilled to semiskilled to skilled factory jobs.

1954 and 1958 all increases were percentages. Another "inequity adjustment," an expansion on the basis of salary figures, was granted in 1958 at the request of the union.

Thus, there can be no doubt that in the negotiations described the union's effect was to expand the salary structure. Other unions have placed similar demands for unleveling increases, but generally without quite the same degree of success achieved by the union in the above account.

The experience of one of these other companies included an interesting twist—the union temporarily reversed its charges that "leveling" had taken place. Salary compression had been an early issue between the union and the company. In 1956, however, after analyzing salary data provided by the company for the past 10 years, the union concluded that, contrary to its prior insistence that there had been a growing compression, the salary structure had *not* undergone any systematic change, at least until 1953. The salary relationships between engineers at various experience levels had remained relatively constant between World War II and 1953.

The union published these findings which contradicted its own previous pronouncements. The reaction from the membership was immediate and critical. Why had the union reversed its position, especially when it did not serve the union's interests? Did this not remove the need for the union? The union president answered:

> One of the most important reasons why . . . [The Association] is certified by the NLRB is that this status provides us with a legal right to salary data. Through an analysis of these data we can learn what the true facts are rather than what we fancy them to be. Once facts are established, however, the professional approach requires that we adjust our viewpoint and our actions to be compatible with those facts. Such a rational approach to the salary question is one of [The Association's] most important traditions. So, in this case [The Association] simply presented the facts as they were revealed by these studies.

The union did conclude, however, that compression had occurred after 1953. To be sure, the principle of percentage increases had long before been established; but new hire rates had now become the culprit, advancing more than general increases and thereby reducing the spread between the bottom and the various other experience and skill levels. In the 1956 negotiations the union made unleveling proposals based on the lag of general increases to starting salaries. The union requested that general salaries be pegged exactly to changes in the starting rate for engineers in order to prevent further compression from this source. In response, the company stressed its intention to deal with the unleveling problem through the merit system. The union did not approve of the idea inasmuch as it had no confidence in the ability of several hundred supervisors to achieve new salary relationships systematically.

In 1957 negotiations the union requested that 10% of the 13% which was required to eliminate accumulated compression after 1953 be given in two parts in a two-year contract. The company offered "a disappointing 2%" for unleveling. The membership accepted, but the union publication warned:

> The overwhelming acceptance vote on the offer is not interpreted as being enthusiasm for the unleveling portion of the offer. It is interpreted as an acceptance of the Executive Committee's analysis and recommendation for indulgence. Of the 10.6% who voted "no," 44% gave as their reason that the maximum amount of the unleveling was too small, 20% that the blanket increase was too small, 18% that the unleveling did not begin low enough, 12% that the money used for unleveling should have been distributed to the lower salaried engineers instead of the higher salaried ones, and 7% other reasons.

In other companies as well, compression continues to be a popular issue with the membership of professional unions;[6] but it is not so important a factor in collective bargaining as it was in the early and middle 1950's; the unions have largely made their point, and starting salaries have stabilized somewhat in recent years.

Consequences of Salary Expansion

Conceding that the unions' influence has been to expand the salary structure, has this effect been a favorable or an adverse one for the companies? It must be acknowledged that the narrowing of rate differentials after World War II was common among most if not all competing engineering organizations; and that the narrowing of engineering rates was a part of a leveling process occurring among and within virtually all income groups during the same period.[7] Managements referred to these prevailing trends in industry when rejecting the unions' remedies for the compression that had occurred. Regardless of the merits of the unions' arguments, the companies felt they could not get out of line with competition. Thus, to the extent that the unions have obtained increases in progressive percentages they have placed their respective companies out of line ahead of competition in the higher brackets, at least temporarily.[8]

The effects of the expansion on internal aspects of salary administration are just as important. To determine these effects, we would first need to know the optimum salary structure for a given company, that is, the ideal spread between

6 The professional societies, too, have deplored the decrease in the ratio of 5-year, 10-year, and 15-year salaries to starting rates. See National Society of Professional Engineers. *A Professional Look at the Engineer in Industry,* Washington, 1955, pp. 48–50.

7 See, for example: Harry Ober, "Occupational Wage Differentials, 1907–1947," *Monthly Labor Review,* Vol. 67 Number 2, August, 1948, pp. 127–134; L. G. Reynolds and C. H. Taft, *The Evolution of Wage Structure,* New Haven: Yale University Press, 1956.

8 This moderate reversal of the trend toward narrow differentials in unionized engineering departments was not completely out of joint with broader developments in our economy. According to Reynolds and Taft (op. cit., p. 325) the early 1950's saw a slowing down of the narrowing process and a stabilizing of occupational differentials.

the medians of the 25-year salaries (the salaries of engineers with 25 years of experience) and the starting salaries, between the medians of the 20-year salaries and the 10-year salaries, and so on. This would presumably require more basic knowledge of many sorts. It will be useful to review some of the preliminary questions that would have to be answered as well as the implications of tentative answers to these questions.

First, precisely what functions do higher salaries have as monetary and status incentives for eliciting engineering effort and encouraging individual development? If salaries are, in fact, important incentives, the increased salary differentials are correspondingly beneficial to the company.

Second, how important in the minds of the engineers is congruity between the two status factors of experience and salary? If engineers as a whole believe that experience ought to be accompanied by higher salaries, the expansion tends to enhance the morale of engineers generally.

Third, what are the differences in the way the younger versus the older, the inexperienced versus the experienced, engineer can enter into the engineering manpower market? In terms of the relative value to current and alternative employers, only the recently graduated engineer would have the same value to two employers. The one- or two-year engineer, having passed through that unproductive training period and having been initiated into industry, may generally be worth almost as much to another employer. But for the 15-year engineer it is different; he may have accumulated his experience in a way that fits his current company's needs more fully than any other; with the result that he is worth less to another employer than to his present one.[9] Thus, from the demand side the older, experienced engineer is at a disad-

9 In Chapter VIII, "Layoff Procedures: Rating Plans," we shall note that rationalization of the engineering task and specialization of skills make this difference between an engineer's worth to two employers less marked today than in the past.

vantage in the manpower market. It is the same for the supply side, when one considers that the older and more experienced engineer has more job rights and community roots and is consequently less mobile. If this analysis is based on valid assumptions, it follows that the increased rates at the top of the structure have little justification competitively, from the companies' point of view.

Fourth, what are the differences among the supply and demand situations in the two or more somewhat distinct markets for engineering manpower; for example, 5-year engineer talent and 20-year talent? Perhaps with the routinization of certain engineering jobs the mix of engineers required would include relatively more junior engineers. Still, in the early stage of a complex defense electronics project a greater proportion of experienced engineers may be required. If the latter case is the one that exists in a particular company, management will be under more pressure to keep its experienced engineers, and the expanded salary structure will operate to the company's advantage.

Fifth, what are the relative "worths," or contributions to the product, of the typical 2-year engineer and the typical 20-year engineer? Is the state of the art so dynamic that recently trained graduates have an advantage over the engineers with long experience in handling certain engineering assignments? If it is, salary compression rather than salary expansion may be appropriate, from the company's point of view.

None of the answers suggested above is conclusive, much less weighted, and so we cannot state whether in net effect the expansion works out to the companies' advantage, or to their disadvantage.[10]

Summary and Conclusion

The engineering unions have been a factor in bringing

[10] Spokesmen for the companies studied were not certain in their own minds, either.

about more formal salary administration;[11] indeed, they have been active, purposeful agents in this regard.[12] Nevertheless, in many ways the companies' practices still do not conform to the formal policies, a condition which underlies much of the difficulty encountered in this area under collective bargaining. Job descriptions are now generally made available to the engineers and may even be agreed upon and incorporated in the contract. Job evaluation plans have been established, requiring companies to justify the grading of jobs in terms of various job factors. On the one hand, advantages from these changes accrue to the company in terms of equity in salary treatment and administrative control. On the other hand, the explication of job assignments, duties, and responsibilities has given occasion for employee and union grievances, leading to certain restrictions on supervision's flexibility of assignment and affecting its promotion practices. Engineers will rarely, if ever, object to an assignment outside their occupational classification. Grievances, whenever they occur, have as their purpose reclassification or promotion of an individual to a higher rated position, or reclassification of a position to a higher classification. Only a few agreements deal with job posting or other procedures governing promotions.

The unions' influence on the differentials within the salary structure is reasonably straightforward. They have reversed the narrowing trend by first obtaining percentage

[11] The findings of this research are consistent with E. Robert Livernash's general observation about collective bargaining and the wage structure, "As a broad total influence, collective bargaining appears to be associated with more logical wage-structure policies and improved wage structure administration." *New Concepts in Wage Determination,* (G. W. Taylor and F. C. Pierson, eds.) New York: McGraw-Hill, 1957, p. 171. Also see Slichter, Healy, and Livernash, op. cit., Chapter XIX, "Evaluated Rate Structures."

[12] The official positions of engineering unions to demand job evaluation contrast with the official position of other unions which, with very few exceptions, have been in opposition. See, for example, William Gomberg, "Trade Unions and Industrial Engineering," *Handbook of Industrial Engineering and Management,* W. G. Ireson and E. L. Grant, editors, New York: Prentice-Hall, Inc., 1955.

instead of flat general increases, and later adding sliding scales to restore some differential lost. More recently they have tried to offset the leveling effect of hiring rates which rose faster than the amount of the general increase. Whether the expansion of the salary structure is to the companies' advantage or disadvantage remains an open question as far as this research is concerned.

CHAPTER VI

Merit Budget

In certain respects the subject of merit budget does not readily lend itself to separate discussion. Merit monies are added to general increases (discussed in a previous chapter) to determine the level of salaries from year to year. An even more intimate relationship exists between merit monies and the individual salary review system (the subject of the following chapter). Certain union-management issues do, however, bridge the provinces of the general and of the individual salary adjustment: Should a greater or lesser proportion of the increases be made through the merit system? Should the total money to be budgeted for merit increases be subject to collective bargaining? Is is proper for management to use the individual adjustment system for purposes other than to reward merit? These issues will be explored in this chapter under the appropriate headings.

How do the merit increase systems normally operate? Recommendations for individual salary adjustment are usually initiated by the first-line supervisors and reviewed and approved by successively higher levels of supervision. The approval of a salary control group may also be required before the payroll department can be instructed to implement the increase. The function of successive reviews is to achieve a desirable allocation of a limited amount of money available for merit increases. What enters into a "desirable allocation" is more the subject of the next chapter. It is the "limited" aspect of merit monies we are concerned with here.

The monies may be limited to a certain amount, usually stated as a percentage of the payroll. The limit may be expressed in one over-all budget for the engineering department, or it may be broken down into budgets for smaller administrative units. "Target figures" are used in place of budgets in some companies, but the effect is substantially the same. In a few instances managers made the claim that their companies did not operate within set limits, that merit money was determined strictly by the sum of "justifiable supervisory recommendation." One called this the "seat-of-the-pants" method. Some companies which were reported to rely upon the "seat-of-the-pants" method may in fact use a more explicit limiting technique. In at least one company, for example, there was conflicting testimony among executives on this point. Such contradiction was understandable inasmuch as the company was careful not to disclose information on this subject to their engineering unions, for reasons that will be examined later.

Merit vs. General Increases

Ignoring for present purposes the question of whether the unions have influenced the total amount of money granted in general and merit increases and consequently the general level of salaries, let us consider their influence on the breakdown of the monies between general increases and merit increases. Does the breakdown involve a conflict of interest between the parties? The unions insist that general increases are required, although not to the exclusion of individual merit increases. Executives representing a majority of the companies avow their preference for a policy of granting all increases on an individual and merit basis.

The Positions of the Parties

One union leader who takes a balanced view of general and merit increases declared:

> After all, it is just as rational and just as professional to superimpose individual salary growth differences upon a changing datum as upon a constant datum. And this is pre-

> cisely the distinction between the proper roles for merit increases and for blanket increases. Merit increases should compensate for increases in an individual's worth due to his own efforts and ability. Blanket increases should compensate for increases in his dollar value as a result of conditions independent of his own efforts.

Other union leaders endorse this statement of the distinction between the proper roles for merit increases and for general increases whenever they base their general demands on changes in the cost of living and starting salaries.

Executives express many reasons for opposing general increases.[1] Refusing to recognize the distinction made by the union officer quoted above, they declare that general adjustments "are just not appropriate for professional employees, who must be compensated on the basis of merit." Some are more specific and object to the "diminished incentive" that results when a part of the engineer salary progress occurs through adjustments made irrespective of his own performance. Another objection is that the supervisors' exercise of discretion is limited to only one part of the compensation scheme. That the supervisors' discretion in the adjustment of salaries is an important element in their relationships with their men can be understood at once. But it will be more clearly perceived in the development of later chapters.

In the absence of general increases, all money would be distributed on an individual basis. According to management some engineers would receive more, some would receive less, and some would not receive any increase. One implication of this is that *during a period of rising living*

[1] Some of these executives would nevertheless agree that the minimums and maximums of the salary classifications should ideally be adjusted periodically and systematically in order to reflect the general movement of salaries. This alternative also presents difficulties under collective bargaining, however, when it is not accompanied by equivalent adjustments in all actual salaries paid because it is regarded by the union as an overt admission by the company of the need for the general adjustment denied. Moreover, those individuals whose merit increases are not adequate to preserve their positions relative to the minimums and maximums of their particular salary range become especially aggrieved.

costs (or starting salaries, if that is the appropriate referent) an individual increase which is smaller than the general increase would have been is effectively a cut in salary. The individual's salary has been reduced relative to his living costs (or to the salaries of new graduates). The advantage of reducing salaries in this way is that the cuts can be administered painlessly. Several managers indicated that it was not uncommon for an individual engineer's salary to get way out of line, creating a situation that required "two-way flexibility" in salary adjustment. The company may have overbid on a man "who didn't turn out to be *that* good." Or they may discover that a man with a high salary has slacked off, although he deserved the relatively high salary when he advanced to it. The remedy for out-of-lineness is a "long dry spell," made possible only if there is a complete absence of general increases. One manager explained: "A man in this profession must progress technically to keep his present salary. If he does not keep up with the technical advancement around him a cut in salary is justified." It should be emphasized again that management was speaking of reducing an engineer's salary in terms relative to purchasing power or the general level of engineering salaries, not in terms of absolute dollar amounts.

The unions certainly reject the idea of a "painless" salary cut. One union president writes:

> This suggestion [painless salary cut] is most shocking because it has as its basis dishonesty and deceit. It also runs directly counter to the fundamental need of individuals to know how they are doing and where they stand.

The Results of Collective Bargaining

The engineering unions have had as their minimum objective the negotiation of general increases at least equal to the rises in cost-of-living or in starting salaries for engineers, depending upon the particular union and year in question. Although further analysis of salary data is required before conclusive statements can be made, it appears that generally over the last ten years the unions have fallen just shy of these targets in negotiating general increases. On the other hand, most of the companies whose representatives state that they would prefer to rely wholly on individual adjustments have granted more than half of the increases to their unionized engineers on a general basis. For more insight into how general increases and the merit budget are related under collective bargaining, let us review a few specific experiences in this matter.

In one aircraft company an industry survey of engineering salaries and the economic package negotiated by its shop union were the important parameters for total monies to be distributed to the engineers during the year, but labor relations considerations were paramount in the breakdown of these monies between general and merit increases. Let us review this matter for the year 1958. What other companies were doing for engineers that year (8.5%) set the upper limit on total monies while the company's settlement with the production and maintenance union (7%) set the lower limit. Initially the company offered the engineers' union a 5% general increase, hoping to retain 3.5% for merit, but finally settled for a general increase of about 7%. The company moved to the higher figure because of the pressure created by the shop settlement for that amount and because "it was along the lines of what was expected by the engineering union." Thus, it was determined that 1.5% was available for merit.

Other managements have more fixed ideas about what would be the minimum merit budget acceptable to them. The minimum may be as low as 2.5% or as high as 4.5% per annum. These managements are loath to negotiate a general increase that will jeopardize their minimum merit budget even if this posture complicates their bargaining relationship with the engineers' union. Sometimes decisions are made in still a different way. The general increase is determined in negotiations and the merit budget is worked out later, but without a specific total figure of general and merit increases in mind. The unions find it convenient to approach the subject in this way and to assume that the companies do also.

One executive representing the above cited aircraft company which gave 7% in general increases in 1958, leaving only 1.5% for merit, complained of the union's influences: his company would "prefer to go the merit increase route." But he did not regard the small merit budget as too serious a circumstance under the conditions existing in 1958 in which the company had engineers on layoff and was not hiring. The merit budget had run 3.5% to 4.5% in previous years when the company was building up its engineering staff. This year it was not necessary to give individual increases.

Managers in other companies argue that it is during such a slack period as this that the general increase is the least desirable. It is precisely when a company is not under hiring pressure that it could afford to be, and should be, most selective in its salary adjustments, strengthening its hold on the better engineers and discouraging the lesser ones.

In 1958 one company which had in the previous five years granted something like 45% of its increases on a general basis made a policy decision that henceforth the company would grant no general increases, only individual increases. It adopted "job performance" as a concept intended to be broader than "merit" as the basis for granting individual increases. Supply and demand, general economic conditions, and how well a man was doing his job were to be "all one ball of wax" under this concept. This company had outlined the new policy to the union in negotiations and took a strong position in its behalf. The union continued to demand a general increase, and eventually succeeded in obtaining a modest one. The company, however, did not abandon its hope of getting away from the general increase practice in the future.

This was the only instance that came to the author's attention where a company tried seriously to substitute individual increases completely for general increases for its unionized engineers. Many do not, however, extend the general increase practice to groups about which they have a choice, for example, to other salaried employees in the same location, or to nonrepresented engineers at other locations. According to management in these companies the general increase monies are added to the merit budget for these employees, although management admitted that sometimes such a budget was not always entirely depleted.

All of this—the sentiments against the general increase, the reasoned objections to it on the basis of its impact, the serious attempt by one company to eliminate the general increase entirely, the preference management shows for the individual increase system whenever dealing with nonunionized employee groups—all of this leads directly to the conclusion that the unions definitely are responsible for the general increases; that is, they are responsible for the fact that the money involved has been distributed on a general basis. Certain other evidence available to the author, however, tends to qualify this conclusion somewhat.

In one nonunionized company with which the writer is familiar the Director of Engineering held strong views in favor of granting engineers general increases that corresponded to changes in general conditions. Although his view was opposed by other management personnel within the company, and his periodic efforts in behalf of general increases were only moderately effective, he was certain that his view was shared by others similarly placed in competing and nearby companies which were also nonunion.

Another company, in which the union representing its engineers was decertified, continued to grant general increases, but with reservations about that method of pay distribution (not the total amount). In announcing the general increase for the year following the decertification, the president of the company said:

> Despite our decision, I still believe strongly—as I have stated in our recent discussions—that a general adjustment is not an appropriate method for compensating engineering and technical people. The individual increase approach can maintain attractive salary levels, and give full recognition to the importance of individual contributions. In the event salary levels fail to keep pace, corrective action can be taken at any time. I believe sincerely that at some time in the future we can adopt such a compensation plan.

Thus, it would seem that managers, with some exceptions, dislike the idea of a general increase, but that this form of adjustment becomes most distasteful to them when it occurs under unionized conditions. The fact that the credit for a general increase in the unionized company goes in large measure to the union is an irritant to managers and affects their attitude toward that method of salary adjustment.

Guaranteed Merit Budget

We have seen that a substantial amount of the money distributed to the members of the bargaining unit is in the form of merit increases. It is not surprising that the unions have taken a direct interest in the over-all amount of the merit budget. They reject the idea that a company can unilaterally set the total monies to be granted in increases and that the union's only role is to negotiate the question of "what proportion shall be distributed on a general basis." The unions' proprietary interest in the merit monies has manifested itself in two ways: (1) insistence that a company is committed at least to maintain, in percentage terms, its historical merit budget, and (2) proposals for a negotiated minimum merit budget or "kitty." A third, less proprietary interest results in recommendations regarding improved criteria for management's use in setting the merit budget.

Historical Precedents and Guaranteed Minimums

Particular concern over the issue developed during 1957 when a cutback by government in defense expenditures simultaneously placed certain additional financial burdens on the companies and relaxed somewhat the general demand for engineers. When the companies reduced their merit programs, the unions protested. Let us examine the experiences in a few companies around this issue during this period.

In Company A, management's failure to maintain the engineers' merit budget at its previous levels figured importantly in subsequent negotiations that resulted in a strike. The company's merit increases, which were staggered so that merit results were announced monthly, had run about 5% of the payroll for several years when in September 1957 it dropped to about 4%. By March 1958 merit increases were down to 3% of the payroll. In January 1958 the union began processing individual grievances filed by those who had received increases but who were complaining about the *size* of the increases. It also filed a union grievance protesting the company's reduction in the merit budget. These grievances were based on the union's contention that by making the merit increases dependent upon economic conditions, as in the union's view the company certainly had done, the company violated the merit concept as it was incorporated in the agreement.

In response, the company officially took the position that *merit* (i.e., meritorious performance) had declined during this period rather than admit the union's charge and attribute the smaller increases to general economic conditions. Further, the company refused to consider the grievances on the grounds that the size of merit increases was not grievable under the contract. When the union requested arbitration on one of the grievances, the company filed in the district court for a declaratory judgment to prevent the American Arbitration Association from proceeding toward arbitration.[2]

Meanwhile, during June and July of 1958 the battleground for the issue passed to negotiations. Earlier that year the union had resolved that the 1958 contract would provide a guaranteed merit kitty. Bargaining items also included a request that the 1957 and 1958 "deficiencies" in the merit program be made up. Negotiations resulted in a strike. According to the union publication at the time, "The sole cause of this strike is the refusal of the company to return to the merit program level it had before September 1957."

Company A's position was set forth in a letter to the engineers on July 15, 1958, during the strike:

> The company *cannot* agree to a guaranteed fund for merit increases.
>
> (1) The general level of salaries for engineers in our industry must influence our salary policy if the company is to remain competitive.
>
> (2) General economic conditions must be important factors in determining salary policy for engineers as with other employees.
>
> (3) The amount of meritorious performance or lack of it cannot be predicted or guaranteed with certainty.
>
> . . . Other unions wanted guaranteed merit increases . . . but they realized management's firm position. . . .

Excerpts from the union publication on July 18, 1958, provide more insight into the guaranteed merit kitty issue:

> . . . the . . . [union] is asking management to stop making a farce out of the whole concept of merit. . . . It has at various times cancelled out general increases by withholding merit increases. At such times, notably during the past year, they have used the merit-raise system to absorb the month-by-month and yearly economic contingencies—while at the same time they insisted on trying to pacify us by doling out

[2] In February 1961 the outcome of the issue was still pending. A Federal District Court had ruled in favor of the company, but the union had in turn appealed the decision to the Circuit Court.

flat general increases. This merely served to doubly negate the principle of fair recognition of meritorious professional performance, of individual accomplishment and advancement. Past comments from personnel inferred that this situation was a consequence of our having "unionized," whereas cause and effect were the other way around.

At another time the union added, "when the company is in financial difficulties let them come to us like gentlemen." The settlement took cognizance of this last point. Although the principles of the merit program worked out to bring the strike to an end did not provide for a guarantee in merit monies, they did include the following statement:

> When the company believes consideration should be given the general business conditions affecting [the company] in arriving at the amount of individual merit increases, the association shall be given access to the information upon which the company is basing their proposed action, and the matter shall be fully discussed with the association.

Some companies have granted the guaranteed merit kitty. During its first contract negotiations in 1951, Company B agreed to distribute an aggregate amount of 7.8% in merit and in certain automatic individual increases, an amount greater that it otherwise would have distributed. In 1955 the amount was reduced to 6%, which still represented the largest of any merit kitty guaranteed by an engineering union agreement. In this company the kitty happened to have incidental value to the company in administering individual increases. The presence of the specific over-all control of merit tended to weaken the case of individual merit grievances processed to arbitration. It is also possible that the large merit budget guarantees operated to reduce the amount of the general increases which could be negotiated annually by the union. Unfortunately the data required to answer this important question are not available.

Company C, which guarantees a kitty of 4.5%, granted the

provision in 1954 although the union had only included the item among its demands for certain "strategic bargaining reasons." The kitty proposed by the union would have also included somewhat lesser percentage guarantees for each section of the engineering department as a whole, a feature that was not incorporated in the provision, nor in the provisions of any other engineering agreements. Commenting on the significance of the merit kitty, the union president late in the summer of 1958 said:

> It hasn't been significant yet, but this year the guarantee may be meaningful. The total of the two semiannual reviews may fall below 4.5%. The company has been giving merit increases at other times. For example, 10% of the bargaining unit have received increases in the last two months. Now the company will claim that all merit increases including those on interim review count toward the 4.5%. We will insist on crediting only those resulting from the semiannual review, which is required by past practice and the contract.

Improved Criteria for Management

Another union, which did not propose any guaranteed kitty, did take Company D to task for "drastically slashing" the merit pool in January 1958 because the company "lacked good reason" for the action. In prior years there had been only small variation in the size of the pool. In the period July 1954 through July 1957 the semiannual merit pool (including classification increases) had only varied between 2.5% and 3.5%, and had averaged 3.0%. The January 1958 merit pool ran about 1.6%. In the union view the company had been "coldly opportunistic" in this matter, "taking advantage of the understandable feeling of insecurity which happened to exist among its engineers at that particular moment." The union reached this conclusion after eliminating other possible explanations: the engineers' work performance had *not* declined, the company did *not* appear to be short of money, it did *not* seem to be preparing for rough times ahead, and finally, the small savings to the company which resulted would *not* improve its competitive position.

Company D's action was cited as demonstrating clearly that under existing practices an engineer's work performance does not determine the size of his merit raise. A union news release contended:

> . . . Although his work performance, relative to that of his fellow engineers, determines his share of the "merit" money available to his supervisor, the company's arbitrary administrative decisions on the size of the whole merit pool exerts a greater influence than work performance.

Remedies of two kinds were sought by this particular union: one for the past and one for the future. First it sought a special merit review which would distribute the 1.4% "deficit" of the January reviews. The normal July review in 1958 was not to be affected by this special review. The company did not negotiate on the special merit review request, as such, but during negotiations it did grant an additional 1.5% over and above the general increase to be distributed "on a selective basis by the company." Was the union responsible for this extra pool, even though the company would not admit to the principle upon which the union's arguments were based? The union believes it was. The company says, "no."

Looking to the future, the union in Company D undertook to educate management on some principles of salary administration. A union release said:

> . . . Each engineer has a right to expect to be paid a salary proportional to his value to his employer. A salary administration suitable for professional engineers should seek to establish salaries according to some appropriate standard. A tabulation of the increases required to maintain conformity with these standards would then reveal the size of that merit pool. The size of the merit pool is a dependent variable; it is the poorest parameter with which to maintain control. . . .

Later, the union president at Company D emphasized that there was no single merit pool figure universally applicable. "One can imagine a situation in which a merit pool of 1% would be entirely appropriate. In other situations, a pool of 10% would be just as appropriate." He did not wish to elaborate this point.

It is readily apparent, however, that differences are appropriate among the merit programs of companies that employ their engineering forces in different ways. For example, it appears that a larger percentage of the engineering work in aircraft companies is routine, and hence offers less opportunities for growth than the engineering work in electronic firms. Aircraft companies require a correspondingly smaller merit pool. Their work, however, is becoming more highly complex as they become more involved in missiles, and the "appropriate" merit pool would be increased accordingly.

Let us return briefly to the question of the guaranteed merit kitty before moving to a consideration of the patterns of distribution of merit increases. Spokesmen for most of the companies which did not have a guaranteed kitty announced that they would not under any circumstances agree to an arbitrary maximum or minimum limitation on merit monies, mainly because it would enable the union to claim credit "even for this part of the compensation scheme"! Evidence suggested, however, that the possibility of claiming some credit for merit monies was not the important consideration underlying the unions' interest in this issue; more important was the need to be able to prevent the company from reducing merit to offset, and thereby virtually nullify, any large general increase obtained through tough negotiations.

Monies for Other Than Merit

Companies have at times been charged by their respective unions with abusing the merit system by using it for purposes other than to reward merit. In one company this issue has arisen recurrently, and has taken several different forms.

The company has been accused of using the merit system (a) to disguise general increases, (b) to induce employees to transfer, and (c) to achieve antiunion purposes. The circumstances surrounding these alleged abuses will be described.

To Disguise General Increases

Early in 1953 the company experienced difficulty in recruiting large numbers of engineers in a tight manpower market, and it became necessary to raise the hiring rates substantially for the positions involved. The semiannual merit review in April resulted in a merit kitty of over 5% of the payroll as against the more normal 2.5% for October 1952. The increases were concentrated in the lower brackets and in the same departmental group (which can be designated group A) where the greater hiring had taken place.

The union pointed out that these raises were used to partially offset the inequities created by the increased hiring rates in departmental group A. Apart from its objection to limiting any inequity adjustment to the lower levels of the salary structure, it did not want the company to pass off any such adjustment increases as "merit."

The union's data showed how increases fell into two categories of departments. In group A, including Flight Control, Radar Armament, and Radar Engineering, increases amounted to 7.75%. Group B included Design and Publications, and they received 2.01%. Corresponding figures for Groups A and B in the two previous reviews were 2.5% and 1.57%, 2.27% and 1.54%. The union rejected the idea implied by management's merit action—that the employees in departmental group B were so unmeritorious.

In its own words the union was chagrined that:

> (1) the advantages accruing to many employees have been overbalanced by discriminatory inequities which should have been equalized by further wage increases; and (2) the union's own prerogatives in helping to define the wage structure . . . have been denied. . . .

When the union filed a grievance on the issue, the company claimed it was not arbitrable and applied to the State Supreme Court for a stay of arbitration. The Court ruled for the company.

In 1955 rumors of an unusual merit review again worried the union. The median salaries of new hires and the medians of all employees in the same job titles were "so far from contract guarantee levels as to make parts of the present contract meaningless." Impressed with the need to adjust the whole salary structure accordingly, the union president wrote the company offering to negotiate the necessary wage adjustments. The company replied:

> It has always been the policy to correct inequities in salaries as soon as there is any indication that this situation exists. . . .
>
> We do not consider the matter of salary increases to be a subject for negotiations during the lifetime of a contract which provides for this subject.

Since the only way the company could correct inequities as soon as they were discovered, without opening the contract during its life, was by correcting them through the unilateral merit review, the union regarded the company's statement as direct evidence that it was misusing the merit system.

To Induce Transfers

In the summer of 1956 union members were again "up in arms," this time "over a thinly disguised attempt to round up volunteers from their ranks by an outright perversion of the merit principle." According to the union, approximately 70% of the engineers in one department were asked to transfer to a new missile plant at Salt Lake City; they were promised salary increases ranging from 6% to 12%, labeled as "merit" raises by the department head, even though he also implied that the men who stayed in the New York plant would not receive them.

When the union grieved, management refused to state whether these increases were "merit" increases or not, on the grounds that it was an academic and hypothetical point at that time. Later, the company in effect proposed that the salaries of the men transferring to Utah not be considered as being on the bargaining unit merit payroll. This would avoid the issue of whether these were "merit" increases (the company now stated they were increases in anticipation of greater responsibilities in Utah), and yet definitely would not be chargeable against the 4.5% minimum merit pool provided for in the agreement. The union executive committee and the grievance committee recommended acceptance of the company answer. But the representatives' council which formulates policy and makes decisions on whether cases should be processed to arbitration elected not to accept. The company then rejected a union request to negotiate a transfer bonus.

The company did not want to place the matter before an arbitrator. According to the union, management stalled the process by raising technicalities and making unusual requests for information. In February 1957, acting on an application filed by the union, a Federal District Court judge ordered the company to proceed with arbitration. In an appeal to the Circuit Court the lower court's decision was reviewed without being changed. The company's appeal to the Supreme Court was not reviewed. The matter finally reached arbitration September 1958. The arbitrator upheld management.

For Antiunion Purposes

The union does not merely regard management as abusing fair and sound principles of salary administration; it alleges that management uses the merit system as an antiunion weapon. The two contentions are not entirely separate. The union leader who wrote the following passage could well have been referring to any one of the earlier "abuses":

> . . . This is a good specimen of the company-dominated, unilateral Merit Review. It has an iceberg-like potential—most of it is out of view—which is not generally appreciated, but no better engine for by-passing, and temporarily rendering impotent, timid unions has yet been devised.
>
> * * * * *
>
> . . . Look what a clever management can do with it. First, it can confound the union. As an organization which exists primarily to advance the economic welfare of its members, the union is supposed to be convulsed if it can be maneuvered into appearing to have *any* objection to *any* process whereby some members will be benefited. And if it protests that all that is desired is to get close enough to the process to see what is proclaimed, pious principles are adhered to, the $64 question can be trotted out: "Do you want to have to lick the boots of a bunch of union politicians to get a raise that you've damn well earned on your own merits?"
>
> Second, with a 100% company-dominated Merit System the company never has to fire anyone. It can just starve them out . . . if the miscreant happens to have incurred the disfavor of some operator in the managerial hierarchy. . . .
>
> Third, the company can try to expand the agreed-upon proposition that merit is to be determined solely by the management into the much more flexible proposition that all salary adjustments come within the province of the Merit Review and are, therefore, out of bounds for the union.

The issues represented in the above discussion were raised in several other companies, but somewhat less frequently and in milder ways.

Summary and Conclusion

The engineering unions exert two important influences on the distribution of monies. The first influence is that of decreasing the amount of money available for merit by negotiating general salary increases that are larger than the company would grant in the absence of a union. The reduction in the merit budget reduces the area of discretion exercised by the supervisor over the salaries of his men, in that way subtracting from the supervisor's authority and status. In addition, general increases decrease the differences in the rate of salary advancement between the various levels of competency, thereby diminishing financial incentive and creating salary injustices. Distributing all monies on an individual merit basis often enables a company to cut salaries painlessly whenever an individual cut is justified in management's opinion, whereas granting increases on a general basis tends to limit the company's flexibility in this respect. Finally, perhaps the most important factor associated with the general increase is the "hunk of credit" which goes to the union because the increases are general and because they are negotiated.

The second important influence has a dual thrust by (1) maintaining the merit pool above a minimum level, and (2) preventing the company from using the individual adjustment system to achieve various administrative salary objectives. Sometimes a company will guarantee a merit kitty contractually; in other companies results along this line are achieved through union surveillance and pressure. Apart from any additional cost to the company, these minimums tend to confer upon the union some credit for merit increases, too. A company often finds itself in the ambiguous position of reducing merit monies because of economic necessities, yet, because the engineers take the "merit" increase system literally, the company is forced at the same time to deny that the system has been influenced by nonmerit factors. Such a posture on the part of the company may nevertheless be costly to the company in terms of its relations with its professionals who say, "We are not fooled." Increases for nonmerit purposes—adjustment of inequities in the salary structure, inducements to transfer, and so on—are also more difficult to distribute through the individual increase system under collective bargaining without damaging union and employee relations.

CHAPTER VII

Merit Review System

We may now turn to the administration of the merit review system as it affects individual salaries. The significance of salary ranges and of the merit review system of increases for engineers derives from the intellectual character of engineering work which cannot be standardized. Pinpoint rates and equal pay for equal work may be appropriate for production and maintenance operations where the work is essentially manual and measurable. But with engineers each is expected to advance technically and creatively at his own unique rate and reach his own ceiling in keeping with his inherent capabilities and ambition. Hence, the need for differential and personal rates of salary advancement.

The merit review system regulating individual salaries has many functions for management, including motivating and rewarding performance and encouraging individualism, competition, and management orientation. Publicly management will stress the justice implicit in rewarding performance differentially, as one company did in stating the "objective" of its merit review program in the bulletin to its engineers:

> The objective of our semiannual salaried personnel rate review is to make certain that employees are recognized and compensated in proportion to their contribution or merit. In engineering and scientific activities such as ours, the quality, performance, and effectiveness of individuals vary widely in many ways. Therefore, recognition and pay must be determined in accordance with the individual's qualities and performance. The key to success in any enterprise, and therefore to our job security, resides with those employees

> who make the most of their respective talents by putting exra effort into their jobs. We are vitally interested in making sure that proper recognition and pay are given to these employees.

Justice and individual treatment are, of course, the features that appeal most to engineers irrespective of their status. Engineering unions have strongly endorsed the merit principle in salary administration. Their criticism of the way a given merit review system actually operates should not be mistaken for rejection of the underlying principle. It is only fair that we let a union leader make this point himself before we examine the attempts of engineering unions to modify their respective merit review systems.

> If past experience is at all indicative, any editorial comment on the subject of merit reviews can be expected to elicit such remarks as "Stop biting the hand that feeds you," coupled with the accusation that the writer is unquestionably opposed to the whole merit idea. Let us therefore state that we believe most emphatically in the merit principle and that it is precisely our concern over its possible abuse that prompts us to examine. . . .

Every company studied had a formal merit review system. Most of these review systems were formalized after unionization but were not products of negotiations between the parties. The systems were of varying types. First, there were many sorts of procedures and criteria used by first-line supervision to arrive at an individual's salary recommendation. Second, different channels for review of these recommendations were used in different companies. Third, the ways in which the results of the review were reported to the individual engineers concerned varied. Fourth, there were many different arrangements for individual appeals and grievances. There were other differences, such as the length of the interval between reviews, and whether the reviews for individuals or groups of individuals were staggered throughout the year or all occurred at the same time. Aspects of each of these elements of the merit review system have been challenged in one company or another by its respective engineering union.

This chapter will first consider a fundamental question raised by the unions; namely, how much information regarding the operation of the companies' merit review system do the engineers or their unions have a right to receive? The next three sections of the chapter will deal with the challenges by the unions to three elements of the review system: criteria used for salary adjustment; review reporting procedures; appeal mechanisms and individual complaints. Finally, two sections—the Point Plan and the Growth Rate Plan—will describe two merit review plans advocated by engineering unions.

Information on How the System Works

The unions have been insistent in their requests for full disclosure of merit budgeting, distribution, and rating techniques. The companies have been equally intent upon keeping this information to themselves. The sparring between the parties about disclosure in two companies offers insight into this issue.

In one company the union, which had represented the engineers for about ten years, asked the company (probably not for the first time) what procedures management used in rating the professional engineers and what bearing these ratings had on salary advancement. They asked for this information in writing. The union explained that knowledge of the basic rating techniques would enable the engineers to better meet management's expectations. The union agreement provided only that the company review the payroll "from time to time" and "grant individual increases based upon merit."

The company advised that there was no single system in either its research or manufacturing engineering departments; that the qualifications for advancements were variable; that any individual could apprise himself of his supervisor's expectations by asking. However, the company took the union's request under advisement.

The company apparently decided to tell the union something about ratings. In the next regular monthly meeting of the parties, management passed out rating forms which essentially required the supervisor to assign one of the following ratings to the man: Excellent, Above Average, Average, Below Average, Unsatisfactory. Management emphasized that the system did not force comparisons or ratings within a particular group; that is, it was possible for all the engineers in a group to receive the same rating. Regarding the interval for rating, management explained that new employees were rated after 4 months, 10 months, 15 months, and 22 months. Beyond two years ratings occurred at irregular intervals.

The union reported this newly disclosed description of the merit system to its membership. Because the feedback which the union leaders received from the members raised some question about the accuracy or completeness of the description, the union called for another meeting with management. In this meeting management stated that in the manufacturing department it did have a definite written scheme for evaluating merit; that an equally definite form also not explained in the previous meeting was in use in the research department. Since individual merit rating is a complex matter and all systems have disabilities, however, and because management is continually changing its methods as improvements develop, it was not in the company's interest to disclose its methods. In any event the company did not wish to make these methods a matter of discussion with the union. With this, the disclosure episode in this company ended.

Another union was only somewhat more successful in its efforts along similar lines. After several years of collective bargaining, this union negotiated a contract clause requiring the company to make known to the union and to the employees "the procedures, policies, and forms that will apply to each merit review" within two days after they have been determined by management. (The contract also provided for specific review intervals and appeal procedures.) The company published (and continued to publish in about the same form for each review) the following description of the operation of the merit review:

Operation of Merit Review:

Engineering Supervisors evaluate all information pertaining to the on-the-job performance of employees under their supervision. This evaluation is based on personal observations, discussions with group leaders or with supervisors in other departments with which the employee is working, and any other pertinent performance information. A personnel analysis guide may be used to assist in determining that all the important relative factors have been considered. (Copies of these guides may be obtained from Engineering Personnel.) After the Assistant Section Heads or Section Heads have evaluated their employees, a meeting is held with their Department Head to evaluate the relative merit of employees in the department. No salary discussions take place at this meeting. Another departmental meeting is held to review the relative evaluations and proposed rate changes of employees in that particular department. Details of work assignments are discussed and, for example, a list may be made showing the relative order of over-all on-the-job performance and present pay for all employees in that department.

The next series of meetings are held between the Engineering Department Heads and their respective Engineering Directors to discuss and consolidate the recommendations. Another conference is then held between the Engineering Departments, the Chief Engineer, and the Engineering Personnel Representative to discuss special problems that may have arisen, to compare each department's recommendations, and to review individually the top people in each Engineering Director's department to assure equitable and proper salary increases among the major departments.

The final step comprises the formal meetings held in the first week of April and October by the Salary and Wage Department and attended by the Engineering Director and his Department Heads, one or more of the Engineering Division top Administrative Heads, and the Engineering Personnel Representative. The individual personnel record of each employee is reviewed once more in connection with rate recommendations. In this way, any unusual situations once more come under scrutiny. This final discussion, accompanied by formal entry of the proposed new rate on the review sheets, completes the steps of the process. After completion of all rate information for the company, the review is approved by the Vice President and General Manager and the new rates become official. No statement or commitment regarding a salary increase should be made to an employee by his supervisor until this time. Engineering supervisors will then promptly inform each employee receiving a merit increase and/or a change in classification.

Thus the company provided the union with a fairly detailed description of the channels for review of individual salary recommendation. It also indicated that a personnel analysis guide, which contained several criteria and with which the union leaders were familiar, "may be used" in some limited way by supervision. The vague explanation of this latter area was clearly deficient in the union's view. In its publication it professed:

> . . . [we know] . . . that there is some form of departmental listing which is a controlling factor in determining which individuals do or don't get merit increases. The company should publish the method of developing this list, and its use, to the membership, in detail. It doesn't. . . .

Either the company did not have a regular, describable method by which its supervisors arrived at their recommendations for salary increases or, if the company did, management preferred not to discuss it with the union. Later it was explained to the engineers that many techniques may actually be used by supervision; that the company policy only required that the supervisor's decisions be made with sufficient clarity that they can be substantiated to his superiors; that if the supervisor uses any aids to assist him in his determination it is not at the direction of his superiors. By the fall of 1958 the union president was finally convinced that there was in fact no more to be explained in the area of individual reviews. "The company apparently does not have a system guiding individual supervisors." Nonetheless, the union would still like to know how the total amount of the merit budget is determined and by whom.

Disagreements such as these have been continuing ones over the years in many of the unionized companies. Typically a union is successful in breaking through the company's "private security system" on merit review to obtain one piece of information at a time. Actually more of this information is acquired vicariously—for example, through a supervisor who "spills the beans" to an engineer when he is passing the buck for the engineer's failure to receive an increase—than is obtained officially from the company during annual negotiations or other conferences.

The great reluctance of the companies to enlighten the engineers regarding the operation of the merit review system would seem to be based on several factors. Disclosing review operation and methods would lead first to union-management discussions, which would be time consuming, and then to union demands for changes, which would be "an unnecessary and undesirable extension of the scope of collective bargaining." Publicizing the intricacies of the review system would also tend to "leave the supervisor standing there with his bare face hanging out," as one union leader put it. That is, if the extent of the supervisor's responsibility for a decision were known by the engineers he reviews, it would not be so easy for the supervisor to blame falsely either other levels of management or certain features of the system. Written descriptions of the system would tend to provide more "handles" for the engineers and the union to grasp in challenging the results of reviews and "more ways for them to try to beat the system." In addition, more publicity would remove one more area in which the supervisor has the status advantage of possessing information not possessed by his subordinates.

One union president, writing in his organization's publication, suggests that there may be a more basic reason for management's secretiveness: the motivating effects of keeping the engineer guessing.

> To understand the company representatives' attitude, it is important to remember the fundamental purpose of wages and salaries. Wages and salaries are a device to command the efforts of individuals and direct these efforts in the ways, and to the ends, desired by company management. In the case of manual workers, where the results of their efforts can be directly observed and measured, it is sufficient to merely offer jobs at certain wage rates.
>
> In the case of mental workers, on the other hand, the problem is more difficult. Mental, especially creative, efforts cannot be so easily bent to the will of the company management as can physical efforts. Thus more subtle means must be used to "motivate" the mental employee to enthusiastically strive to please his supervisor. Thus the mental employee's salary usually depends on his supervisor's subjective evaluation. Of course, the less the employee knows about salaries and salary evaluation procedures, the more he feels dependent upon his supervisor's opinion and the more he strives to please him. The theoretical optimum from a company's point of view would seem to be for the employee (1) to be sure in his own mind that he would be treated fairly and (2) know nothing else about salaries. It is obvious why engineers continually strive to escape this emphasis on subservience through greater understanding of the facts.

Contrariwise, there may prove to be unexpected advantages for managements who disclose their review methods. It was reported in one company that the engineers were favorably impressed when they learned the amount of effort management put into the review process, and the fact that each individual in a department was compared against all others in that process. It is also possible, as heralded in books on Personnel Administration, that employees do better when they understand how they are being judged, notwithstanding the fact that this was not accepted by the managements studied as being literally true.

Criteria Used for Salary Adjustment

The first issue here is, of course, part of the one that has been discussed above, that of disclosure. Generally, the unions would like to have the factors that enter into salary recommendations made as explicit as possible, but companies have made very few concessions in this area. Three contracts do not even mention the companies' methods of adjustment of individual salaries. One company is only committed to "determine what changes, if any, in the rate of employees shall be made as a result of the review." Three agreements provide for the adjustment of individual salaries on a "merit basis." Another for "improved performance and meritorious service." Still another gives merit increases "for above average performance." In another the company grants merit increases "to those whose performance warrants special consideration." One agreement states:

> Salary rate increases are based on merit, including the employee's capacity to handle the range of work of his position classification and the quality and quantity of work being performed. Any merit increase will be of such amount as to make his rate commensurate with his performance as related to these factors.

Only one agreement actually lists the factors to be considered by the company. These are listed in general terms: quality of work, quantity of work, knowledge of work, versatility, attitude, guidance and instruction required, and "other factors which may be significant in specialized types of work or in individual cases." Other companies may in practice use review forms that list the factors upon which salary recommendations by supervision should be based. In some cases these forms are only for the supervisor to refer to as a more or less complete check list.

There appeared to be on the part of some managements studied a weakening confidence in the usefulness of review forms listing and weighting specific criteria. While the tendency cited seemed to be unrelated to the unions' presence, managements could also readily see how explicit factors would be a liability under collective bargaining. Unfavorable merit review reports woud have to be more specific, which would not only require more supervisory time, but would also provide more occasion for merit complaints. Then, too, the complaints filed would be much more difficult to handle. The supervisor would not merely have to justify one over-all judgment; he would have to substantiate several individual judgments, a much more difficult and time-consuming requirement.

Review Reporting Procedures

Sooner or later the individual must learn of the results of the review. Ultimately he will learn the results through his paycheck, and indeed, some engineers are not informed of the results in any other way. The unions have endeavored to establish more elaborate procedures incorporating (a) time limits within which the employee must be informed, (b) an employee-supervisor interview, and (c) a written review report.

Time Limits

Let us trace the evolution of the reporting system under the influence of the union in one company studied. During the first contract negotiations in 1945 the union sought a definite and formal system for handling merit increases. As a part of the formal plan, the union asked that rating reports signed by the supervisor be furnished the employee and discussed with him. The company did not grant these provisions that year, but did agree informally that if any engineer went beyond a year without a raise the department manager would explain why. Several years later a provision was added guaranteeing employees written notification of eligibility for merit increases by a certain date. The next contract provided that notification of status of eligibility for a merit increase would be signed by the employee's supervisor, apparently because the supervisor occasionally disclaimed any knowledge of the final results of the review when he was confronted later by the employee. The employee signed a second copy and returned it to the supervisor.

Notwithstanding these provisions, the employees continued to have trouble with their supervisors' not notifying them by the date specified. The company explained that notification difficulties resulted when the approval procedure, which normally took three months, was delayed. Such unavoidable delays were regrettable and against company policy, according to a personnel official. The union believed, however, that the supervisors were responsible for many delays which were avoidable. One of the merit grievance cases over management's failure to notify an engineer within the time limits went to arbitration (not, however, as the main issue). The arbitrator acknowledged the company's violation of the contract but did not award any penalty.

One other agreement contains a similar provision. Another requires notice, but does not specify time limits. Another obliges the company to give the results of the review only to those who get a raise. This contract provides no definite notification period except "as far in advance as possible of the first payment at the new rate."

Interviews

Employees not only want to be notified of the results of the review, but they also want to know the reasons for the supervisors' decisions. One of their key objectives in the reporting aspect of the merit review system is a mandatory supervisor-employee interview. A broader but related objective—an employee appraisal system incorporating employee-supervisor discussions, even if it is separate from the merit review—will be considered later in this section.

Only two companies were committed by the union agreement to discuss the merit review with the engineers. The supervisors in one were required to give notice within 20 days of the review date, telling the engineer the reasons for the action taken and discussing the engineer's work with him. This agreement also listed the several factors to be considered in reviewing the performance of each employee which could provide the basis for the supervisor-engineer discussions.

Despite this provision, a survey by departments in this company in 1955 showed that it was common for employees to receive no notice of the results of the review, and even more common not to be interviewed by the supervisors. The company explained that this was due to the attitudes of engineering supervisors who are "embarrassed about discussing intangibles." A new performance review interview plan proposed by the union to correct the supervisory delinquencies in this area was not acceptable to the company. Management did attempt, however, to educate their engineering supervisors to the "positive function" of these review discussions and in 1958 could report some improvement in supervisory practices.

Another union agreement gave the employee the right to discuss his status with respect to the periodical merit review with his supervisors "at any time." There was no reguarly scheduled interview, and the employee was expected to take the initiative for discussion. Perhaps a few more engineers were encouraged to approach their supervisors for discussions than would have been without the contract provision, but the arrangement was far from satisfactory to the union, which favored mandatory interviews.

The company refused to require its supervisors to schedule an interview with each employee regarding his review status, insisting that the matter should be left to the discretion of the individual supervisor. Instead, it provided that the engineer could discuss his status with a personnel official if he desired. When this provision was first instituted in 1958, the union hoped that by giving the employee that option the supervisor himself would be more likely to try to satisfy the employee's desire to know how he stood, rather than have this service performed by the personnel staff. At the same time, union officials doubted that the personnel staff could be of any real assistance in the task of explaining that which is essentially the product of a supervisor's judgment. In the fall of 1958 the provision had not been adequately tested.

Many supervsiors in companies that do not have provisions covering the matter do discuss the merit review with their men, but more do not. The supervisor is more likely to have a discussion with a man who received an increase than with a man he denied one, although it would seem that the latter had the greater need. The differences in the practices among supervisors are in themselves objectionable to the union. Furthermore, the situation in which the supervisor is obligated to conduct his interviews with his employees is quite different from the situation wherein an employee may request an interview. One unionist explained:

> The important thing is that the supervisor is forced to sit down with the engineer. It gives the employee a chance (the only opportunity in many cases) to talk about himself. If he had to go to the supervisor, the supervisor would be "asked" and would not feel any obligation. Under our system the supervisor comes to you and he is your guest. The words are less important than the fact that they sit down and talk.

Whether interviews are conducted on a voluntary or mandatory basis there is the further problem of making the discussions meaningful to the engineer, in other words, of obtaining the supervisor's candid appraisal. One engineer made this comment:

> This is a weasel wording company. It lacks candor from top to bottom. The only way to get an idea of how you are doing is to break the code, that is, know what an individual means when he says you are "good."

Supervisors also tend to blame the merit review denial on higher authorities or other conditions beyond their control in order to avoid talking about the engineer or his performance. One measure taken by the unions in recognizing this tendency is to acquaint their members with the various devices used by supervisors to outflank the engineer interested in having an employee-centered interview. The following article first appeared in the monthly publication of a West Coast aircraft engineering union in approximately the form reproduced here. Because of its general applicability it has been reprinted in the publications of several other engineering unions since.

* * * * *

> When the employee says, "I deserve a raise," there are a number of well-defined evasive tactics at the disposal of the supervisor. In many cases he may parry the thrust with a jest. Example: "So do I, Jones, Ho, Ho." This may be more effective if accompanied by a vigorous dig in the ribs. At any rate, even if the parry fails, it starts the interviews on an informal, friendly, man-to-man basis. Supervisors should use caution in administering the dig in the ribs, as it may not be completely understood by the employee.
>
> Another tactic is the postponement. . . . The supervisor looks at his watch and says "Sorry, haven't got time to discuss it right now." Or he may say, "I'd like to go into detail with you on that, Jones. See me early next week." The simple delay is only a temporary expedient. It should be used only with particularly timid employees.
>
> Another method is the Graph and Pattern Approach. This may be used in stubborn cases when the Postponement

routines have failed. The supervisor simply floods the employee's mind with a torrent of statistics . . . salary data, rates of progress, and Average Income of Upper Middle Class Families in West Bean Pole, Nebraska. A phonograph record bearing a typical Graph and Pattern Approach is available for the use of qualified personnel.

There are numerous other effective methods which may be used at the discretion of the supervisor to fit particular cases: The Salubrious Climate Pattern, The Budget Gambit, The Fringe Benefits Pitch, the Lack-of-Education Spiel for use on shop trained personnel, and the Lack-of-Practical-Experience Lecture for college trained people.

If all else fails, there is always the Upper Management Decision Discussion (the term *discussion* is used in the general sense—the employee should never be given the opportunity to counter-attack). . . . In this pitch, the supervisor represents himself as a White Knight attempting to storm the Gloomy Citadel of the Evil Ogres (his superiors) to secure raises for His Men. This lecture has been known to wring a tear from ten-year employees, but it must be used sparingly to prevent trauma.

Let us turn briefly to what we have referred to above as the broader but related objective of an employee appraisal system. Several companies have an appraisal procedure which is intended to be separate from the merit review. The distinction is clear as far as the contract is concerned, but in practice the employee does think of his supervisor's appraisal as being related to his salary experience. The story at each of these companies is similar. The supervisors become lax, some do not discuss the appraisals with their men, others completely fail to rate their men. Individuals complain to the union, a few may even file grievances. The union takes up the matter with the labor relations or personnel people who approach engineering management to do something about it, or who put pressure directly on the supervisors. For a period the supervisors become more conscientious in conducting their appraisals and interviews, and then they revert to their former laxness. Since the appraisal is intended to give the man a reading on himself, to facilitate employee counseling, and to identify training needs—all management objectives—personnel staff and top engineering management generally agree with the union that the appraisal is a good thing.[1] In fact, they use the contract as a club over the head of supervisors to get them to make the appraisal and the interview, saying in effect, "see, we've got to do it."

Written Reports

The interview does not always adequately fill the employee's need to know how he stands; hence the third reporting feature sought by the union: the written report on the review, including the supervisor's evaluation.

One union requested in negotiations that a written evaluation be given each employee at merit reviews. Urging the necessity for this provision, the union submitted evidence of the breakdown in frank and honest reporting under the present system:

> One . . . engineer . . . turned to the [union] Merit Review Committee to investigate his merit standing when he did not receive a raise. . . . During the interview, his department head stated that this man had always done a superior job on his assignments which were routine, but that he was tech-

[1] The assumption that the appraisal interview achieves informative and motivational purposes was firmly held by the union officials and the personnel managers in the companies studied, but was not necessarily shared by the author of this study. Some authorities seriously question whether an appraisal interview system is in fact functional or dysfunctional for a company. For a critique of performance appraisal, see Douglas McGregor, *The Human Side of Enterprise,* New York: McGraw-Hill Company, 1960. For example, Professor McGregor suggests on pages 84–87 that the interview may do serious damage to the relationship between the supervisor and the subordinate, that the interview accentuates the subordinate's dependence and "thus readily arouses latent anxieties and hostilities," that expressed desires by a subordinate to know where he stands should not be taken literally, that feedback about behavior is usually at a time too remote from the behavior itself in order to be an efficient stimulus to learning, and so forth. Unfortunately, data to test these hypotheses were not collected as a part of this engineering study.

> nically incompetent for performing the more complicated engineering tasks. Therefore, he did not merit an increase in salary. The department head also stated that the employee had had this position explained to him many times. However, the employee had no recollection of being told anything except such pat phrases as, "The [union] negotiated too large an increase this year, and there just isn't enough money left for adequate merit increases," and "Don't worry, you're doing a fine job and you will undoubtedly get a raise next time." Written merit rating sheets would have eliminated this misunderstanding between a valuable employee and his supervisor.

The company rejected the idea on the grounds that written records would discourage the free, oral exchange of views between employees and supervision which, it pointed out, was already permissible under the agreement. Merit reviews in this company were not grievable and, in the union's own words, "This would represent a step in the direction of a grievable merit system; it would give the union something to take before an arbitrator." These documents would be of value even within the company's present appeal procedure.

One agreement requires written reasons for merit denials from the *supervisor* at the time of the merit review. Under earlier contracts requiring only that the reasons for denial be reported by the "employer," such reports were issued on standard forms and were meaningless to the employees. The contract change forced the supervisor to make this explanation himself. As if to substantiate the fears expressed by the other companies, the written report procedure had its main significance in the way it contributed to merit grievances. The effect of such a procedure is to put the burden of proof on the company.

Appeal Mechanisms and Individual Complaints

No union has indicated any desire to be in on the initial determination of merit increases, but generally unions have insisted upon the employee's, and sometimes the union's, right to challenge management's decision. Four agreements specifically set forth that merit increase decisions may be the subject of individual grievances, although one precluded arbitration. A fifth contract makes any disagreement by the *union* with the decision of management as to the employee's eligibility for a merit increase subject to the grievance procedure. Five other agreements contain no such provisions but do not appear to preclude merit grievances. Finally, one agreement did exclude merit grievances:

> . . . It is distinctly understood and agreed that such merit increases are at the sole discretion of the employer and failure to receive such increases shall not be deemed a grievance subject to the grievance and arbitration machinery. . . .

The agreement established an alternative appeal mechanism. An employee who has not received a merit increase in any four consecutive reviews (three consecutive reviews for certain occupations) may request that his case be referred to a joint company-union committee for "consideration." The committee consists of three union representatives, the dissatisfied employee's immediate supervisor, the head of the department, and a representative of the personnel department.

Sources of Merit Complaints

There are at least eight distinguishable sources of merit complaints: (1) personal antagonisms; (2) disagreements as to whether certain factors should be considered, such as attitude; (3) differences of opinion as to what degree of "merit" is required for an increase; (4) disagreements as to whether a man's potential capability or his performance on his current assignment is the proper basis for merit determination; (5) differences in evaluations of performance or in weighting of factors; (6) inconsistencies in management evaluations for different purposes; (7) faulty communication between supervisor and employee; (8) failure to follow the reporting procedures of the merit system. Once a merit grievance is filed it often brings into play several or all of these problem areas. Let us examine briefly each of these sources of merit complaints.

Personal Antagonisms. One of the bases most frequently cited by the grievant for a merit complaint is personality conflict. If the supervisor is clearly discriminating against a man for no other reason than because personal antagonisms exist between them, the company probably will overrule the supervisor. However, antagonisms are usually manifested in work behavior as well, perhaps because the supervisor directs the less desirable assignments to his antagonist who in turn responds by working somewhat less diligently. Antagonisms may also be accompanied by consistent disagreement between the engineer and the supervisor about what line of analysis should be used in solving problems assigned to the engineer. Where performance appears to have been affected by a personality conflict, the cases are resolved in the supervisor's favor more often than in the employee's.

Relevance of Factors. What factors should go into merit considerations? The unions challenge the appropriateness of such factors as "attitude," "ability to get along with other people," and lateness, on the grounds that if a man's on-the-job performance does not suffer he should not be penalized for any personal deficiencies in these particular respects. Such factors have been dropped from revised appraisal forms in some instances. Certain statements by management spokesmen in several other companies would tend to indicate that the union has persuaded them in some degree on this point.

Some companies clearly do not accept the union's view on these factors, however. Supervision insists upon disciplined behavior and correctness in attitude, penalizing employees through the merit review if they do not measure up. The union will not challenge supervision if in its opinion the employee's performance has also suffered. One grievance chairman described a case he had recently handled in which the engineer would do only what he was told and in general presented a poor appearance; that is, he took the "army routine." When he protested the denial of an increase, the union refused to support his grievance. There are many cases which are not as readily settled. While an engineer's attitude may not be *important to* his work, it may be *indicative of* his work —the quality and quantity of his output. Research and development work does not lend itself to measurement, and other observable (albeit intangible) factors such as "enthusiasm" take on great import. For most managers attitude was important in and of itself. A few mentioned the need to be able to encourage that "extra loyalty" toward management and the company on the part of engineers.

Degree of Merit Required. What degree of "merit" is required where that word is not elaborated in the agreement? Must performance be outstanding or just satisfactory to warrant a merit increase? Grievances occasionally raise this issue, especially when an older employee is involved. The company will admit that a man's performance is "satisfactory," but will then take the position that merit increases are only awarded for meritorious service, despite the fact that the company does not adhere to this standard among younger engineers where manpower competition is felt. Many companies may actually adhere to the criterion of outstanding performance in principle, but they apply it in practice only when the grievances arise from other sources. The inconsistencies in the companies' position in such grievances are often exploited by the union. In at least one case an arbitrator "could find no basis in the agreement for the company's position that a man must do 'outstanding meritorious work' to become eligible for a merit increase."

Capability versus Current Performance. A man's abilities to handle more complicated assignments may increase over time while he continues to perform the same level task. Should he receive a merit increase on the basis of his increased capability? Or should his merit progress depend upon his performance on the present job? When this issue arises in a merit grievance, the union will ask that the employee not be penalized because the company fails to use him to capacity.

Disputed Evaluations and Weighting. Difference in the evaluation of performance is common in merit grievance discussions. The supervisor may state, for example, that the man does not accept responsibility for a job and follow through on the assignment, to which the grievant, often supported by his fellow engineers, will answer that he does not have these faults. Or the supervisor may believe that the man took too long to complete a particular project; that he is prone to distraction from the main line of thought; that he is disorganized; that he needs continual supervision; and so on. The engineer may disagree that these are fair evaluations, or he may object to the weighting they receive.

Inconsistencies. Management's several evaluations of an engineer may differ one from another. If the reports on an engineer's performance review for retention or counseling purposes is glowing but his salary is not advanced accordingly, he has the basis for a grievance. Regardless of how vigorously the company protests that the reviews are for unique purposes and are separate matters under the agreement, the company's position is vulnerable whenever inconsistencies between the reviews exist. In one arbitration ruling the arbitrator disagreed with the company testimony that a rating and comment for retention purposes was "perfunctory and not relevant" to the merit review. These reviews and ratings were made by the same supervisor and, in the arbitrator's judgment, "could reasonably be expected to have some relationship one to another."

Faulty Communication and Failure to Report. Faulty communication is an important source of grievances. The engineer will not know the basis for his supervisor's merit decisions, even though the supervisor may believe that he has informed the man of his weaknesses. Similarly, many merit grievances are filed by engineers because the supervisors are delinquent in notifying them of the results of the review. The absence of a notice is seldom a favorable sign, and the engineer who has been passed over will take advantage of the supervisor's reporting error under the contract as an occasion to challenge the merit decision.

An Illustrative Case. One actual merit grievance case containing almost all of the above points can be used for illustrative purposes:

> The grievance occurred in a commercial division of an electronics firm involving over 100 engineers engaged in engineering work from advanced development to product planning. It was filed by a Senior Engineer, whom we shall call Handley, during the summer of 1955. He had received his last merit increase, a 7% raise, in June 1953. When he was reviewed again at the regular interval 13 months later, July 1954, he was notified by his supervisor that he was not deemed eligible for a merit increase. Under the contract whenever an engineer is denied an increase he must be reviewed again after three months. However, Handly was not notified until June 1955 and only then after he had contacted his union representative who in turn spoke to his supervisor. The June 1955 notification slip did not state clearly whether or not Handley was eligible for an increase. However, in conversation with the union representative the supervisor finally agreed to initiate a merit increase for him.
>
> In August Handley received another notice, stating that he was not eligible for an increase because his salary was

sufficient although he was considered of superior ability. The Senior Engineer was certain that three levels of supervision had initiated and approved an increase for him, but refused to use this information in the grievance proceedings because to do so would have violated a trust and prove embarrassing to his supervisor.

During August discussions on the complaint, the chief engineer stated that according to his philosophy of the merit system an average man does not merit an increase—a man must be of superior ability, especially if he is near the top of the bracket. When it was pointed out that the grievant was doing the same thing today he was doing 10 years ago, the union interjected that this was not the fault of the man. Another debate centered around whether the Senior Engineer had been put in for an increase in June.

The grievance discussions were resumed in mid-September. Management could now outline several reasons why Handley did not deserve an increase at the present time. The grievant was a "good engineer," but had "leveled off" in the technical ability; he had also developed a tendency to "slide out from under responsibility and try to place it on someone else." The union asked management how long this situation had existed. Management estimated that it had been brought to the grievant's attention in 1950 for the first time.

Management cited a recent example of difficulty with Handley. A motor for which he was responsible was "giving trouble" on the production line. The chief engineer stated that he should have "picked it up." The union disagreed that it was his sole responsibility and thought that supervision should have "tied in," since it had been brought out by management that the supervisor was aware of the motor situation but just stood by and watched. The parties finally agreed that both the engineer and the supervisor might have been at fault in this case.

According to management the Senior Engineer also had a tendency to digress to side issues and to follow details to a minute ending.

The comments entered on the engineer's retention review

form also mentioned these characteristics. Otherwise, the review results were better than the appraisal of the man developed by management during the merit discussions. This fact tended to support the grievant's case. Furthermore, it appeared that the supervisor had not taken time to discuss these matters with the engineer during the last several years.

At the conclusion of these discussions management agreed to review the man very closely again, continue to discuss the results with him, and advance his salary at the sign of improvements. All the parties—employee, union, and management—were satisfied with the outcome of the grievance case.

The Dynamics of Appeal Mechanisms

The particular complaint described above reached the formal grievance stage. A few do, but in most companies many more complaints are handled informally. In an even greater number of cases the engineer will go so far as to contact his union representative and complain about being denied a merit increase, but will be reluctant to take the matter to his supervisor. According to one grievance chairman: "The typical engineer will have a high opinion of his own technical competence, but he is embarrassed to appear greedy about money matters. He also fears that the supervisor will hold it against him in future review if he challenges the supervisor's judgment."

Another union official distinguished between engineers of varying lengths of service and their reasons for reluctance to process merit complaints:

> Young engineers are simply afraid to speak up to their supervisors. Older engineers are generally content enough with their salary that they don't want to rock the boat for a merit jump. Although there are exceptions to this statement, the grievances generally come from the engineer with 3 to 10 years who has both the confidence in his ability to do the work and some courage to speak up.

Even with the middle service employees, however, the grievance chairman practically has to "con the guy" to get him to take up his grievance with his supervisor.

Merit grievances processed by the engineering unions seldom resulted in a retroactive adjustment. More often they concluded with a compromise, such as a promise for an early review date for the next review. An important product of most grievances was a full discussion of the employee work record.

The unions have had even less success in arbitration than in the preliminary steps of the grievance machinery when merit matters were involved. One union took the issue of merit denials to arbitration four times (several separate and different cases each time) between 1955 and 1958 without a single success. On each occasion a slightly new twist in the situation gave the union hope that the arbitrator might rule in its favor. In 1958 the union appealed three cases. In one of these cases, according to the union publication, the arbitrator decided in favor of the company because the supervisor had a past record of fair merit review and appeared to be acting in good faith in the present instance. Generally, the arbitrators have ruled that it is a "pure judgment feature of supervisors," and that only evidence of "poor judgment, discrimination, and so on" would justify a reversal.

When one grievance chairman was asked if a supervisor's decisions in awarding merit increases were influenced by the knowledge that his decisions might be reviewed, the chairman commented:

> The total effect of the grievance procedure has little effect on the distribution of merit increases, which is more affected by personal attitudes. Sure, the supervisors try to be honest and give the better man a little more than the less competent man, but he does this only within small ranges—small differences between the best and the average. The supervisor will take the amount of money he has available and go through the group distributing it in such a way as to minimize discomfort. He will, for example, apply his knowl-

> edge that the older engineer, even if most deserving, is more satisfied with his salary and is less likely to resent or complain about no increase. Believe me, he is more concerned lest he alienate his personal relationship with individuals than he is about the grievance chairman showing up.

Many managers agreed that the prospect of grievances had little, if any, effect on the supervisors' merit recommendations. Other managers indicated they were in doubt as to whether there was an effect or not.

Following the comment quoted above the grievance chairman stated:

> Supervisors are not rough enough. They are chicken hearted when it comes to telling a man he's not doing a job, or what he is failing to do. Most of the time spent in grievance sessions is consumed trying to get a supervisor to tell the man these things.

This last comment applied with equal force to the experiences under the contract which precluded grievances, but which did provide an alternate appeal mechanism. According to a spokesman for this company, the review by joint committee has brought about a closer relationship between the supervisors and their personnel.

> Many times the supervisor will not discuss a definite problem with an employee, and the employee flounders. At the committee meetings the job of the personnel department is to get the supervisor to give his reasons for merit action fully and frankly. At the same time, the presence of the union bolsters the individual so that candor can be used on both sides.

This candor presumably works to the benefit of all concerned. In one case the company derived some unexpected goodwill from a joint committee session. The union expressed itself as being very favorably impressed with management's preparation and presentation of their merit reasoning.

It is probably unnecessary to state that there is no single

engineering union approach to merit grievances. Some unions vigorously solicit and process merit grievances. A few do not want to get involved in any way in individual merit review complaints. One union leader said he did not dare press for grievance rights on the merit system because the union members were opposed to union involvement.

This section and the preceding sections have treated aspects of the merit review systems commonly advocated by the unions and currently in use in some companies. Two approaches to merit review that have been advanced by certain unions are of interest here even though there is no actual experience under these plans to report. One, which we may refer to as the Point Plan, was later instituted by the company in 1959. The other—the Growth Rate Plan—had not been accepted by the company upon which it was being urged.

The Point Plan

This plan resulted from negotiations between Company A and its engineers' union in 1958. Entering negotiations in the summer of 1958 the union listed its "musts" for a new merit review plan:

1. Right of association to question amounts of increases to engineers.

2. Standardized and understandable performance rating form with a standardized weighting for the several performance characteristics on which engineers rated.

3. Rating form broken down into enough detail so that a supervisor can fix attention successively on the individual aspects of the engineer's performance without being distracted by the other factors. (This will end the present slovenly procedure, where the supervisor is expected to form an over-all judgment of the engineer's performance with no intervening steps. In addition, it will enable the individual engineer to question the supervisor in detail as to where his performance has fallen down on the particular factor under discussion.)

4. It must explicitly recognize that an engineer cannot be held responsible for poor planning on the part of the company which results in his being assigned work beneath his classification, and guarantee that he will not suffer in his merit increases as a consequence of such an assignment.

5. The increases must depend absolutely on the scores received on the performance rating, reducing as far as possible the amount of subjective judgment which must be performed by the supervisor.

6. Employee's increase must be based on at least two performance ratings.

7. The engineer must be given the opportunity to examine and comment upon any performance rating used to determine his merit increase.

The proposed rating form included the following general performance characteristics, each with several specific aspects:

I. Communication
II. Organization, Scheduling, Planning
III. Producing Results
IV. Technical Competence
V. Judgment, Understanding, Manner of Approach to Assignments
VI. Work with Others
VII. Professional, Personal, and General Characteristics.

Each aspect of each general characteristic of the man's performance was to be given a rating from zero to four. However, the supervisor had to decide which specific characteristics were very important, moderately important, and not important in each engineer's assignments. The ratings were to be weighted by factors of eight, four, and zero respectively. The maximum attainable score for any individual was equal to 1,000. It was a stated requirement that the average engineer at any salary level would receive 500 on each performance review. (The detailed performance rating form and instructions for computing rating scores under this proposed plan appear in Appendix B).

The outcome of negotiations represented a compromise. The company did not accept the union's plan, but it promised in writing to institute a formal merit review program in approximately six months. The plan was to be developed by the company, not subject to negotiation, although the company agreed to consider any constructive plan the union might advance.

Meeting pursuant to this commitment, engineering management and personnel officials expended considerable effort to come up with something that would be acceptable to all concerned. Just before the plan was reported to the union, an executive who played a principal role in the development of the plan commented: "We were very pessimistic about the entire project at the outset, but now we are much more enthusiastic. We surveyed all of the rating forms in existence. Now we think we have something that will be a challenge to management."

He outlined the factors that would be covered by the plan as it was generally conceived at that time. The plan consisted of three parts:

I. Management's Assigned Objectives
  A. Technical excellence
  B. Time and cost schedules
    1. How well does he meet them?
    2. Does quality suffer under pressure?
    3. Does he contribute to cost control in use of expense accounts, testing facilities, etc.?
II. Assignment Capabilities
  A. Performance on the job assigned (Or ability to perform a given job assigned to him)
III. Professional Actions
  A. Engineering-supervisory working relationships
    1. Contribution to the planning of the work
    2. Supervision and follow-up required
    3. Response to job irregularities that impose on personal convenience, such as overtime and travel

B. Effectiveness in dealing with other individuals and groups
   1. How does he contribute to accomplishments of others?
   2. How does he use contributions of others?
C. Contribution to engineering profession
   1. Stimulation of others
   2. Morale
   3. Company reputation
   4. Advancement of others

A supervisor would not rate a man on traits, such as his attitude, for purposes of merit increases, a feature of the plan that represented a concession to the union. However, an executive cautioned:

> The engineers do have to recognize one thing—they are still working for someone. About one transfer for personality reasons is all we will stand for. We want to keep the concept of boss, despite the fact that the engineers don't like this authority.

The company had not decided how to weight the scores of the men on each of the three areas. It was considering assigning a weight of unity to I and III, and a weight of three to II. II also required variable weighting to give two men who performed similarly on comparable jobs different final scores if one had considerably more experience than another.

The company's plan incorporated most of the "musts" listed by the union during negotiations. Two features, however, were missing. First, only one rating was specified during each review period, not two as the union requested. Second, there was no guarantee that an engineer would not be handicapped if he was assigned work beneath his capacity or his classification. In fact, part II of the company's plan clearly was based on a man's performance on his present assignment, not his personal capacity or the work level of his classification.

Company A realized that it faced a problem in establishing and administering the plan, especially in coordinating the efforts of the several hundred supervisors in many divisions who had the responsibility of rating thousands of engineers.[2] A training program was planned to include every member of engineering management to enable them to use the plan properly. In a concluding comment the executive stated:

> Yes, I believe it is a good idea with or without a union. Under the plan the manager has to be pretty specific as to a man's assignment, and his responsibility. Then he will judge as to how the man performed against them.
>
> These are just principles of good management. It is true that engineering management is more willing to accept the extra work involved because it has been demonstrated that the engineers want something along these lines. It is not simply a case of personnel foisting something on them.

Growth Rate Plan

For one union representing aircraft engineers in Company B a merit plan based on growth rate curves has become a key objective. The union has campaigned on behalf of the idea among its members, their supervisors, the company's staff personnel, other professional unions, and professionals

[2] In February 1961 a check was made with the union to learn about how the employees had reacted to the plan and about other subsequent developments. What the union leader reported can be paraphrased as follows:

"When the plan was explained it appeared to have real merit. We regarded it as a laudable attempt to measure a man's job performance. Problems developed, however. First, supervisors were not trained to use the plan; many didn't even understand it. Second, many engineers were not prepared for it. It was, after all, the first time they had had such candid opinions expressed to them. I would say it was those who didn't like how they were evaluated who were upset about the plan, and disapproved of it. In September 1959 we processed a grievance over what we thought was an instance of misapplication of the plan. The company's reaction was to loosen the plan, to give their supervisors more latitude. We not only objected to the change in the plan, we were concerned about the way the change was made, unilaterally by the company. Therefore, we went into negotiations in 1960 with the demand that management not be allowed to change the plan unilaterally. As it happened we were forced to strike over that issue, but that's another story. . . ."

in general. The growth rate plan is not a substitute for the point plan such as the one described above. The point plan centers on the comparison and rating process, whereas the growth rate plan concerns the conversion of ratings into salary increases. The plans represent a difference in emphasis based on a difference in judgment as to which part of the merit system is the more important.

The union at Company B did not challenge the company's fundamental basis for making merit review decisions, which was essentially the subjective judgment of immediate supervision ranking engineers on a totem pole according to value to the company. It was not interested in any scheme to make this evaluation process more objective. The union president wrote in the organization's monthly publication:

> Under our present organizational arrangement (assignment of tasks to groups, individual designs never objectively evaluated unless they fail dramatically, no particular effort to assign individual responsibility, etc.) evaluation of engineers is going to be largely subjective. These evaluations will be as good as, and only as good as, the supervisors who make them. Any effort to disguise this fact by complicated, sometimes mystic, procedures is more likely to result in poorer rather than better evaluations.

What the union was proposing was simply a different way to convert the supervisor's subjective judgments into merit increases.

The union president explained the plan:

> . . .We are proposing that each supervisor assign each engineer an *annual growth rate* instead of a discrete, one-time salary increase. This growth rate would be punched on each engineer's payroll card and he would automatically receive the specified increase twice a year. Then every six months each supervisor would review the progress of each engineer, just as at present, to see if his work performance warranted changing that annual growth rate, either up or down. The

growth rate punched in the payroll card would then be changed accordingly. . . .

The growth rates to which engineers would be assigned could correspond to the company's historical salary growth curves by deciles or to some idealized set of growth curves.

The advantages to the union were described or implied in the same publication:

> At present, each engineer is considered for a merit raise a month or so before each semiannual review. If his salary happens to be above the minimum for the next higher classification and below the maximum of his present classification, he would be considered for a reclassification raise. Some engineers receive a merit raise at each semiannual review period. Others may only receive a raise every one and one-half or two years, or even less often. The primary variable in salary growth is the frequency of the raises; the secondary variable is the size of the raise itself. Thus a smaller than average raise each year is the growth rate equivalent of a larger than average raise every year and a half.
>
> Herein lies a serious shortcoming of the present system. An engineer cannot really evaluate his rate of increasing ability until he can plot his salary growth curve for two or three years. Even more important, he is unable to detect a change in his growth rate until after from one to three years at the new rate. This makes it very much less likely that he will recognize the need for him to change something, his job, his attitude, his technical knowledge, etc., as soon as he should. [Under the growth rate plan an individual always knows where he stands.]
>
> Another shortcoming of the semiannual merit review concerns transfers. If an engineer transfers a short time before a merit review period, he usually is passed over at that period. No matter how conscientious his new supervisor may be, it is very difficult for him to place a recently assigned engineer on the totem of his entire group. Most transfers are made for the company's convenience and they should not interrupt an engineer's salary progress. [Under the union's plan . . . the

company could keep an engineer on his previously established growth curve for a predetermined period of time to give him a reasonable chance to establish his competence in the new position.]

Another shortcoming is that the present system permits, perhaps even encourages, a casual attitude among supervisors concerning merit reviews. If a supervisor isn't sure what increase an engineer should receive, he can make a guess and then make a correction at the next review. If he later believes that the earlier increase was too small, he can recommend an extra large one next time, and vice versa. A supervisor would be very much less willing to have to tell an engineer that he was being assigned a growth rate of, say, $35 per month annually, change it to $30 six months later, and then change it back at the next review. These changes would have to be explained in terms of changes in the engineer's performance.

There is also a psychological disadvantage inherent in the present system. A merit raise has too much the connotation of a "present" rather than a natural consequence of the engineer's continuous increase in capabilities. . . . In fact even the word "merit" carries the connotation of something. . . over and beyond the call of duty rather than normal growth. [These disadvantages would be eliminated under the growth rate plan.]

The union believed that there were other advantages. The supervisor could more readily separate the effects of business conditions from individual performance. If it became necessary to cut the merit pool, individual increases would be cut automatically, without shifting anyone from one curve to another. It would be easier for engineers to get classification promotions. The man's growth curve would determine when he passed from one classification to another. It would only be necessary to argue which growth curve was appropriate.

Some disadvantages were anticipated by the union, supervisors, and upper management. Those possible disadvantages conceded by the union, along with the union's counter arguments, were listed in its monthly publication:

> The following could be disadvantages of our proposal:
> 1. An engineer might be assigned a particular growth rate and then be forgotten. Presumably the company would continue to require each supervisor to prepare a semi-annual totem pole. Thus any discrepancies in the relationship between his engineers which might arise would manifest themselves and he would take the required corrective action. Besides, each engineer would be free to discuss the situation at any time.
> 2. It might cause a supervisor to be reluctant to assign a zero growth rate to any engineer and thus result in raises for undeserving engineers. This might happen at first, but they would quickly upset his totem pole relations and he could not long put off taking the appropriate action.
> 3. It would tend to make reclassifications automatic. Actually, they are nearly automatic now in most instances. However, in the event that an engineer's growth rate caused his salary to reach the maximum in his classification and his superior did not believe he should be reclassified, the supervisor would either have to suspend the engineer's increases pending reclassification or permit the engineer's salary to exceed that maximum, a procedure already permitted by our contract.
> 4. It would be difficult to fit new hires into the system. Some special provisions would have to be made for new hires. They could be assigned a temporary growth rate or could be merit rated as at present for the first six months or first year.

Other objections were expressed by a significant number of the engineering supervisors who were surveyed by the union for their opinions about the plan. On the one hand, they were concerned about the effect of the plan on engineers' attitudes: below average engineers would tend to be discouraged, reduce output, and perhaps quit; others might have a false sense of security by regarding the assigned growth rate as a guarantee. On the other hand, the supervisors were worried about the extra administrative load that might be required. Finally they thought that, in practice, juggling of growth rates would be entailed to accommodate the ever-changing judgments of supervision; this would defeat the purpose of the plan.

The first of the supervisors' objections was elaborated by other management persons. They were opposed to the degree of candor that would accompany the assignment of growth rates. They believed that engineers do not *really* want to know how they are doing unless they are doing well.

Whether these anticipated advantages and disadvantages would actually result if the plan was introduced is an open question with respect to this research. It can only be said that they are plausible. Growth rate curves have been used in nonunionized companies, notably in two companies well known for the high quality of their engineering and research departments. They were also being used to some extent in a few of the unionized companies studied, although the unions concerned are not aware of this latter fact.

What is said elsewhere in this study regarding certain other personnel plans under unionized conditions holds true for this plan—the demand to rationalize, formalize, and make explicit is greater under unionized conditions, but the risk of doing so in terms of union influence or interference is also correspondingly greater. Hence, paradoxically, the management at Company B may be less willing to experiment with growth rate curves than it would if it had no union with which to contend.

Summary and Conclusion

Dissemination of information about merit budgeting, distribution, and rating has often had the consequences feared by management. It has been the basis for individual grievances, union-management discussions, and union demands. It has tended to weaken the supervisor's position, first, by publicizing information for which he previously was the chief source, and second, by removing any doubt as to the extent of his responsibility. In addition it has, presumably, removed a motivating element in the engineers' environment by eliminating secrecy, although an improvement in morale may be an offsetting influence resulting from the same factor.

Adding to the administrative load of supervisors are the duties to notify engineers of merit increases (sometimes in writing), to interview engineers about the factors entering into the merit increases, and to supply the engineer with a written evaluation. Middle and upper levels of management endorse some of these provisions as sound supervisory practices, although the supervisors themselves often resent the obligations imposed upon them and are lax in their administration. The rest of management joins the supervisors in opposing these procedures when they open the door to grievances.

When the company specifies the factors that enter into merit recommendations, this specification makes the decisions more vulnerable to merit grievances. Even when the factors are not set forth as such, reference to a particular merit criterion may give rise to union protest. Union objections tend to limit direct consideration of engineers' attitude, for example, despite the fact that for management's organizational purposes attitude might be quite important. Their appeals of merit decisions influenced by personal antagonisms as well as those arising from faulty communications between the supervisor and the engineer are frequently successful and, incidentally, to the net advantage of the company. Also the unions are many times charged with responsibility for the substitution of "satisfactory performance" for "meritorious service" as a standard for merit increases, but management itself is basically responsible for this substitution.

The above challenges and others made by the individual

engineer and by the union regarding individual merit recommendations tend in themselves to remove merit from unilateral control by management. Most merit grievances, however, do not lead to reversed decisions. Nor have arbitrators been inclined to award merit to the engineer in disputed cases; they preserve these increases as "pure judgment features of supervisors." Still there is the possibility that the threat of grievance action bears on the supervisors' merit recommendations at the time they are initiated, although the scant evidence available on the point suggests no such influence.

On a different level, the engineers have made broad contributions to a reconceiving of the merit systems. One proposal, a point plan based on weighted factors, would make the merit evaluations more explicit and, hopefully, more objective. To repeat an earlier point, these very features tend to make the supervisors' recommendations vulnerable to challenges through the grievance machinery. Another proposal would rationalize merit advancement practices by the assignment of individuals to growth rate curves. The logic of this proposal commends itself. The chief disadvantage of the proposal to the company might result from the apparent certainty of an engineer's future increases which is suggested by a given curve. This *appearance* of certainty might impinge upon the engineer's incentive.

A more general comment should be made before concluding our treatment of compensation in Part I. Recall the discussion in previous chapters regarding publication of salary data, disclosure of position descriptions and evaluation data, union access to information about business conditions upon which a company bases its decision to cut its next budget; and the discussion in this chapter about information on the operation of merit systems, merit criteria, reporting procedures, appeal mechanisms. An important point which emerges is that the engineering union forces an open versus a secret salary system. Thus far, our attention has been directed toward analyzing and documenting the specific effects associated with the union's interest in each of these matters. More often than not the "specific effects" described have been difficulties for management. However, the general consequence—and it is not as readily documented—is that management has been forced to *develop policies* in the compensation area, resulting in much sounder salary administration. The stronger feelings of "privacy" about compensation matters which typically exist in white collar groups had permitted the non-unionized employers to cover up inconsistencies of all sorts. Therefore the spotlighting of compensation practices and the subsequent development of policies which accompanied the onset of collective bargaining probably were more dramatic occurrences in the engineering departments studied than those which are usually experienced in the newly unionized production department.

PART III

Impact on Personnel Administration

CHAPTER VIII

Layoff Procedures: Rating Plans

THE engineering unions, born during or after World War II, were concerned about the huge layoffs predicted for the postwar period. Although generally these postwar layoffs did not materialize immediately, at least not in the proportions expected, the initial union agreements were written during this period and reflected the engineers' concern. In recent years additional factors have contributed to the emphasis on layoff procedures which engineering unions have placed in their bargaining proposals. These factors may produce changes in the relevant contract provisions in the future. The provisions which will be discussed in this chapter and the following one, however, are in most cases almost identical to those written in the unions' first contracts.

There is no single typical layoff provision among the agreements of the companies included in the study. A few contracts provide for detailed layoff procedures; others contain only a statement of policy. Some contracts emphasize seniority, whereas others make no mention of it. This chapter contains, first, an analysis of the basic interests the engineers and their unions have in controlling layoffs, and second, descriptions and analyses of two rating and ranking systems governing the order of layoffs. The elaborate systems for rating and ranking engineers for layoff purposes will be treated in considerable detail because they represent marked departures from the collective bargaining arrangements of other employee groups and because they epitomize the engineers' approach to the important matter of employment security. The next chapter will consider other methods adopted by engineering unions for controlling layoffs.

The Engineers' Interest in Layoff Procedures

Employment Security

Engineering unions have become especially interested in layoff policies during two periods—1947–1948 and 1957–1958. Sizable layoffs occurred in 1947–1948 in several of the companies studied. Then again in 1957–1958, for the first time in a decade, many of the engineering departments made substantial reductions in force. As a result of these experiences, several unions have placed layoff demands near the top of their bargaining objectives. The engineers' interest in layoff policies is not, however, attributable solely to temporary circumstances. Fundamental changes occurring in the conditions of the engineers' industrial employment have prompted them to revise their attitude toward job security.

The instability associated with employment in the research and development defense industries included in this study is one factor. Further, in the aircraft companies even the commercial engineering forces are believed to be quite vulnerable to large-scale cutbacks.

Routinization and specialization are two other factors enhancing the importance of job security for engineers. In many instances the lower rated jobs have been routinized so that engineers performing these jobs can readily be replaced with minimum training or break-in periods. Thus, a single engineer's value to the company does not increase during his tenure with the company in a manner that inherently provides substantial job security. Specialization of the man has a similar effect. Even where the job has not been deskilled through routinization, but has been narrowly defined instead, the engineer may find that as a specialist with specifically defined qualifications he is interchangeable within that specialty to a greater degree than the generalist was within the engineering function several years ago. Thus, an employer will be less hesitant to release the specialist during a temporary reduction because he knows that another engineer with the same specialty will be able to fill the position with a minimum break-in period required to acquaint him with the company's products. Furthermore, the narrow and specific talent the engineer develops may not be required by his employer on an indefinite basis. The specialty itself may even become obsolete in that industry. The above conditions have developed in certain industries. For instance, the mass employment of engineers in the electronic and aircraft industries can be contrasted with the conditions of some other industries in which a few engineers become intimately acquainted with a particular company's product and the company's unique way of performing the engineering or research task. The mutual dependence of the company and the engineer under the latter conditions provides the engineer with considerable job security.

Specialization bears on an engineer's interest in job security in another way—in job seeking. This was borne out during the layoff of engineers by a very large aircraft company in 1957. Engineer job-seekers with one specialty, such as servomechanisms, were not fitted for most other jobs, and reportedly experienced more difficulty than the generalist in landing another job.

The changing state of the arts also works counter to any concept that job security should increase with experience or length of service. Several persons interviewed suggested that the training the college graduates now receive better equips them to deal with the problems of the missile age than does the experience of the long-service engineer. Consequently the engineer may not have the security of knowing that his worth to the company is increasing with each passing year. His value may be declining! When one considers that the company is invariably paying substantially more money to the long-service engineer than to the short-service man, the former may be thought of as particularly vulnerable to layoffs, unless some strong cultural norm or contractual agreement protects him.

Another condition today, this one affecting the somewhat shorter service employee, results from the mass education of engineers and the mass hiring practices of large engineering departments. Companies find great variations in the quality of the engineering talent they hire. In 1957, after seven years of a tight engineering market, the demand for engineers slackened, at least temporarily. The several companies which had to reduce their forces at this time laid off the "deadbeats" hired during each of the preceding seven years. Most of the individuals laid off were surprised at being classed as "deadbeats" and placed first on layoff. They argued with considerable justification that if their performance reviews and merit progress were "par," as they consistently were, they should not be "summarily dumped" after several years of presumably satisfactory service. The feeling of insecurity in such a situation is shared by many more engineers than those who will actually be affected in a future layoff.

Operating in the opposite direction, to reduce the interest in job security provisions, has been the generally high level of demand for engineering talent, always providing alternate opportunities for the individual engineer. There is no guarantee, however, that the demand for talent in the next decade will be as brisk as it has been in the past. Moreover, engineers in the future may be less interested in opportunities *elsewhere*. As the engineers who entered the profession in unprecedented numbers after World War II grow older and establish community ties, they may become relatively more interested in the specific jobs they hold, and relatively less concerned about opportunities generally.

Actual evidence that the high level of demand for engineers could slacken came in 1957 and 1958, chiefly as a result of sharp cutbacks in defense expenditures. The July 31, 1957, issue of the *Wall Street Journal* reports on one of the first signs of the change in pace:

DOWNEY, Calif.—Is the great engineer shortage ending?

Not everywhere, to be sure, but there are some definite signs the demand for the slide rule operators is easing. And perhaps more meaningful, events in this Southern California town show how quickly a shortage can become a surplus. The situation that's emerging here—engineers actually walking the streets in search of jobs—is little short of amazing in an era accustomed to think only in terms of a "critical engineer shortage."

Here's what happened in Downey. On July 10, in an economy move, the Air Force suddenly canceled the Navaho guided missile project on which more than half a billion dollars has been spent over an 11-year span. North American Aviation's Downey plant had been the work center for the Navaho, and the reaction was swift; layoff orders for 12,000 workers, including more than 1,000 engineers. More than half these employees already are off the job; others will be laid off in coming weeks.

Organizational Security

Layoff provisions are more important to the engineering unions themselves than is conveyed by the above discussion of the engineers' interest in employment security—layoff is an area of critical conflicts of organizational interests. A few unions frankly admit that they place high priority on controlling managements' layoff authority because it is a technique for protecting active unionists who might otherwise be among managements' first choices for layoff. In that way layoff provisions contribute to the security of the union itself. Likewise, several managers spoke of the organizational aspects of layoff provisions, but from another point of view. Their comments can be summarized as follows:

Whether the unions' right to participate in the selection

of employees for layoff is implicit or explicit, such participation is untenable. Straight seniority, obviously, is not a practical basis for selection of layoff sequence for engineers. However, in the absence of such a hard and fast rule, judgments about individual abilities and specialties, about future manning problems, and about current and future technical difficulties become necessary. Such factors must be differentially weighed in each circumstance. An intimate working knowledge of the past, present, and anticipated working circumstances is required, which cannot be gained by the union leaders through short or sporadic "conferences."

Bilateral selection means agreement by *both* parties. Regardless of the explicit language, if bilateral participation is involved, and disagreement in selection of layoff employees results, the union gains another device with which to assert "rights," and cause dissension. Also, such "bilateral participation" (really the right of checkmate short of legal action) places the union in a position of wielding considerable power and influence over individual employees, especially those who are junior in tenure. This becomes a club in the hands of a union representative. People do what he tells them to, because in the absence of rigid rules, he can grant or withhold his support or maneuver to have any one individual laid off when the work force is being reduced.

This influence has special significance if a contract does not provide compulsory union membership. Power in the hands of the union representative in layoff circumstances provides a substitute impetus for an engineer to join the union. Union officials will fight for a loyal supporter and an avid union member, and, at best, will ignore a nonmember who perhaps personally opposes them or their theories.

The situation described had not become an important phenomenon in any of the unionized engineering departments studied; the managers quoted above were expressing the *fears* they had about what could happen if the union shared control of layoffs.

Descriptions of two ranking and rating systems governing

order of layoffs in two companies and an analysis of them follow.

RATING SYSTEM A

The layoff formula in the union contract incorporates (a) retention ratings based on the company's evaluation of worth (this rating being subject to the grievance procedure) and (b) points accumulated for months of continuous service. Supervision assigns the retention ratings to employees during March and September of each year, using a range from 60 to 120 points. The supervisors are further required to discuss the rating with each employee. Lists of retention ratings are made up for each job classification, ranking employees on the basis of the average of their last two retention ratings, and are distributed to union representatives after each rating. In the event of a layoff, only ratings established more than 60 days prior to the date of layoff are used, unless there are no prior ratings for an individual.

When a layoff situation develops, the employees with the lowest retention ratings are those termed "eligible" for layoff. The number on the list of "eligibles" is somewhat greater (usually 20%) than the number actually to be laid off. This is where length of service counts. For each month of seniority of each of the employees on the eligible list one point is added to that employee's average retention rating, producing a "modified" rating. The names on the eligible list are then rearranged in the order of their modified rating, and layoffs are made from the bottom of the list.

The system was applied to surplus—to layoff, transfer, or downgrade—over 500 engineering employees, reportedly, in 1957 and 1958. Men were typically laid off in groups of 15 to 30 at a time, and during the layoff period nearly all the occupations represented by the union were affected. We shall analyze the various elements of the contract provision and the administration of the provision during these layoffs with a view toward answering the following questions: What are the intended functions of the retention rating system? How well does the system operate? What are the consequences of the system for the employee and for the company?

The Rating Process

The two parts of this provision—the periodic rating process[1] and the application of the rating arithmetic in a layoff situation—may be distinguished for purposes of analysis. The purposes or functions of the periodic rating process would appear to be: to ensure that ratings are made in advance of the layoff situation; to give the engineer advance notice of his standing; to encourage communication between the engineer and his supervisor; to provide a means for an engineer to appeal his supervisor's evaluation of him; to increase the objectivity of the evaluations; to increase the consistency among supervisors of these evaluations. After each of these purposes has been explored, a few special problems arising in the application of the ratings will be analyzed, including the necessity to make provision for employees doing specialized work and the difficulty in securing waivers of the contract provision in special cases.

Advance Rating. An obvious purpose of the system is to require management to determine over time and in advance of a layoff situation the relative worth of each individual, in order that that evaluation, modified only slightly by the seniority factor, might be the layoff determinant. These ratings occur, year in and year out, whatever the prospects for a layoff.

Successively higher levels of supervision must meet and

[1] The rating process is separate from the company's merit review, which is also conducted semiannually. It is also unrelated to the "employee appraisal," another type of individual review recently initiated in this company for counseling purposes. For several years the retention review was termed "performance review," but this led to confusion with the merit review. The confusion developed because the employee expected the results of the two reviews based on "performance" to be wholly consistent.

agree in the process of ranking all the engineers in each classification drawn from many geographically separate departments. The extra administrative load placed on engineering supervision, a group which is rather stingy with its time for such work, must be an onerous thing for them, especially during the many years when no layoff is contemplated. Whether the supervisors benefit from the evaluation-rating practice, and the engineering department gains from the interaction among its various levels of supervision in this rating process, is necessarily a matter for speculation. In these terms of company benefit alone it may be worth the time and effort required. It is true that during the years when no layoff was in sight all levels of engineering management were lax in conducting the ratings. Still, the considerable amount of personnel changes—turnover, transfers, upgrading—does require that the ranking be revised with some care every period.

One group within management wanted the layoff provision changed to lower from 60 to 30 days the time limit which must elapse before the latest list could be used. The company never recommended the change during negotiations—"we didn't want to ram it down their throats." Nevertheless, the fact that an individual engineer's relative retention worth to the company may change significantly within six months, as the requirements of the projects change, creates difficulties for the company in actual layoff situations. In fact, it is in layoff situations that manpower requirements are likely to be subject to the most drastic changes. This problem will be explored later in this section.

Advance Notice. A second purpose of the retention rating system is to apprise the individual of his relative standing regarding layoffs. Apprisal occurs in two ways: from the supervisor during a discussion of the rating and from the union representative who receives an official copy of the retention rating roster issued by the company after each review. On the one hand, one might consider that the union channel for obtaining this information tends to strengthen the individual's orientation toward the union. On the other hand, the periodical rating and ranking by his supervisor for job retention purposes reminds the engineer of the degree to which he is dependent upon his supervisor's approval for his job.

Other questions of impact can only be raised, not answered, by the present research. How does the knowledge of his retention standing affect the engineer's motivation on the job and his identity with the company? How does the retention information influence the engineer in his career planning decisions with respect to: (a) seeking employment elsewhere (if the marginal engineer is prompted to look for another job, is this generally to the current employer's advantage or disadvantage?), (b) obtaining a transfer within the company, (c) attempting to negotiate a larger merit increase. (On the last point, it can be argued that the engineer who realizes he does not have job security will insist upon more salary to compensate for the lack of security. If, notwithstanding his low ranking, he is nevertheless currently making a contribution in excess of his salary rate, he is in a position to take a short-run point of view in negotiating an individual increase. A contradictory view is that the engineer who realizes he is regarded as expendable will depreciate his own personal bargaining power and will not attempt to secure much in the way of individual increases.)

Communication. Another function of the system is to accomplish some "communication-understanding" between the supervisor and the employee. The provision states, "After the completion of such rating the company shall discuss with the employee his retention rating." These "required" interviews, like those for other reasons in this company and in other companies, frequently do not actually take place; and when they do, they are seldom very productive.

Even if candid discussions between the supervisor and the engineer do not occur, certain minimum information is nevertheless communicated. The man learns his relative standing in his classification, a rating which the engineer may take to indicate real deficiencies in his performance, or apparent deficiencies. Further, the man may learn of the relative standing of other individuals in his own classification and use this knowledge to substantiate any suspicions he may have of favoritism or discrimination. This information may become the basis for antagonisms between individual engineers, as well as between the lowly rated engineer and his supervisor. Finally, the man learns of changes in his relative standing. He may be given the reasons for the changes during the interview, or he may grieve to learn more. The hope is that as a result of the rating and any discussions he might have with his supervisor, the employee will be in a better position to improve his performance.

Right of Appeal. A fourth function of the system is to create an avenue for the employee to appeal the supervisor's decisions. The provision enables an employee to obtain a revision in the rating assigned by his supervisors through the grievance machinery. An individual can grieve within 30 days of rating. Any changes that would result from the grievance must amount to an improvement in the rating of 10% or it will not be implemented.

What is the effect of having the ratings subject to the grievance procedure? Certain tentative conclusions can be given concerning the approximately 200 grievances since the first contract, based on the author's analysis of a representative sample of 56 grievances. Almost all the grievances have occurred during periods when layoffs were actually contemplated—half of them in 1946, one-fourth in 1957–1958, all but a few of the remaining in 1947–1949. Thus the appeal feature for ratings is significant only in layoff situations. How were the grievances resolved? The grieving engineers were able to get an increase in their rating in one-third of the 56 cases examined. In some instances the grievance answers tended to give the individual some better idea of why he was evaluated as he was. In a few cases the grieving engineer had outlined in detail his own evaluation of himself. Does the grievance feature encourage political activity on the union's part? It is significant that in almost every case the union has supported the claim for higher ratings. Does the grievance feature tend to cause the engineer to look to the union in these matters? The answers to grievances are recorded "as a result arrived at by mutual agreement."

Objectivity. It is further expected that the rating system will make the supervisor's layoff retention decisions objective; that is, free from biases based on isolated experiences which happen to be fresh in mind, free from personality clashes, and so on.

The effective rating is an average of the last two ratings, and the importance of the "incident fresh in mind" at the time of either review is diminished accordingly. Because an individual's rating will be known to that individual and to other individuals, the supervisor probably becomes more conscientious in his ratings. The supervisor will be judged by others above and below him in the organizational hierarchy on his rating ability, and therefore he will be more, rather than less, inclined to rate the man in a way that is likely to agree with the evaluations of others. Thus, the supervisor will be pressed to subordinate his own sentiments in order to rate a man according to a broader consensus of worth. Of course, there is the risk that in subordinating his own feelings, the supervisor may be merely substituting a broader popularity also based on elements other than technical competence.

One could argue that the tendencies described above operate with or without the formal rating system. They do operate without the system, but less strongly. If no formal system of the type being discussed here exists, only a few individuals are affected when a layoff occurs; and a man may be laid off within a few days (or hours!) after he knows he is to be affected. Accordingly, it is possible under such arrangements for a supervisor to "take care of" a personal friend, or to get rid of an antagonist without too many repercussions. It becomes clearly quite another matter under the prior rating system to have to go on record on each and every employee twice a year, whether there is a layoff in sight or not.

Consistency. Finally, it is expected that the formal rating process with its successive steps will result in retention decisions that are more consistent among supervisors. Let us take an example—Design Engineers B. The first-line supervisor makes the rating of his Design B's at the group level; these ratings are then combined with the ratings of other Design B's at the department level, subsequently on a project basis, and finally on an organizational basis. At first the parties also used a rating form that required the supervisors to consider and weight identically the same criteria—quality, quantity, ability, potentiality, dependability, and attitude. The company discontinued using the form because supervisors were not using it as intended. They were determining the total rating which they thought was appropriate for an employee and working backward to make it come out right. Used in this way, the weighted form did not actually contribute much to consistency among ratings. However, the form was discontinued for an additional reason—the factors gave the union a handle for grievances. Recently, the union proposed that a form with weighted factors be used once again. The proposed form differed from the one used earlier in that it did not include the factor "attitude."

Application of Ratings

The application of the retention ratings in administering a layoff also presents problems, probably more tangible problems than those arising from the rating process alone. Some of the controversies that developed between Company A and the engineers' union in the layoffs of 1957–1958 can be used to illustrate these problems.

Employees Performing Specialized Work. The layoff provision of the agreement contained a section allowing the company to exempt certain employees from the retention listing system who filled jobs requiring qualifications not possessed by other company employees. The company is required to show which employees are assigned specialized jobs under this section at the time it furnishes the union with the list of the results of the retention ratings.

In the fall of 1957 the company invoked "the intent" of the section by retaining several individuals with special abilities who were otherwise subject to layoff. These employees had not been designated as assigned to specialized jobs before the layoff situation developed. Accordingly, the union filed grievances complaining that such employees had been retained out of retention order.

One case, typical of the others, involved a Design Engineer A who was low enough on the retention list to be included on the scheduled layoff list. He was retained by the company because of his specialty in the field of aircraft fuel systems and tankage. The engineer was responsible for the preliminary design and development of various aspects of fuel systems, such as integral tanks, flexible tanks, fuel systems, component apparatus, and fuel distribution systems. He had been employed by the company two years earlier to do this type of work. In his prior employment he had had 13 years of active continuous work in all aspects of aircraft fuel systems. The company concluded that in view of the manner in which project fuel system design was accomplished in Company A, the work could be handled only by an engineer with comparable experience or specialized qualifications. It had no other employees who could meet either of these requirements.

The union protested the company's "eleventh hour" designation of such persons otherwise slated for layoff. Further the union insisted that it had the right to carefully screen each case of a specialist designation. The company denied the grievances and managed to keep these contested individuals on the payroll.

Was the failure to have these engineers properly designated merely an oversight on management's part? Or are there reasons for management to be hesitant about classifying an individual as "performing specialized work" when no layoff is contemplated? To single out an individual who is otherwise a Design Engineer A and classify him separately will call the employee's attention to the importance of the specialized work he is doing and hence make him "harder to get along with"—for example, more insistent upon rapid merit treatment. Furthermore, to single out and to give him special treatment evokes the question in the minds of others who believe their work is specialized, "Why am I not similarly treated?"

Waivers. Later, in situations like the one cited above as well as other general situations, the company used the individually signed waiver rather than the section of the agreement which exempted employees performing specialized work. Under the waiver practice, the company calculated the modified seniority list from the retention and seniority factors, decided which employee from the affected group it "must" retain for business reasons, and asked an engineer on the "eligible" list but not in the affected group to waive his retention right in order that the "required" employee might be retained.

First, the frequency of the waiver requests and, second, the types of situations requiring waivers suggest respectively the magnitude and the quality of the effects of the contractual layoff system. The most conservative estimate of the number of waivers sought by the company was 25, out of layoffs numbering several hundred. The same company source thought that of these the company had obtained about a dozen. Situations requiring waivers are of at least three types: manpower requirements by general function, specific task completion, and field service assignment.

The first type of situation occurs when a layoff strictly by the modified seniority list will create an imbalance among functional areas represented by the remaining engineers. Several cases of this type occurred in the Design Engineer B classification which utilized only one retention rating roster, and yet included engineers performing work in many general functional areas, such as Hydraulics, Electronics, Structures, and Mechanical. In one case the lower end of the layoff list included too many Design Engineers doing electrical work and too few doing structures work. If the layoff were carried out according to that list, it would be necessary to put men experienced in structure design on electrical design work. The men who would be transferred could do the job but much less efficiently for some time. To avoid a loss in efficiency, the company secured waivers from structural designers not otherwise on layoff who admitted they could not immediately perform the electrical work in the quality and quantity required by management. Thereby, the company was able to retain the electrical designers.

The second type of situation develops when an individual who is up for layoff is needed to finish a specific task which he could complete within a few weeks, whereas another man, even a generally more qualified man, would require several months. In an example of this type, a man scheduled for layoff was doing an aircraft canopy job with a deadline a few weeks hence; it would have been impossible to get the job done on time if the man were laid off as scheduled. The company obtained a waiver, holding this man out of line, temporarily at least.

In the third type of situation, a man who is on field service assignment is scheduled for layoff according to the list. Should the company bring him back and lay him off, replacing him with another employee not subject to layoff? The company takes the position that it will not return the men for layoff whenever the geographical distance is great or the time until the field service employee is returned to home is short. The company will lay him off when he gets back.

The union, for its part, did not have a well formulated policy with respect to the company's waiver practice. It recognized that "the semiannual predetermination of rank order of retention does not always jibe with specific operational requirements at the moment of layoff." But it also took "the determined view that the waiver procedure is conducted wholly outside the perview of the contract," and thought that "it could probably be thrown out either in arbitration or in an unfair labor practice because it involves negotiation between the company and an individual wherein the individual is asked to negate certain rights given him under the [union's] contract." However, the union was reluctant to eliminate the practice completely because it was often to the employee's advantage to sign a waiver. That is, if the individual knew he could not perform well in the new job, or if he realized that he would be in the next group laid off, he might for one reason or another prefer to leave earlier.

The administration of the waiver procedure—the "crude" way in which these waivers were obtained from employees—did provide the union with an opportunity to attack the company on the issue. The union wrote in its newsletter:

> . . . Personnel have been given the "little room filled with high powered supervisors . . . little you all alone . . . decide in ten minutes" treatment. It is most offensively employed when a company representative thrusts a waiver in front of

an employee with remarks to the general effect that, "You know you can't do this job, it is the one you will be assigned to, and if you can't cut the mustard within one week we'll fire you!"

For a long time the union could only voice objections to what it regarded as unfair pressure tactics since none of the individuals signing waivers would initiate a grievance on the subject. In September 1958 the union got its test case. A Design Engineer B, whom we shall refer to as Smith, was "voluntarily terminated" for inability to perform work to which he was assigned after he refused to sign a waiver. Then he requested that his "wrongful termination" be rescinded.

The case arose as a result of a surplus of Design Engineers B in mid-September. Strict application of the modified seniority rating would have included for layoff seven employees performing a continuing assignment which required an electrical background and experience. Smith was among the seven on the modified seniority list next in line above the layoff list. The company judged that Smith, who was not an electrical design engineer, did not have the ability to perform the assignments, and this was explained to Smith. When Smith refused to sign a waiver he was assigned a specialty job in the electrical function. At the end of the second day he stated to his supervisor that he was unable to perform the assignment and requested to be laid off. Management reminded him that he had refused an earlier opportunity to be laid off; that it was no longer a layoff situation and Smith would have to be terminated for inability to perform the job should this prove to be the case. Three days later he was offered the opportunity of voluntarily terminating or being discharged. He chose the "voluntary termination," but grieved for reinstatement. In this case the union was successful in gaining from the company a reversal of a previous action: Smith was reinstated without loss of pay.

Meanwhile several discussions between the company and the union had led to certain promises on the company's part:

that it would endeavor to notify the union of all prospective waivers with the reasons therefor three days in advance; that the names of persons to be contacted would be submitted to the union; that the person would be given a personal interview explaining the problem, after which he would be given the opportunity for a personal interview with the union representative; that he would be allowed not less than 24 hours to decide whether he wished to sign; that the individual refusing to sign would be allowed time to prove his performance in the new job varying with the complexity of the position; that waivers would not be requested from any personnel other than those considered for layoff in the first step of the procedure. These conditions tended to make the waiver practice more palatable to the union.

Nevertheless, shortly thereafter the union requested the company to completely cease and desist its waiver practice. It claimed that the company had several alternatives available to it to meet its need to retain qualified personnel to accomplish the work. First, the company could use the classification of "employees performing specialized work" exempting the necessary employees from the layoff procedure. The company did not want to apply this section broadly for reasons suggested previously. Moreover management thought that it would not be fair to give the relatively lower ratings to those persons who were generally better performers but not currently engaged in a specialized task. Furthermore, if management actually tried to apply the special provision in such a way as would meet the needs of a large layoff, the union would undoubtedly raise serious objections.

The second alternative, according to the union suggestion, was for the company to give personnel who were needed for particular reasons higher retention ratings, thereby reducing their vulnerability to layoff. However, there was no way for the company to predict one year or even six months in advance who it would be necessary to retain in order to complete a certain project in the event of a layoff. Furthermore, even to try to take these matters into account would alter the whole concept of the existing rating system and would multiply the effort required of supervision to complete the ratings. It would be more difficult for employees to understand the basis for the ratings and would certainly give rise to more grievances over ratings.

A third suggestion offered by the union was that whenever a particular functional skill was in short supply, such as electrical, separate classifications could be established. The company regarded this as administratively unwieldy. It is doubtful whether the union actually would have agreed to much subdivision of the existing classifications, since any narrowing of the seniority unit tended to defeat the purpose of the layoff provision.

A fourth suggestion was that the employees on the modified seniority list who were out of reach of a scheduled layoff should also be offered the opportunity of voluntarily taking layoff in place of the people scheduled for layoff who were required by the company. In the company's view this would tend to defeat the purpose of the retention ratings system; namely, to keep the most valuable employees the longest. It was unreasonable to think that the company would deliberately make it easier for its better employees to look around for a better position.

Although the union was not able to force the company into any of the alternatives it suggested (recalls began replacing layoffs at about that time), the foregoing discussion illustrates the many dilemmas encountered under the rating layoff system.

General Comments on Rating System A

Company A also faced other issues in administering the layoff provision, such as those concerned with the right to transfer engineers from other nonunionized divisions into the bargaining unit and the right to return supervisors to the bargaining unit. These issues will be considered separately in the next chapter, however, since they were not related to the rating system.

The agreement allows for two important contingencies for the company—temporary layoffs and emergency reductions in force. Layoffs not exceeding 15 days may be made on the basis of operational requirements of the company without regard to the contractual procedure. Similarly, during an emergency layoff occasioned by the cancellation of contracts, the company may first lay off the employees directly affected for the time necessary to implement the contractual procedure.

A spokesman for Company A commented generally on the layoff procedure:

> It is O.K. Certainly management would like to have its own way, with no questions asked, but then if the employees had no recognized rights that would be bad for morale. Our procedure is a compromise. It also is a check on supervision.

In making this last point, he went on to contrast the procedures at Company A with the processing of a layoff in the engineering department of another (nonunionized) company in a related industry. It was reported that supervision in the latter company was haphazard in its layoff decisions; also, that the friendships that had developed between supervisors and certain engineers became important in these decisions. Thus, engineers who had developed good relationships with their supervisors were kept in preference to more qualified engineers who had not. The spokesman for Company A continued:

> You might say that with a little foresight the supervisor can do this under our system. That's true to a certain extent, but inasmuch as the rating can be reviewed every six months, it's less likely to happen.

Rating System B

The Formula

The order of layoff in Company B, as in Company A, was determined by a formula specified in the union agreement. At Company B an employee's retention credits were based upon educational background, length of experience, continuous service, and company evaluation. The company was obliged to take certain steps to avoid layoffs (these requirements will be discussed in a later section), but if it became necessary to lay off employees with more than 12 months' service, it had to make such layoffs strictly according to retention credits within occupational classification, subject to the proviso that the employees remaining had the skill and ability to perform the work then required to be done.

The layoff provision received its first test in 1957 when layoffs were necessary in several divisions of this company. A description of the clause that was in effect during these layoffs follows. The changes negotiated in the procedure in 1958 will be considered later.

Retention credits were based on a point system as follows:

A. A maximum of 60 points for educational background, experience, and continuous service as follows:
   1. Two points for each year's study at an accredited school toward a bachelor's or other degree in engineering, mathematics, or physical science with the following maximums—bachelor's degree, 8 points; master's degree, 10 points; doctor's degree, 14 points.
   2. 1/6 of a point for each month of continuous service with the company or an affiliate as an engineer or engineering supervisor.
   3. 1/12 of a point for each month of continuous service with the company or an affiliate in occupations other than engineer or engineering supervisor and 1/12 of a point for each month of employment as an engineer or engineering supervisor with a company other than the employer.

4. 1/12 of a point for each month of employment as an engineer or engineering supervisor with the company or an affiliate prior to the commencement of continuous service.

B. A maximum of 40 points for skill and ability, computed in accordance with the employee's service review plan. There are 10 job rating factors in the service review.

1. quantity of work
2. quality of work
3. dependability
4. job attitude
5. adaptability
6. job knowledge
7. judgment
8. initiative
9. organizing ability
10. effectiveness in dealing with people

Each of the 10 factors takes on a value from 0 to 4 according to the following table:

Unsatisfactory	—0
Fair	—1
Good	—2
Very Good	—3
Excellent	—4

The total of these values yields the number of points for skill and ability. Service reviews are conducted semi-annually for some employees, annually for others.

Point Ratings in Practice

Thus, potentially 60% of an employee's retention standing (a maximum of 60 points) is derived by fixed factors in which the company has no discretion. Only 40% is based on judgment factors. How important was each of the three factors —education, service experience, and company evaluation— in practice?

On the basis of certain reasonable assumptions about the composition of the bargaining unit in terms of the engineers' varying length of experience and service, it can be estimated that well over half of the engineers fell within a range of 15 points for the service and experience factor. The narrowness of the range is due to the fact that the company's engineers were predominantly short service engineers without much prior engineering experience.[2] The point of this type of analysis is that since in practice the spread of the service plus experience points was small, the company was in a better position to minimize the influence of these factors by the way in which it distributed evaluation ratings. Of course, the older engineers with from 10 to 20 years' experience, who constituted a 20% minority of the bargaining unit, probably had service plus experience points that ranged between 15 and 35 points and thereby did have a significant edge over the younger engineers, an advantage that very likely would not be wholly offset by differences in evaluation.

The next question is how did the company distribute evaluation ratings? Or, over what range did the evaluation ratings fall? The following table represents the distribution of ratings published by the union in March 1958:

Rating	*% of Total Engineers*	*Percentile*
10–14	1.2	1.2
15–19	17.7	18.9
20–22	32.2	51.1
23–24	15.1	66.2
25–29	28.4	94.6
30–34	5.2	99.8
35–39	0.2	100.0

Except for less than 1.5% of the employees at the extremes, the company was using only a range of 20 points out of the 40 points spread available to it. If the company was interested

2 Three-fourths (77%) of the engineers at Company B had less than 10 years' total engineering experience: 6.5% with 1 year, 10.5% with 2 years, 11% with 3 years, 9.5% with 4 years, 8% with 5 years, 7.5% with 6 years, 10% with 7 years, 8% with 8 years, 5% with 9 years. Similar figures were not available regarding number of years' service with Company B.

in minimizing the influence of the fixed factors in determining the order of layoff, it was defaulting on one opportunity to do so. There are at least two reasons for this tendency to default, one procedural and the other "natural."

Procedurally, there is no over-all requirement in the agreement or in company policy that there must be a certain spread between the top and the bottom rating. "Naturally," the tendency is for supervisors to rate all the men "a little above average." It was explained to the researcher:

> The supervisor has to live with the men, and doesn't want to antagonize them if he can avoid it. Nor does he want to discourage any of his men by a low rating. Furthermore, to give ratings over a wider distribution takes more effort than the supervisors are willing to devote to this sort of thing.

And it is a fact that "this sort of thing" has not been of much consequence during the long period when no layoffs occurred. One other point should be mentioned: the original purposes of the service review were to facilitate employee counseling and employee development; accordingly, it included factors, such as "job attitude" and "effectiveness in dealing with people," that were more appropriate for these purposes than for layoff. It is not surprising that the supervisors developed the attitude toward rating that they did, and that the pattern of rating emerged as described above.

The effect of the narrow range in evaluation ratings is to enhance the value of the fixed factors. This point can be nailed down with an illustration. A typical engineer at Company B might have a B.S. degree (8 points), about five and one-half years' service with Company B (11 points), no other engineering experience (0 points), and a service review rating of 19 (19 points). Management's evaluation of this engineer, indicated by its service review rating, is that he is among the lower one-fifth of the company's engineers. His total points would be 38. Another engineer in the same classification with three years' less service at Company B might have been given a service review rating of 23, indicating that the company placed him in the top half of the engineering force. This engineer's total retention credits would be 36. The less senior but significantly higher evaluated engineer would be the first of the two to go out the door. If the company chose to use a wider distribution of service review ratings, however, the difference between the engineer evaluated as lower one-fifth and the one evaluated as upper half could be more than 4 points.

The ratings were applied in an actual layoff only to a handful of persons at one location. The other reductions during 1957 and 1958 were accomplished by laying off engineers with less than one year service.

Regarding the single instance wherein the retention credits determined the order of layoff, a company spokesman commented:

> We had no employees with less than one year's experience. We gave notice to 15 men at our location, going strictly by the retention ratings. Of those laid off or transferred only a few would have been in the group removed without that provision. In fact, there were some engineers with longer service and higher salaries that management would have preferred to lay off. With this experience the retention rating system is being policed very closely.

Comparison with Company A System

Several differences between the Company B service review and Company A's retention review should be noted. The service review at Company B performed the dual purposes of counseling and of layoff ordering, whereas the Company A rating governed layoffs only. The service review included specific job factors, equally weighted, whereas Company A's retention review did not, although it did at one point in the history of the plan. The engineer at Company B could appeal the service review rating to the second level of supervision, but he could not file a grievance; hence, management maintained unilateral control of the ratings. At Company A the ratings were subject to the regular grievance machinery. The union at Company B, in contrast with the one at Company A, did not receive a list of the individuals and their ratings, which could in turn be made available to those members who were interested to see what ratings other individuals received. In 1958 negotiations the union at Company B did propose that the company compute the bottom 25% of the list of employees twice a year, rank them in order of their total retention credits, and inform them of their status. The company rejected the idea.

At Company B the first and second levels of supervision established the ratings within their group. In contrast to the system at Company A, there was no mechanism for integrating the rankings and ratings of all the engineers in a given classification through review of the ratings by successively higher levels of supervision. The fact that one group in Company B had an average rating of 20.6 and another had an average rating of 23.5 probably reflected more than differences in the quality of the engineers within these groups; it undoubtedly represented differences between the general level of standards used by the individual supervisors in the two groups. In view of the tight distribution of the ratings, such differences in the general levels of ratings among groups could be quite significant in a layoff.

The Revised Formula

The union obtained certain important changes in the retention credit formula during negotiations in 1958. The formula continues to be based on a total of 100 points, allowing 60 for education, experience, and continuous service. The rate of the accumulation of points for continuous service and experience, however, has been revised upward from 1/6 and 1/12 point per month respectively to 1/5 and 1/10 point per month. The service review has been discontinued. The maximum 40 points for skill and ability which were determined under the service review are now based on two measurements, each with a maximum of 20 points.

One measurement is a newly devised rating plan that will serve the dual purpose of determining merit increases and retention credits. The plan was not available for analysis at the time of the field visit to Company B although it is known that the new plan eliminated "trait" factors.

At the union's insistence, the other measurement is based on the relationship of the employee's salary to that of other employees of the same number of years of engineering experience. In each of several occupational classifications, also broken down into four promotional classifications, point scores are allowed for the position of the engineer within the rate range of his occupation-promotional classification with relation to that of other engineers in that classification. The range between the minimum and maximum yearly salaries of the classification are divided into categories for that purpose so that a progression of salary groups is established with point values of from one to twenty distributed among the salaries within these groups.

This latter procedure is intended to measure a concept called Engineering Value or Career Value. The assumption is that the relative position of a man's salary with respect to other engineers of the same experience level in his classification is a reasonably accurate indication of management's true evaluation of his worth to the company. If this relationship does not hold already, the union would force management to adjust the engineer's salary to conform with its (management's) evaluation of the man. In the short run, adjustments would only be made upward, of course. Those who would stand to benefit most from this would be the competent but more timid individuals who are not able or are not inclined to bargain for their share of merit money. Also by this measurement the engineer whose recent performance is not rated as highly as his past performance would not be as vulnerable to layoff as he would be if his skill and ability rating were solely dependent upon his present supervisor's current evaluation. Assuming that his relatively good performance in the past was matched by relatively good salary progression, placing his current salary high among others with similar experience, he has thereby accrued some security to help tide him through the current layoff situation. But the company may be just as sharply handicapped by this concept: judging from the actions of other companies in a layoff situation, the engineer who somehow got ahead in the salary game but who is performing below par currently is exactly the man that management would most like to cut, since he represents the least value for the money.

Both measurements of the new rating plan tie the company's evaluation of a man for retention purposes closely to its appraisal of the man for compensation purposes. Referring to these types of measurements a union official stated:

> The company cannot tamper with this system without paying for the privilege. If they think a man is unusually valuable, and wish to retain him during a layoff, they have to pay him what they think he is worth. No more slap-on-the-back, the high service review, but no money.

Another advantage claimed by the union for the new skill and ability measurements was that they would be more sensitive, and would result in a wider distribution of points. For example, the Engineering Value concept forces an even distribution over the full range of 20 points. This would seem to be to the company's advantage as well, if it prefers skill and ability to have more influence in the order of layoffs.

The union advanced one other concept in these negotiations which was completely unacceptable to the company. It was proposed as a third measurement of skill and ability. The concept was simple: that salary is a measure of an engineer's value. The engineer with the minimum salary would receive 0 points, the engineer with the maximum salary, 20 points, and the engineer with the median salary 10 points. Essentially, this tended to reward both length of service and unusual salary progress, but especially the former since much of the total salary progress is, in practice, a function of the passage of time. This is probably among the reasons why the company rejected this part of the union's proposal.

The engineering unions in several other companies have patterned their bargaining proposals on layoff after one or the other of the two rating and ranking plans discussed in this chapter. One plan which appeared to be patterned after the Company B plan, however, differed in one important aspect. According to the president of the union proposing the plan, points for skill and ability based on merit and performance were to be *cumulative,* and hence actually would be more a measure of length of service than of relative ability. To date, no other formula plans have been negotiated but the unions will certainly continue to show an interest in them.

Summary and Conclusion

The interests the engineers and their organizations have in controlling layoffs have essentially the same dimensions as those of the production worker.[3] The engineers want an equity in their present employment—that is, they desire rights based on tenure and other specified job inputs as protection against arbitrary release. Also, they desire certainty—they want to know in advance what their status is with respect to layoff. The engineers' union as an organization seeks to control layoffs also as a matter of self-preservation; it must prevent its officers and members from being the first to be dropped. Analysis in this chapter also indicates that conditions are changing in such a way that collective bargaining offers a more effective means of providing the engineers with employment security. Nevertheless the approaches adopted by some professional unions to solve the problems

3 See Sumner H. Slichter, *Union Policies and Industrial Management,* p. 98.

of job equity and certainty are unique and deserve special attention.

The order of layoffs in two companies are governed by rating plans that incorporate both ability and seniority. The rating plans assign specific weight to seniority, which represents a departure from managements' unfettered layoff practices and probably favors the long service employee. This would appear to be particularly true in Company B where the supervisors' use of a narrow range of evaluative ratings enhances the relative importance of seniority. The weight attached to seniority was not looked upon with favor by either company, though they did not report it as an important disadvantage during the layoffs implemented under their respective plans.

Each company was forced to lay off men whom it would have preferred to keep, and to retain men it would have preferred to cut, but seniority was seldom the culprit. The undesirable choices were often forced upon the companies because of the way they assigned their own ability ratings, not because of the influence of seniority. The ratings assigned prior to the layoff frequently were not appropriate when the layoff occurred, either because the rating had never been appropriately assigned or because conditions had changed to outdate the ratings. One company required special dispensation for employees performing work that only those particular employees were qualified to do. It also employed a noncontractual device, the individual waiver, to regain some of the flexibility lost by the union contract, particularly where the company desired (a) to maintain an adequate staff with experience in a general functional area, (b) to complete specific tasks, or (c) to fill out field assignments. While the company's needs were partially met by the dispensation and by the waiver, these needs were also partially compromised because of the constraints placed upon the company by collective bargaining. The union's objections to the waiver practice, based especially on the manner in which the waivers were administered, tended to restrict a liberal application of the waiver. Apparently management had to employ harsh or forceful tactics in obtaining some waivers, with resultant damage to employee relations. The union then secured limits on such tactics which tended to further weaken the company's ability to obtain waivers.

Just as the product of the ratings—the order of layoffs—contain disabilities for the companies' operations, so do some of the administrative trappings of the rating process provided by the collective agreements. Both plans feature (a) periodic ratings, which add to the administrative load when no layoffs are anticipated; (b) advance notice to engineers of their standing for purposes of layoff, which may enhance the feelings of insecurity of some engineers and the feelings of security of others (there is no valid means of ascertaining the secondary effects of an advance notice in terms of a man's application to his work and his identity with his present employer); (c) supervisor-engineer communication, which may result in more understanding, or which may add to antagonisms; (d) objectivity, a constraint on the supervisor, which may be to the net advantage of the company. Company A's plan was designed to attain a greater degree of consistency among supervisors on layoff evaluation. It also enabled the employee to appeal a rating through the grievance machinery, thereby bringing the union into the rating procedures; a process which has resulted in a moderate number of rating revisions. It cannot be stated whether these specific revisions operated to the company's advantage or disadvantage. One final comment on the effects of one rating plan: by making the rating subject to appeal and by injecting the union into the reporting process, the ratings tend to make the engineer less dependent upon his supervisor; in the opposite direction, the periodic rating process continually reminds the engineer of the extent to which he is still dependent upon the supervisor for his job security.

Thus, we see in these two companies an attempt to devise

a formula to govern layoffs with a sincere effort made by the parties to balance their respective needs and interests. In an innovative manner characteristic of the engineering participants in collective bargaining, they have endeavored to synthesize concepts of seniority and ability, and to let an individual know where he stands in advance of a layoff situation, but without eliminating all of management's flexibility when a layoff does occur.

CHAPTER IX

Other Layoff Procedures

THE PREVIOUS CHAPTER discussed the formula approach to layoffs. Now we shall turn to other means that engineering unions have utilized for governing layoffs or for minimizing the impact of layoffs on engineering employees. The agreements in two of the companies studied place emphasis on continuous service. A third agreement calls for rigorous man-to-man comparisons before an individual is selected for layoffs. Several agreements merely try to make management's layoff process more explicit and insist upon the right to grieve management decisions. As an adjunct to this effort most agreements call for minimum notice of layoff to the individual and to the union. Another stresses the need for the company to exhaust all alternatives to layoff. Others govern recall and place limitation on management's right to hire during a layoff. In some instances severance pay has been negotiated as a substitute for job security. Finally, super-seniority for union leaders during layoffs is provided for in many union agreements. Each of the above approaches to controlling layoffs will be the subject of a separate section of this chapter.

SENIORITY CLAUSES

The two companies discussed in the preceding chapter had layoff clauses allowing some weight for the seniority factor. Other agreements included in the study merely mentioned seniority as a factor to be considered if other factors were equal. Some agreements did not even include mention of seniority in this connection. Two agreements, however, required the companies to lay off by seniority within occupational classifications, reserving to the companies "X" list provisos of 5% and 10% respectively. We shall refer to these last two companies as Company C and Company D.

Company C

The contract discussed below covers a multiplant operation but is applied on a plant-by-plant basis. In many plants the bargaining units include all general salaried, nonsupervisory employees. According to the agreement, the first to be affected by a reduction in work load will be the least senior employee on the position affected. He has bumping rights: he may replace the least senior employee in the next lower level of his occupational ladder within the seniority unit. There are two exceptions to this rule: first, certain union officials have superseniority, removing them from layoff vulnerability; second, the company may designate two employees or 5% of the employees in the bargaining unit (whichever is greater) as exempt from layoff because of the outstanding abilities they possess. Management's list of outstanding employees must be made up in advance.

A manager at one of the engineering operations employing 150 engineers discussed this seniority provision in the latter half of 1957. He referred to the seniority provision as "The principal factor in the union relationship affecting the company." Conditions at that time required a reduction in the engineering staff of at least ten men. The manager could identify the first ten men he would "like to fire" but this group did not happen to coincide with the ten least senior engineers. On the one hand, three of the engineers that the manager regarded as particularly eligible for layoff on the basis of ability had eight to ten years' seniority; the others that management thought should be released were in the range of two to five years, engineers who had been employed during the period 1953 to 1956 "when anything alive was hired." On the other hand, most of the ten least senior men were "quite promising." Each of five engineers hired in June 1957, and still in their six months' probationary period at the time of the interview, was regarded by this manager as "outstanding or above average," although he did not believe one could be perfectly certain of an engineer's capability during the first two years of his employment. At any rate, he was loath to let these relatively new hires go.

The contractual list of "outstanding" employees was of no assistance to the company in this matter; in fact, the one that was current at that time did not include *any* engineers. Because the engineering staff was seldom affected by layoffs, the company could get more frequent benefit from the X list by designating employees in other (nonengineering) positions generally more sensitive to reductions in force.

Still, at the time the discussion with this manager took place, he thought there was one "saving" factor—the flexibility of the union leadership's attitude in administering the agreement:

> We have sensible union representatives. The engineers pick their leaders from among the best engineers. We can meet with the engineering general representative, explain to him that a man is deadwood, that he will not be promoted in the future, and that he would be advised to look elsewhere. After we know that the union representative understands, we sit down with the man involved and explain the situation to him. The man usually can be persuaded that it would be better for him to find another job.

What, then, are the net effects of this provision? It should be remembered that only one instance is cited. In other plants with different union leadership the contract may be more strictly enforced. Even in this instance, it is doubtful that the company will attempt to handle in the manner described above any more than a couple of the ten individuals the company would like to remove. It is one thing to persuade a man to resign voluntarily; it is another matter to ask a man high up on the seniority roster to take layoff out of turn. (Keep in mind that the waivers under the practice at Company A were secured from engineers next in line for layoff on the roster.) If a man will not take layoff out of turn, the company might attempt to terminate him. As a minimum deviation from what would otherwise occur in the layoff situation developing in 1957, the company would undoubtedly delay implementation of the layoff until the five new hires were no longer in their probation periods.

One aspect of the transaction referred to above by the manager is that management would be compelled to obtain the union officials' understanding in this matter before proceeding. Is this relationship one of mutual understanding? If so, what is the other half of the transaction? Unfortunately, the question cannot be answered on the basis of the research in this company.[1]

Company D

The contract in Company D provides that seniority would govern in layoffs. Employees with less than three years' seniority are permitted to use their seniority only within their occupation. Employees with three or more years' seniority can displace a less senior employee in a lateral or lower labor grade anywhere within the bargaining unit, provided, however, he has the ability and can perform the work of that employee. The company can select and retain in each occupation engineers with less than three years' seniority in an amount equal to 10% of the total number of engineers in each occupation after layoff.

This *clause* is less severe from the point of view of management than the clause in Company C in many respects; for example, an employee with less than three years' seniority cannot displace into lateral occupations or bump into lower grades. Also, the X list is about twice as large and does not have to be drawn up until the layoff occurs. More importantly, however, the union in Company D takes a much

1 The usefulness of the concept of "transactions" in a situation such as this one, however, is supported by the research of Melville Dalton. See his article "Unofficial Union-Management Relations," *American Sociological Review*, October 1950, pp. 611–619.

stricter view of contract application than does the union in Company C. Thus, excepting the 10% X list, Company D was effectively committed to a layoff system based on seniority, with all the attendant problems such as those that seemed at first to confront Company C.

Other Companies

A few other companies are required to lay off first all employees still in their probationary period in the event of a layoff. The personnel manager of one company, which has a clause that requires the company to cut all employees with less than one year's service before any other employees can be laid off, described the effect of this requirement as it was applied to a small reduction in force in one operation: "We had to cut back 11 men. We were obliged to lay off men hired within the last year regardless of how promising they were, rather than the marginal employees we would prefer to let go." He identified four of the "marginal employees" that would otherwise have been the first to go. One had been with the company five years, another eleven years.

The unions representing the engineers of at least two other companies have tried unsuccessfully to negotiate seniority plans similar to those at Companies C and D.

Man-to-Man Comparisons

The first section on seniority dealt with the extreme use of seniority to govern layoffs. The agreement of Company E, which is the subject of this section, goes to the other extreme —omitting any mention of seniority. Instead, the provision features man-to-man comparisons as a prerequisite to layoffs; they are essentially the only contractual part of the layoff procedure.

Company E

The relationship between Company E and its union was one approaching cooperation. The union itself assumed a very conservative and professional posture. These conditions were manifested in the union's layoff policy, a policy which was not at variance with the company's objective in this area. The union president asserted publicly and privately that it was the union's objective, also, to have layoff determined by "straight value to the company."

Further, the union leader had no quarrel with the clause which stated, "After . . . comparison, management shall determine which employees shall be retained." It was all right for management to have the say on who was of the greatest value to the company. This "say" was apparently to be final in practice inasmuch as the union president stated that the union would not be disposed to challenge management's decisions if arrived at properly—that is, through the proper procedures.

Under the collective agreement, this procedure involves essentially the following steps:

1. Management will determine how many engineers of each occupation shall be laid off.
2. They will identify all engineers having these or related occupations.
3. They will appoint a management review committee.
4. This committee will review the performance, educational, and experience record of each of these engineers and compare them with each of the others.
5. They will then decide which of these engineers possess the greatest ability to perform the required work and to maintain or improve the efficiency of the company.
6. Finally, these will be the engineers retained.

An idea of the amount of effort this procedure entails can be gathered from the experience of a separate division of the company employing about 1,000 engineers who are covered by an agreement containing an identical layoff provision. In August 1957 the company decided to lay off five men in the four classifications deemed by management to be overstaffed. For each of the four classifications, management created an analysis group of five supervisors who as a group were acquainted with all the employees in the classification being reviewed. Each group screened the personnel records and pulled out the files of the employees in the classification to be affected and ranked them, considering several factors, including formal evaluation and potential for growth. A member of one of the analysis groups reported that his group had spent 40 hours analyzing the records of 70 people considered for layoff in order to lay off one man. The group then wrote a memorandum to demonstrate that the man had been duly compared with other comparable men. Another manager in this division commented, "It would be an impossible task if we were to have a substantial layoff."

In the second half of 1957 it began to appear that the company would be forced to carry out a substantial reduction in the engineering force in its main divisions employing over 6,000 engineers. No major layoff developed, but a small one was initiated in late summer. In this instance the effect of the union, backed by the contractual requirement on procedure, was to prevent the layoff. The comments of company spokesmen corroborated the following description of this situation given by the union president:

> A member reported to the union office that he had received a two weeks' notice of layoff. When we checked with the company it was apparent that the procedure stipulated in our contract had not been followed in the selecting of this man for layoff. They had not made a man-to-man comparison of all other employees in his occupation. After we called this to the attention of management and started processing a formal grievance, management issued instructions that this layoff notice be cancelled and that four other engineers in our bargaining unit who had already been laid off be recalled. It simply was not worth it for the company to check the records of several hundred men in several locations just to lay off a few men.

The significance of the provision is better appreciated

when the company's actions within the bargaining unit are contrasted with its actions at an out-of-plant site, where both represented and nonrepresented engineers were assigned. In the proposed layoff at that site, direct line supervision was granted full permission to lay off nonrepresented engineers. To lay off represented engineers at the same site would have been a major operation involving teams of line and staff management.

The company moved to meet the problems encountered under its contractual commitment in three ways. First, it undertook to weed out and "release" those marginal engineers whom it might otherwise have "laid off." Second, it "war gamed" a layoff. Third, it undertook to develop new techniques for implementing the contract.

The first point is that the company was discouraged from "culling" the marginal performers and then calling it a "layoff." The union agreement at Company E makes it more difficult to lay off a man than to terminate him, since there is no discharge clause requiring the company to demonstrate just cause, and since the union leadership was known to favor a policy of higher minimum performance standards for the company's engineers. Further, the union did not oppose the selective release of the marginal producers acquired during the previous several years. For these reasons, it was to the company's advantage to let a man know whenever it actually considered his release a permanent layoff, and not a temporary one. The formidable layoff clause also probably prompted the company to consider terminations for engineers it might otherwise have decided to lay off.

Letting the man laid off know he is actually being terminated and not merely laid off has its potential disadvantages for the company. The man is less likely to remain unemployed and available to the company in the event that the company should have some unanticipated demands that would require a reinstitution of a "warm body" hiring policy. This drawback would be important if a large percentage of the engineering force is involved. Another disadvantage to candid terminations might be its adverse effect on morale of other engineers, although this is by no means a foregone conclusion. According to the union president, the engineers he represents share his own desire that the company do more culling, be more selective. Perhaps, then, the morale and the incentive of the remaining engineers are heightened by the terminations.

The second response of the company, that of war gaming a layoff, illustrates the way in which the union can prompt a company to do more advance planning. By simulating a layoff the company put itself in a position to accomplish a real layoff, if one became necessary, under the current contract language, and with the techniques currently available to management, and in the short period of time available.

The union proposed that the company go further along these lines by making it an annual practice to war game a 30% layoff. Without trying to distinguish between individuals whose abilities were nearly equivalent, the parties could be reasonably sure that this 30% would include those who would actually be affected in a 10% layoff. The union included another feature—employees would be informed roughly of their layoff standing. After taking the rough cut of 30% the company would notify those engineers in the remaining 70% that if a 10% layoff were to occur *that day* their names would not be on the eligibility list from which those to be laid off would be chosen.

The union felt strongly about the advance notice feature for reasons similar to those supporting the ranking systems discussed in the preceding chapter. The engineers at Company E had been unnecessarily uneasy during the entire layoff scare in 1957–1958. Even first-rate engineers were nervous because they did not know their standing. The union charged that it was this insecurity on the part of the whole force that enabled the company to get away with an "infinitesimal" merit increase in December 1957. The uncertainty of the situation was advantageous to the company in other ways. For instance, a manager asserted that after a 10% reduction in the engineering force of another company had been effected, output at that company increased 10%. The union made another argument in behalf of its proposal: Just as 70% of the engineers could rest easier with this knowledge, the 30% could begin preparing intelligently for "any eventuality." From the company's point of view, this preparation—job hunting, for example—distracted the engineers from their work.

In rejecting the union's war gaming proposal, which went much further than the company's own practice, management also took the position that it would damage morale to inform a man of his low standing. It was repeated time and again by management people that the engineer is only interested in knowing where he stands if his standing is favorable. He is not *really* interested in knowing if it is unfavorable.

One chief engineer at Company E advanced two additional arguments against the ranking of the war gaming plan:

> No man should be identified at a point because there is no point. Conditions are constantly changing; different projects have different requirements. Furthermore this constitutes an unproductive preoccupation. It is better that a man work toward professional objectives and not be concerned about his specific position and layoffs.

The third way in which the company responded to the union challenge in the layoff area was to step up consideration of methods of implementing the provision. Many informal union-management sessions were devoted to this subject. The company came up with a skill inventory system classifying engineers by major and minor skills into about 100 occupational specialties. This would facilitate identification of the employees who must be compared whenever a reduction in certain work is made. Individual IBM cards contained information regarding the employee's education, experience, and informal performance rating by supervision, all of which would be of further assistance in making preliminary comparisons. This system could be used for other purposes, including transfers.

Other Companies

After observing the administration of the provision in Company E, the union at another company requested a similar provision. The union president complained at the manner in which recent layoffs at his company had been conducted: "I don't doubt that the company made some effort to compare individual ability, but the comparisons were certainly most superficial."

The company did not accede to language requiring man-to-man comparison because of the "added burden" it would impose upon management. This company already employed a rank-order system to identify those eligible for layoff, but did not adhere to the order strictly.

Another company did not commit itself to complete man-to-man comparisons before a layoff, but did adopt this practice on a limited basis. After a supervisor had picked the men from his group to fill his quota, the engineering personnel staff jointly with the second level of supervision compared all men in the group who were *less senior* than the engineers picked. Management adopted this practice to avoid grievances in this area and to be sure that their decisions were ones they could support should grievances arise.

Spelling Out Layoff Policies and Procedures, Rights, and Obligations

Criteria

A majority of companies do not have anything that approaches a layoff "plan" spelled out in the agreement. These companies are even reluctant to put their present practices in writing, much less further commit themselves to continue the present practices. They are afraid that they would be opening the flood gates to grievances, or worse yet, from their point of view, joint control of the layoff process.

Generally, the agreements in these companies contain a statement to the effect that ability will be the controlling factor, but that seniority will be given consideration. Still, for several of the unions such a statement regarding ability was not sufficiently definitive. Failing to obtain a more specific provision in negotiations, one union filed a grievance around a specific layoff of several employees, requesting that management furnish it with the criteria used in making out the layoff list. The company refused.

In the company just mentioned, the union was particularly annoyed because the company did not use written merit reports. The fact that the union would expect such reports to bear on layoff decisions may have been one reason the company did not make them in writing. The following is a statement by one engineering administrator who had just previously processed the surplusing of nine engineers with service ranging from two to nine years, all of whom had a record of at least "normal merit progression."

> It's strange, when you get into a layoff, a supervisor will want to get rid of a man on whom he has been submitting glowing reports and to whom he has been giving merit increases regularly. The review sheet will show no need for improvement but now the supervisor will say he was sloppy in his work, irregular in attendance, and so forth. . . .

The apparent inconsistency between a company's merit evaluation and its layoff evaluation of certain employees was one of the most common phenomena encountered in the field research.

Grievance Rights

In almost all the agreements the employee has the right to grieve in connection with the layoff provision, but in one agreement the question of whether seniority has been given due weight is specifically denied. There have not been a large number of "serious" grievances in this area; still, one must conclude that grievances or the threat of grievances affect managements' layoff behavior.

Company F is a case in point. The union agreement lists certain factors to be considered in evaluating ability, performance, and conduct. They are:

(a) The results of previous reviews of performance.
(b) The employee's ability to perform available work, as compared to the ability of other employees who are available for such work.
(c) The employee's versatility.
(d) The employee's capacity for development and future advancement.

A manager at this company described the processing of grievances under this provision as "most harassing." During a recent layoff when eight grievances were processed, the supervisors were "hard put" to testify about relative incompetence. As a result, two of the men won their grievances (although after winning the point they quit!). Four other grievances were compromised; the men were given transfers or were permitted to take lower rated jobs rather than be laid off. The other two grievances were withdrawn by the employees involved.

The layoff provision also contains another significant clause that entitles an employee who is notified that he is to be laid off to "a full explanation from his supervisor of the reason for the action taken." Thus, even without filing a grievance, a step that engineers are loath to take, the engineer can put the supervisor on the spot.

As a consequence of the use of grievance machinery and this supplementary right, the supervisors tended to base their decisions on objective criteria, such as education and length of experience; they were less eager to make decisions based on the very subjective criteria which the contract listed as controlling.

Management at Company F also set up an internal check to prevent layoffs that contained inconsistencies which could be embarrassing to the supervisor and the company if the decision were grieved: if a man who had received merit increases in the last two reviews was picked by his supervisor for layoff, management would overrule. There were "a few" such instances in the 1957 layoff.

It is a mistake to convey the impression that the union solicited the grievances or even supported them vigorously. They did not. On the contrary the union leaders typically were neutral, sometimes rather apologetic, according to one source. If an engineer is actually shirking his duties, his fellow engineers are the first to know. A representative of the company conceded, "The union has paid more than lip service to the notion that an engineer must earn his salt."

Similarly, union representatives at this company were generally surprised and favorably impressed with the degree of preparation the management personnel had made on the individual layoff cases that came before the grievance committees and the other joint special committee created to discuss layoff problems.

A management spokesman commented:

> Is it wasted preparation? It takes one kind of effort to convince yourself a layoff decision is right. It takes additional effort, a different kind of effort, to convince another party the decision was the right one, or even to defend the decision satisfactorily. Yes, if we had our preference, we would spend 40% less time on layoff preparation and administration.

Notice and Consultation

The agreements in most companies require the company to give the union and/or the individuals affected minimum notice of layoff. A few require the company to discuss the layoff with the union before it is effected.

The layoff provision in one engineering contract consisted almost entirely of such requirements.

> In the event of layoff of more than two weeks' duration, the company shall give the secretary of the [union] one week's notice thereof.
>
> * * * * *
>
> The company agrees to initially discuss the question of the employees to be laid off in a department with a [union] departmental committee composed of not more than three (3) members, two (2) of which shall be from the department affected.
>
> After such initial discussion a [union] departmental committee may request a meeting with a company committee composed of four (4) management representatives from at least two (2) other major engineering departments. The [union] committee in these subsequent discussions shall not exceed four (4) members, two (2) of which shall be from the department affected.
>
> These discussions shall take place before the company notifies the employees who are to be laid off. The company may give notice of layoff to employees five (5) working days after initial notice of the layoff has been given to the appropriate [union] departmental committee. Employees shall be given not less than two (2) weeks' notice of layoff, exclusive of paid vacation time off, or two (2) weeks' pay in lieu of such notice.

The company was not bound by this union agreement in later layoffs during which the advance notice, pay, job rights, and tenure considerations were voluntarily administered by the company; but a spokesman for the company stated that, in any event, the company "could not have operated over a long period" under the clauses.

Another company is not required to give notice to the individual prior to layoff but is required to give the union a list of those whom it proposes to lay off "as far in advance as possible," and to consult with the union at its request prior to the layoff. In practice, this company submits its layoff list to the union immediately prior to the layoff.

In a third case, the company is obliged to give employees at least two weeks' notice, and to furnish the union with a list of the employees to be laid off. In practice the company occasionally gives notice to the employees and the union as much as three weeks in advance. On the other hand, the company is not bound by the minimum notice clause if the layoff results from the termination or amendment of a government or other production contract.

The agreement in another case requires the company "whenever possible" to give the union three weeks' notice of proposed layoffs accompanied by a list of employees to be laid off, but in no event should notice be less than five days. This company gave the minimum notice when certain layoffs resulted from a decision to discontinue an entire department in several steps. The company explained, "Earlier notice would have disrupted the work of the department."

Many arguments against the minimum notice requirements are offered by the managers in the companies studied. "It creates a lag between the layoff decision and the reduction in payroll that is sometimes costly." "It encourages the employees to file grievances, and provides an opportunity for union activity." "You don't get any production out of a man during his notice period." "It damages the morale of the entire group, encouraging even employees not affected to do some job hunting." Finally, "Conditions change so rapidly in this business [aircraft and missiles] that a layoff pending several weeks might not materialize after all."

The companies applied similar reasoning to the unions' requests for discussions on the prospects of layoff. Early in 1958 with many companies reducing forces as a result of the cutback in government defense expenditures, the engineering unions in other companies wanted to be "let in on" the thinking of their respective managements. Generally, the companies refused to discuss layoffs until a specific cut was announced. The personnel manager in one company explained:

> The layoff had been considered for some time, during which utilization—the work load and personnel—was analyzed. A very complex analysis was made in January. We could not discuss layoffs with the union during this period without taking the risk of affecting the behavior of the men under our analysis. Hence, our refusal to meet with the union to talk about layoffs.

Chafed at such refusals, for whatever reason managements have, the professional unions develop many ingenious means of obtaining internal company information regarding managements' layoff thinking. This information is passed on to the membership as the best available information. What is the effect on the engineering force of the dissemination of this type of information? First, it can be said that the predictions made by the unions as to the number to be laid off in 1957 and 1958 greatly exceeded the number actually affected. Do we conclude that the engineers thereby obtained an exaggerated view of the impending layoffs? Perhaps, but it is also plausible that in the absence of the "best available information" provided by the union the employees would have imagined even greater layoff prospects and experienced even more insecurity.

This latter view tends to be supported by the facts of one case, wherein management kept the union apprised of layoff prospects. In the midst of a period of uncertainty the union published this extraordinary statement:

> Concern about layoffs among [the company's] engineers is greatly exaggerated, we believe. The *worst* foreseeable condition which seems at all possible would be a release of about 1/6 (of the engineering force) . . . during the next year. It would appear that there is at least an even chance that no more than 1/60 . . . will be released. [The company's] backlog, which seems to be in no danger of reduction, is about the largest in the industry. . . . In summary, the basis of the

concern of the engineers in the bargaining unit appears to be emotional rather than factual.

MEASURES TO AVOID LAYOFFS

In addition to whatever concerns the unions might have with respect to the order of layoff, many attempt to ensure that management has exhausted all alternatives before implementing the layoff. Three agreements contain a statement on this order: "The employer shall make all reasonable efforts to avoid layoffs." Many of the contracts were more specific, naming one or more of the types of "efforts" the company was expected to make.

The first of these companies that we shall consider was expected under its 1957 agreement to take the following steps prior to a layoff affecting employees who had at least one year's service:

1. Return all design and development engineering work to the group affected.
2. Make any possible transfers within the plant.
3. Lay off all employees with less than 12 months' continuous service.
4. Gradually reduce the work week of employees in the occupation and group affected in the plant.

Steps 1, 2, and 4 were not unconditional guarantees; they were required of the company only "in so far as practicable and consistent with efficient operations." They became the subject of disagreement in the fall of 1957 when the company laid off several engineers with one to five years' experience.

The company did call back two subcontracts. Others could not be called back, without costly duplication of effort and/or damage to an important relationship with the subcontractor. The union representatives believed that under the agreement the company was obliged at least to review the outstanding contracts with them, which management refused to do. It was afraid that even this step could prove embarrassing to the company.

No transfers within the plant were possible in this particular layoff; also it happened that there were no engineers with less than a year's service. Next, the company was obliged to consider a reduced work week. The personnel manager discussed the problems connected with this move.

> Under the contract we had to consider a reduced work week applied to "employees in the occupation and group affected in the plant." The union was interested in defining the "group affected" as broadly as possible. We took the opposite position since we were not interested in reducing the work week for any employees, much less for the entire plant! Keep in mind that this was not simply a case of being overstaffed; this was an expense reduction, and at the time it appeared to be, of necessity, a permanent one. Because of the fringes and overhead that continue for every man on the payroll regardless of the number of hours he works, personnel expenses don't go down as fast when you merely reduce the work week.
>
> There were other things to consider. A reduced work week might eventually result in the loss of half of the engineering force, especially the better half which could quickly get a good "full-time job" elsewhere. Also, there is the problem of schedule fit with the other support groups at the plant. Many nonbargaining unit groups must work the same hours as the engineers, in the interest of efficiency. Finally, there is the question of differential treatment; can you reduce the work week for layoffs for one group and not do so for another without a cost in terms of labor relations or employee relations?

Despite its misgivings, management did reduce the work week somewhat, to 39 hours the first week, then to 38 hours, at which level it remained for several weeks before it returned to 40 hours. This reduction applied to 19 engineers. This "technical" reduction in the work week was viewed by the union leaders as nothing more than a superficial attempt to comply with the letter of the agreement.

In negotiation in the following year the union tried to

write into this short work week clause a more specific requirement. It was not successful. In fact, management was able to eliminate the requirement completely. It must indeed have been troublesome for management. The union was also defeated in its efforts to eliminate the "loophole" words "whenever practicable."

Normally, the layoff procedure involves some transfers within the location affected, as management adjusts the personnel to lay off the "least qualified" (by whatever criteria are applied—ability, seniority, education). The unions become interested in how this transfer process is accomplished. The leaders in another union, dissatisfied with their company's efforts in this direction, took it upon themselves to find proper niches for 18 employees surplused by the elimination of one department. The union established a "Job Coordinator" to investigate and determine where the employees would best fit.

According to the union publication:

> . . . [there was] one added roadblock—increased resistance on the part of departmental supervisors to accept these people into their groups. Once again the machinery ground to a halt. The association then took the next step; . . . [the president of the company] was contacted to verify that what was happening was under his personal cognizance and blessing. As it developed he had, apparently, not been aware of the severity of the problem, and the reaction was one of increased activity. The Employee Relations and Technical Administration Departments were seemingly permitted to take a stronger hand in placing people. Management made the further gesture of retaining persons on the payroll through vacation, until their cases could be decided upon. Yeoman service on the part of . . . Tech Personnel, . . . Tech Adm., . . . Labor Relations, plus the continued efforts of . . . [the union] resulted in the placement of 16 of the 18 Publications Engineers. . . .

Many of the unions cover engineering operations in several divisions located in the same general area. These unions are interested in having all the possibilities of interdivisonal transfers systematically explored before any man is laid off. Thus, unions have negotiated this as a precondition to layoffs.

The provision in one agreement requires that before being notified, an affected employee up for layoff will be considered for placement in other engineering positions as follows: first, in an available job in the same unit, subject to his ability to perform the work involved; second, in other jobs presently performed by other employees in comparable work groups in the same division, on the basis of relative ability; third, in an available job in another division, subject to his ability to perform the work involved; fourth, in other jobs presently performed by other employees in comparable work groups in another division, on the basis of relative ability. An employee displaced under this provision will be given similar considerations for placement in other jobs. Thus, the bumping concept operates area-wide based on "straight ability." Since job priority is based on ability, the provision is not objectionable to the company in principle. Nor is it likely to become troublesome to administer: the system is wholly within management's hands; the engineer does not even apply for an opening or to displace a less able employee. Nevertheless, even this limited provision represented a concession to the union, and it was opposed by some members of management who thought it would "restrict their freedom." Industrial relations officials were generally a little more sympathetic with the union on this point "inasmuch as there are 650 supervisors making decisions on individual and independent bases."

In a company unionized in only one of its divisions located in an area containing several divisions, the positions of the parties on the interplant transfer issue are reversed. Management urges company-wide "seniority" or employment rights, and the union objects. In one of the companies with retention ratings incorporating length of service (Company A, preceding chapter) this issue deadlocked the parties for several weeks in negotiations and almost resulted in a strike. The company wanted all company employees, without regard to where they were hired, to be permitted to transfer to and from the unionized division with full seniority rights. The union's position was that employees transferring into the bargaining unit should have seniority dating only from the date of transfer for purposes of layoff. They did not want to have the unit subject to the possible influx of engineers from another division replacing bargaining unit engineers in a general layoff situation. The company did not want to shut out any possibility of general transfer activity and for obvious reasons: one of the other divisions was engaged in a highly speculative line of weapons systems; if it were suddenly cut back, the company wanted to be in a position to retain the best engineers from each division.

The company's position prevailed to the extent that transferees from other divisions were permitted to compute their seniority from the date of hire. However, the company continued to agree to an even more important limitation on wholesale interdivisional transfers than the one concerning the right to count length of service. We shall examine this limitation in the next section on recall.

Recall and Hiring Under Layoff Conditions

Many managements enjoy considerable latitude in determining the order of layoff. This also holds true for the order of recall which is normally required to be based on the same criteria as the layoff. Where layoffs are based on fairly specific measurements, the recall order automatically approximates the reverse of the layoff. The layoffs based primarily but in a general way on skill and ability present a different problem. Managements with clauses of this type have usually assumed that when considering whom to recall they are allowed to make a fresh evaluation of skill and ability in the light of the specific tasks to be performed by the recalled engineers. In at least one instance the union challenged this assumption, filing a grievance against the company for not recalling in exactly the reverse order of layoff. The agreement was silent on this specific issue. The union lost the case in arbitration.

A related issue also deserves attention. Is a company permitted to hire new engineers while the company has engineers on layoff? This issue is of special importance to an engineering department. Listen to the engineering administrator in one aircraft company:

> Even when we get into a situation with declining engineering manpower requirements we want to leave the door open to hire new talent. For an engineering department to survive in this business it is necessary to continually *increase* its capability.

Under the engineering agreement at this company the company recalled engineers who had been laid off within the past two years, on the basis of ability, before adding new engineering employees to fill jobs within the bargaining unit. The effect of this rule was that some men who would have been placed on layoff status were released instead. The engineering administrator quoted above said:

> To keep the association off our neck, we have to release the men rather than lay them off. We might want to hire back some of the men later if the need arises and the market is tight, but right now we would rather be free to go out and hire. Hence, we have to terminate these guys.

Another company manager indicated that termination was more realistic:

> Under the pressure of demand in recent years we have hired many lower qualified engineers. Also, the complexity of the work has increased and many of those who had the level of skill to perform before are now getting over their heads.

The engineers who "are getting over their heads" were generally the longer experienced engineers who had no formal engineering training. Apparently several hundred of the two types mentioned were thereby "released," not laid off. Further consequences of this condition are similar to those mentioned in connection with Company E where the company also terminated instead of using the layoff, albeit for different reasons.

Another company is even more restricted in hiring during layoff conditions. Employees must be offered the opportunity to recall or transfer back into their previous classification before the company may hire. Furthermore, if any employee on recall is able to do the work in another classification within a period of time equivalent to the probationary period for that job, he has preference over a new hire. This company had not had any layoffs that provided a basis for judging the impact of this provision.

A few agreements made special provision for the companies when truly special hiring needs were involved. One agreement provided:

> The company and the union recognize that from time to time the company must bring into its organization inexperienced engineers with academic training. . . . It is further recognized that from time to time the company will employ engineers and scientists with especial college training who have little or no actual engineering or technical working experience. When these employees are placed on work which their education has qualified them to perform, at the discretion of the company, a reasonable number may be exempted from layoff during their first two years of employment.

The problem with this provision would be obtaining agreement between the company and the union as to whether truly special hiring needs *were* involved.

The union that represents only one of several divisions of a company regards transfers from nonorganized divisions into the represented division as similar to new hires. Hence, the agreement with one company fitting this description (mentioned in the preceding section) prevents transfers into job classifications in that division for which there is a recall list. One exception is allowed: employees with very specialized qualifications can be transferred in.

During 1958 the parties had an opportunity to test the meaning and strength of this provision. The company transferred an employee into the Design Engineer A classification at the unionized division at a time when engineers in that classification were on recall. The union viewed this as an obvious violation of the agreement, but failed to induce any of the employees on the layoff list to file a formal grievance at the time. A grievance filed by a union representative on behalf of the union was denied on the grounds that he was not affected personally.

It was not until another layoff occurred in that classification several months later that an individual "affected" was willing to file a personal grievance on the matter. While there were several technicalities surrounding this grievance which tended to weaken the union's case, the grievance nevertheless provided the union with an opportunity to voice certain apprehensions:

> The company's interpretation of the agreement insofar as allowing it to transfer employees when there is a recall list would leave a large loophole for finagling. A department could transfer a group of employees with low modified seniority ratings to another division, then surplus a group of employees having modified seniority ratings, and then transfer the first group of employees back from the other divisions, completely ignoring those employees on the recall list.

The company responded that no finagling was involved in this case. The transferred employee was merely being returned to the organized unit from which he had transferred seven months earlier. He was being returned as a result of a particular need for his qualifications and experience on an assignment, namely, coordinating design activity on electrical design installations. If a nonpermanent transfer from the organized unit was involved, as it was in this grievance, the company wanted to be able to assure the employee that he would be able to return in the future if he accepted the assignment.

Layoff Preference for Union Representatives

About two-thirds of the contracts give union officers and group representatives preference over other employees during a layoff. A typical clause of the so-called "superseniority" clauses in these agreements:

> During a layoff representatives shall not be laid off if there is work available in the group they represent which the representative can perform in a satisfactory manner.

Typically the individuals given "superseniority" constitute about 3% of the bargaining unit, a not entirely insignificant percentage. The actual effect of this provision depends in part upon the extent to which union positions are filled with the less competent engineers. There was no reliable evidence available on this point.

Layoff Pay

Several of the companies guarantee severance pay or layoff pay to the engineers based on length of service. The more liberal provisions written in the contracts call for one week's pay per year of continuous service to a maximum of twelve weeks' pay.

A few unions advance the principle of severance pay based on length of service as a substitute for a layoff plan based on seniority. One union leader expressed this view:

> First, the plan would penalize the company for fluctuating employment.
>
> Second, it would penalize the company more for laying off senior employees. The more senior employee has a higher

base rate multiplied by more weeks. This might discourage the company somewhat in its tendency to lay off the senior employee. At the same time, it still has the decision as to whom it does lay off.

Third, the notion of *layoff pay* progressive with length of service is acceptable to the average engineer whereas *layoffs by seniority* are not. Thus, we can get the support of the membership for this proposal.

Paradoxically, certain actions on the part of the union sometimes result in individuals *not* receiving layoff or severance pay. It happens thusly: faced with the contractual requirements placed on the company in connection with layoffs, the company decides to release marginal employees rather than place them on layoff status; the marginal employee prefers to "resign voluntarily" for the record rather than be terminated, but the contract does not allow severance pay for resignations, only for layoffs and terminations for lack of work.

Summary and Conclusion

Engineering union contract provisions (in addition to the rating plans discussed in the preceding chapter) have had the effect of altering the order of layoff that management would have followed had there been no union. Superseniority provisions applying to union officials have this effect. So also would the seniority provisions contained in two engineering union agreements except that to date such provisions have been tempered, in one company by an "understanding" attitude of the union leaders with respect to its application, and in the other by a substantial X list—10%. Grievances under the union agreement, especially if it sets forth specific layoff criteria, have led to reversals in layoff decisions. The grievance procedure also affects layoff decisions in a secondary way: Because the more subjective criteria of skill and ability which are supposed to govern layoffs under the agreement are more difficult to support if challenged in the grievance machinery, the supervisors tend to give more weight to the objective criteria of education and length of service. A company's layoff decisions are also affected if the contract restrains or limits its ability to transfer engineers from a nonunion division to a union division.

The decision about whether to lay off or not is sometimes influenced by collective bargaining. Where rigorous man-to-man comparisons are a prerequisite to layoff, the company may forego a small layoff altogether rather than involve itself in the lengthy and time-consuming comparison process. Another type of provision insists that management exhaust certain alternatives to an impending layoff, each with its own particular disadvantage to the company: (a) return outstanding subcontracts, which action may adversely affect relationships with subcontractors; (b) make all transfers possible, which may involve more administrative effort than the results are worth to the company; (c) reduce the work week, which may result in the loss of the better engineers and in scheduling complications.

At least two companies took steps to terminate marginal employees who might otherwise have been placed in layoff status; in one case the terminations were made to avoid man-to-man comparisons; in another to avoid placing the released engineers on the recall list which would have prevented the hiring of new engineers for a two-year period. Continual hiring is essential to an engineering department which must improve continually for competitive reasons. In the case of marginal engineers there is probably no disadvantage to the company in having the status of the released engineers clarified. However, a company would limit its ability to recover its full force if it used the same procedure with engineers whom the company might desire to rehire in the future.

Other aspects of administering layoffs under collective bargaining lead to union and employee relations difficulties. First, unions have spotlighted apparent inconsistencies between layoff decisions and prior merit evaluation with the result that the engineers' morale has been damaged and their confidence in management weakened. Second, minimum layoff notices specified in many agreements result in less production during the period of the notice, and provide an opportunity for union activity and individual grievances. A third point is that most managements believe that the union leaders tend to alarm the engineers falsely about layoff prospects. Because of this belief managements often reject union requests for joint discussion of layoff prospects. Managements' fears may be ungrounded because a better informed union may be less likely to alarm their members unduly about layoffs.

Some miscellaneous advantages may accrue to the company as a result of definite layoff provisions. The effort required to make man-to-man comparisons may result in better layoff decisions. Layoff provisions may provide the impetus for advanced manpower planning by the company, although not to the degree desired by the union. A skill inventory technique for improving layoff decisions was adopted by one company partly as a product of collective bargaining. In a few cases the quality of managements' thinking reflected in layoff grievance or discussion has favorably impressed the union leaders, with the desirable result of improving employee relations.

In the preceding chapter we noted that the rating plans were uniquely designed for the engineering organization. So, too, are the provisions discussed in this chapter calling for man-to-man comparisons and explicit criteria, whereas most of the other layoff provisions are similar in concept and purpose to provisions frequently incorporated into other union agreements.

CHAPTER X

Hiring, Promotion, and Transfer

IN THE two preceding chapters we have seen that one manpower function—reduction-in-force—has become an important subject of collective bargaining with professional unions because it bears directly on the critical issue of job security. The manning functions which are the subject of this chapter and treated in separate sections are recruitment and selection, promotions to supervisory positions,[1] and transfers.[2] Managements' tasks in these areas have been made more difficult by the unions in certain minor ways.

RECRUITMENT AND MAINTENANCE OF FORCE

The fact that a given company's engineers are unionized is one among many factors that engineers consider in thinking of employment in that company. Graduating engineers who believe that there is something inconsistent between their newly earned professional status and union representation prefer not to compromise their professional status by joining a unionized company. The views of the engineering graduates about unionism are derived in part from their predominantly middle class background and from the anti-union attitudes of the engineering professors who counsel them about industry. Other engineers who are more pragmatic are nevertheless similarly influenced. They take the presence of the engineers' union as *prima facie* evidence that

1 Recall that promotions within engineering ranks was treated in Chapter V, Salary Structure.

2 Discharge, also an important manpower function, is the subject of a separate chapter.

something is wrong with the treatment of the engineers in the organized company. Why else would they need a union? Given an otherwise equal alternative, an engineer with this attitude will not choose to work in a unionized company. The views outlined above are only partially shared by the engineers who have been out of school for a few years because, according to one recruiter, "They no longer have stars in their eyes."

Almost every unionized company offered evidence to support its contention that the presence of a union hindered its recruitment activities. An intramanagement memorandum in one midwest company in 1957 carried the following statement:

> Recruiters at colleges have reported increasingly frequent comments from college officials to the general effect that they view with suspicion, even alarm in some cases, any company where professional employees are unionized. The importance of this factor has become increasingly apparent during the present shortage of technically-trained men. The existence of [the union] . . . has undoubtedly been the deciding factor in the decisions of some men who have refused employment offers for. . . .

The recruiter for another company reported an unusually small turnout at one campus where the unionization issue had been recently publicized. Another said that well over half of the graduates interviewed asked whether the company had a union.

Most engineers who are not members of engineering unions receive much of their information about the unions through the unions' public relations activities. The unions carefully include most of the libraries and faculties of the engineering schools throughout the country on their publication mailing lists. Much of the content of these publications is concerned with conditions in the engineering talent market and with salary surveys in particular, topics which are of interest to both the engineering college senior and to the employed engineer. As a result of these efforts, many engineers become more sympathetic toward the unions and hence less likely to reject employment at a company because it is unionized; other engineers merely bcome more aware of the company's unionized status. Moreover, the full content of the unions' publications is such that the potential employees also become apprised of the vulnerable points in the company's employee relations, and therefore still less favorably disposed toward the unionized company.

The leaders of engineering unions also visit engineering colleges to appear before student groups whenever possible; probably the appearances by union leaders has much the same effect on student attitudes as those of union publications. These appearances have caused some companies to publicly express concern.

Another type of union publicity is unique. An advertisement that appeared in the *New York Times,* Sunday, May 6, 1956, encouraged engineers to consider certain conditions of employment before they selected their future employer. It asked: does the employer provide tuition refund, furnish statistical data on salaries, assure the individual of periodic merit review, provide the engineer with a channel to make his feelings known to top management? Inasmuch as these advantages were guaranteed by union contract at the company organized by the union making the advertisement, the ad urged the engineer to investigate that company. A spokesman expressed management's belief that despite the positive tone of the ad, it would scare off more good engineers than it would attract.

One company with a union shop agreement was at a serious disadvantage in recruiting engineers, especially among highly qualified engineering and scientific personnel.[3] The

[3] No other engineering contract contained a union shop clause. The companies are resolutely opposed to the union shop for engineers, and the unions by and large have not made an issue of it, a few union leaders even being avowedly against compulsory union membership as "a matter of principle." However, there are a few maintenance of membership provisions; and there

union shop agreement was an important reason for a long and bitter strike in 1953 which resulted in a slight modification of the union shop clause to exempt employees hired for pay in excess of $10,000 per year.

The unsolicited publicity surrounding strikes or public demonstrations by engineers may have dire effects on the recruitment program of the company involved. In a curious way it may have an impact on the recruiting efforts of other unionized companies. For example, a recruiter for a company that had not experienced a strike reported that six to eight candidates who had previously worked for another company where the union had been out on strike declined employment with his company because of the mere presence of the union. In another company, recruitment efforts suffered after it became nationally known that the union representing its engineers had affiliated with an AFL–CIO international trade union. As a result this company experienced a much greater rate of refusals from students than it had in previous years, and was completely boycotted for a short period by one of the best engineering schools. Typical of dozens of answers from engineers being sought is the following letter:

> I have received your invitation to complete and return your application for employment form. I also understand that engineers employed by your company are unionized. Inasmuch as I am not interested in representation by such a union I am returning your application form. . . .

Various responses are offered by company recruiters to the union-based queries or objections by engineer applicants. Whenever one recruiter is confronted during an interview with a question about the union, he rejects the idea that the engineers' organization is a "union"; it is "an association of gentlemen who exchange ideas." Another stresses the pro-

---

have been union demands for a compulsory "service fee" whereby all members of the bargaining unit would pay a minimum fee to the union (or to a favorite charity if they prefer) for services rendered; engineers would not be required to join the union.

fessional approach to merit review and layoff taken by the union in his company. Except for the case of the one company with a union shop, the recruiters emphasize the point that the engineer may join the organization or not as he chooses.

Curiously, a majority of the companies that confessed considerable handicap in recruitment did not admit that the quality or quantity of engineers recruited had actually been affected. Indeed these companies with unionized engineering forces probably were among the fastest growing engineering companies in the country. Apparently the manpower requirements in unionized companies were met by expending more recruiting effort.

Naturally, the unions do not admit that their presence, their strikes, or their affiliations obstruct a company's recruitment. This view is expressed in excerpts of a letter from the president of an IUE affiliated engineers' union (Company A) to the president of another union contemplating affiliation with the UAW (Company B).

> Thank you for the information keeping me abreast of developments at [Company B]. The threat of the company's inability to hire first class engineers in the event of affiliation with an international union within the AFL-CIO structure was also expressed at . . . [Company A], but the . . . report [accompanying the letter] should conclusively prove that the reverse situation exists. As a matter of fact, since our 13-week strike in 1955 and . . . the affiliation of the IUE on February 1, 1956, [Company A] has undergone an expansion like none other in its history. We have as you can see doubled our staff including many top-notch specialists. Contrary to the dire predictions, [Company A] since our affiliation, is healthy and apparently extremely desirable to both new graduates and established "first class" engineers, even in the midst of this "critical shortage."

The prevention of quits, like recruiting, is important in maintaining an adequate engineering force. Certain actions affect the turnover of engineering personnel more directly than they affect recruitment. For example, one company complained that the union materials distributed to new employees created an unfavorable impression during the employees' initial period with the company.

Strikes influence both recruitment and turnover. Each of the companies which had experienced a strike could directly attribute a number of quits to the strike and social tensions which accompanied it. A dramatic example is provided by a strike in 1955 which cost one company 127 engineers, including 24% of the engineers in the Associate Engineer Grade, 25% in the Engineer Grade, and 28% of the Senior Engineers. Perhaps the engineers quit because of the union's presence, or because of the company's labor relations policies, or because they could not remain out of work. In any event, the quits were related to unionization.

Closely related to recruitment is the selection function, which seems to have been slightly affected by unionization. Two specific types of company reactions are noted. First, there is the expressed desire to detect and to avoid hiring "hot rod unionists." One company even refuses to consider hiring any engineer previously employed by one unionized company whose engineers were characterized as being "conditioned to class consciousness." This company has also been "fussy" about the engineers of another unionized company. Second, there is the expressed desire to keep out less competent engineers who want the protection of a union. One company, which weighted seniority heavily in layoffs, was particularly alert to this problem.

Promotions to Supervisory Ranks

Regarding promotions to supervisory positions, one important question must be asked, "Has the fact of unionization cut off the engineering force as a source of supervisors and future managers?" Not one manager in any unionized company indicated that this had resulted in his company, despite the fact that the representatives of nonunionized employers interviewed before the study unanimously stated that this would be an important consequence of unionization of their engineers.

Another important question is, "Has union membership, activity, or leadership affected promotions to supervisory ranks?" There were a variety of responses to this question on the part of managers and union officials. The management spokesmen were careful, naturally, not to admit to any bias in promotion practices that would make them vulnerable to a charge of an unfair labor practice. Within this limitation a few companies admitted that particularly militant and obnoxious characters had by their behavior in their union role jeopardized their chances for becoming supervisors. A far greater number of comments by both union leaders and managers were made to the effect that, if anything, there is a "positive influence" of union leadership experience which "slightly accelerates advancement into management ranks." One manager in an electronics company said: "A man develops administrative capabilities more rapidly and also comes to the attention of management—if he 'has it' he won't be overlooked." Agreeing with the above statement, one labor relations executive in an aircraft company added:

> When I look at the number of promotions from the union's executive board I feel responsible. After seeing a guy perform for several meetings I urge the man's superiors to promote him to a supervisory job if he seems to have it.

In almost every company one could find a steady stream of ex-union officers entering supervisory positions. Although no reliable statistics were developed on this point, there were indications that a larger than otherwise normal percentage of employees who have been union officers subsequently were promoted to managerial positions. Indeed, the president of one of the larger unions, who was not a full-time official, said that he had bid for the president's job partly because he thought it might help his chances for advancement to management.

Transfer

The engineering unions attempt to influence transfer policies in two ways: first, by preventing employers from transferring employees against their will, and failing this, by minimizing the disadvantages associated with such forced transfers; second, by facilitating transfers for individuals who request them.

Forced Transfers

Transfers "for the convenience of the company" are generated by the constant change in the nature and organization of the engineering departments. There are extensive changes when the engineering function is undergoing major reorganization, a common occurrence within the past few years in several of the companies studied. These forced transfers meet with an engineer's opposition for any of several reasons: he may be doubtful as to why *he* was picked for transfer; he may prefer his present assignment to the one to which he is being transferred; he may be uncertain about how long it will be before he can return to a preferred assignment; he may believe his salary progress will suffer; he may be required to change residence. The unions' concern for these friction-generating situations is evident in the solutions which they have proposed for the forced transfer problem as it has developed in several companies.

During a union-management meeting in one company in 1956, the union cited cases where "loaned men" had not been treated as well as the union thought they should have been. The union stressed the importance of motivation as a determinant of the individual engineer's performance; if he feels that he is being transferred or farmed out because he is not highly regarded in his own area, his work in another area will suffer. He should therefore be informed of the transfer and be given definite time limits to the transfer. The union urged that the company reduce the extent of the loan practice by relying more heavily on floater groups which had been used to some extent in the past, and suggested that such groups could utilize versatile and capable men, or men without an assignment preference. The union also objected to the practice of having a man who is loaned for a long period continue to be reviewed by his former supervisor, who could not know how the man was progressing, and who had naturally lost some interest in the man; the union contended that because supervisors tended to favor men currently working for them a loaned engineer should be reviewed by the man for whom he is working. There were no explicit changes in company policies or practices resulting from these discussions, but the company indicated it did "make some additional efforts to accommodate" the union on the above points.

The experiences of an aircraft company point up even more clearly the problems inherent in large-scale transfers of engineers by management. Several years ago a crisis developed in the allocation of manpower to the urgent rework required on a long-range bomber. Engineers on other projects had to be diverted to the rework project. To complete the rework project the company applied a quota system to each functional area of aircraft engineering. Supervisors were asked to send those men whom they needed the least. Only a few engineers were interviewed and asked how they felt about the transfer. The union alleged that even then, some of the engineers who objected to the transfer were moved anyway. Many of the engineers were incensed with the perfunctory manner in which they were transferred. The union representative said, "It was all too apparent to them that they were pawns." The union leaders admitted at the time that they could not see an alternative to the draft, considering the time available to get the rework project under way; however, they did urge management to "look at the *engineers'* problems, and then take steps to minimize them."

In a meeting with the company called by the union, the union asked that the company enter into an agreement to return the transferred men to their former jobs within 10 months. For any temporary assignment longer than 10 months the union asked the company to guarantee the previous merit rate progress of the individual engineers involved. Thus, a man would have some assurance that his professional development would not be interrupted for more than a year, and that his salary progress would not suffer as a result of the transfer.

As a result, the chief engineer made an address to a gathering of engineers in which he gave them verbal assurances that the transfers were temporary and that the engineers would soon be returned to their previous assignments. In addition, each individual affected would have his name encircled in red and supervisors were to be instructed to take care not to let the transferred man suffer financially as a result of transfer. Though this action was not synonymous with the union's proposal, it did represent a recognition of the engineers' needs as they were expressed by the union. What was the effect on management of this attention to the engineers' anxiety over transfers? If it encumbered management in its allocation of the engineering manpower, it was not significant enough to be reported.

In the period after the bomber rework situation occurred, a sizable amount of transfer activity continued in connection with divisionalization of the company's operations and the buildup of certain divisions. The union continued to receive calls from engineers who were being transferred from one project to another against their wishes. Unlike the rework transfers, these transfers were largely permanent. After discussing several specific cases with the company, the union began to look for a general solution to the problem of unwilling transfers, recognizing that the task was made more troublesome because of the "rather well developed conflict of interest [which seems to exist] between the company's business needs and some of the engineers' professional needs." The union, in its publication, described the conflict of interest in this way.

> The two *extremes* are rigid and uncompromising. On the one hand, the company makes firm commitments for delivery several years ahead and these commitments must be met. The company has the prerogative of assigning its employees where they are needed and it pays for this prerogative every other Thursday. On the other hand, an engineer has nothing to sell but his ability and experience. He gets his ability and experience largely from his work assignments. If he receives a permanent work assignment which does not contribute to the field of specialization which he has chosen to follow, he owes it to his career to move to another company.

If the basic conflict of interest was unavoidable, there were certain aggravating conditions over which the company had some control. For example, management's practices of manpower allocation came in for criticism in the union's publication:

> . . . we are working in a mass employment situation. When personnel men have to sluice hundreds of engineers from projects which have passed their manpower peaks into others which are still building up, it is only natural for them to develop the "warm body" complex. There just simply are not enough personnel men available to devote the amount of time required to make good placements under these conditions—at least not while using present techniques. It is so much easier and quicker to use force, if necessary, rather than to find out what each new man can do best, find ways to eliminate objectionable features of certain jobs, and generally adjust the attractiveness of various jobs to the manpower [sic] needs.

The mandate for management to "find out what each man can do best" was later recognized in the establishment of a professional skill code which provided an inventory of technical capability available in the company. Thus, "what each man can do best" is determined for transfer purposes on the basis of the nature of his education, work experience, and supervisor's judgments. The inventory also contains information on the man's preferences as to work assignments. All the information is coded on IBM cards and kept current by periodic review.

The skill inventory was an idea that had been tossed around by management for several years. Nevertheless, a review of the sequence of events leading up to the plan suggests that the union can claim considerable credit for its introduction. After the union raised the issue in negotiations in 1957, the company invited the union to formulate a detailed proposal for such an inventory to be inaugurated on a trial basis. Nothing came of the idea in 1957, but the following year, when it became necessary to improve the procedure for selecting persons for layoff under the contract, the skill coding idea was developed by the company into a plan that could be used for transfers as well as layoffs.

In another company, changing work loads led to transfers of individuals and, in some situations, whole groups from one location to another. The union surveyed the individual engineers' transportation problems, attitudes, and other problems in accomplishing the move, and concluded that several engineers would resign if the transfers were carried out as planned. The union followed through with efforts to keep the company from requiring the individual to sacrifice his own best interests.

Regarding the final factor which may disconcert the engineer (a change in residence) some unions have obtained provisions allowing an engineer to refuse a transfer to another location, while others have been able to obtain minimum notices of transfers to new locations.

Thus, we see that in several instances the unions have addressed themselves with a limited degree of success to the problems associated with the transfer of engineers for the convenience of the company.

Refused Transfers

The second type of transfer problem occurs when an engineer is "locked" into his present job and cannot obtain a desired transfer. The unions have attempted to prevent such circumstances from occurring; when they do occur, they have tried to lend assistance to the individual whose transfer is blocked.

In contrast with the problem of unwilling transfers, the refusal of a company to transfer an engineer usually does not involve a conflict of interest between the individual's professional needs and the company's business requirements. This is suggested by a typical statement of transfer policy objectives:

> A. The company's objectives with respect to employee requests for transfer are:
> 1. To utilize the highest skills of each employee consistent with company requirements.
> 2. To assist employees to work more effectively by eliminating, when possible, personal problems which may be solved by a change of work assignment.
> 3. To encourage employees to develop their abilities by making available to each employee company-wide consideration for utilization of skills and experience.

The difficulty is more likely to arise on the level of the immediate supervision. Review of such cases in several companies indicates that the supervisor of an engineer requesting a transfer may block the transfer for one or more of several reasons. First, the supervisor may want to keep the man because he is already experienced in the work. If special, difficult-to-replace skills are involved, the supervisor's personal interest may parallel that of the company's. Second, the supervisor may not be well liked by his men and thus be forced to reject transfers in order to prevent a mass exodus which might be regarded by management as a sign of poor supervision. Here the interests of the supervisor and the company do not coincide, but the supervisors frequently have in the personnel or manpower control department an essential ally, because the functions of the staff officials in these departments obligate them to keep even the poor supervisors supplied with engineers, by "force feeding them," as one union official termed this practice. As a result these staff departments are of no help to the engineers who request transfers to escape poor supervision. Third, the supervisor may, out of spite, block the transfer of an individual toward whom he has a personal antagonism. This type refusal is not in the company's interest and will normally be remedied by the personnel staff if it comes to their attention. Fourth, the supervisor may be guilty of "empire building," a universal game not unique to an engineering organization. One manager outlined the empire building game in the engineering department in this manner:

> The company encounters great difficulty in making a manpower forecast. Only first and second levels of supervision have the essential knowledge. Because of natural tendencies to protect themselves against contingencies and to enhance their own importance, supervisors will pad their requirement in numbers and in quality. The managers know this and when they receive the supervisors' estimates, they subtract a certain percentage. It's a game between the levels of management, each trying to discount the other's behavior.

This same manager went on to state that the union performs a function for the top management team by processing grievances on the subjects and by otherwise calling top management's attention to instances of surplus talent.

Let us consider a typical case of empire building occurring in an aircraft company where this behavior has been an important phenomenon during the period of the tight engineering manpower market. (Sometimes the surplus manpower situations were created by company policy for purposes of bidding on government contracts; at other times they were not supported by company policy.) A union official reported:

> This engineer in tooling, known as an average guy, called me and said he wanted out of his group. There was not enough work in that group and he had found a job elsewhere in the engineering department. He had located the job through a supervisor in his car pool. Word came back to him that his transfer was refused, because "nobody transfers out of Muller's group." I contacted Maxwell in Labor Relations and he called Muller [the man's supervisor] who said that he had a lot of work. Then Maxwell called the man's prospective supervisor and gave him hell for giving the man encouragement to transfer. Maxwell declined my suggestion that we go to Muller's group and judge for ourselves whether he was loaded with work. In this particular instance the engineer entering the complaint was willing to stand up for himself. The next day I learned that the man had received a transfer although not the one he had requested.

This case illustrates the technique of bringing a complaint to the attention of higher management, and it also contains a clue as to why the technique is not more effective: an official from the labor relations department went to the supervisor involved to learn "the facts" surrounding the complaint. In this case the supervisor apparently reversed himself to avoid having his own manpower practices investigated. More often than not the supervisor does not reverse his position, and the labor relations official relies upon the supervisor's version of the case.

The individual engineer has at his disposal another technique for pushing through a transfer request—the threat of quitting. This technique is a genuine alternative for the engineer who is frustrated in his present assignment. But how effective is the threat of the individual to use his ultimate bargaining weapon, his resignation? Often it is *not* effective, even if the engineer involved is a very good engineer, for if the supervisor, who is attempting to prevent the transfer, believes he is going to lose the man, he often becomes indifferent about whether the man leaves the company or merely leaves his group since the results are the same as far as the supervisor is concerned. If a personality clash is involved, the supervisor might prefer that the engineer not be placed within the organization.

The unions have sought other solutions to the transfer problem, including a contract clause providing for freedom to transfer. However, generally after lengthy discussions the parties more or less agree that there is no basic conflict between the union and the company; and that the present company policy is adequate in theory, though often not so in practice. In at least one instance, the company agreed to send out a memorandum reminding supervisors of the procedures which should be followed in processing transfer requests. Certain relevant statements of their policy and procedure included:

> Employees may request transfers to other departments, types of work, or shifts in order to solve compelling personal problems or to make better use of knowledge or skills. . . . The company will arrange transfers when the basis for the request is well founded and such action is not to the material disadvantage of the company.

One company announced a new transfer policy in a letter mailed to the engineers' homes in the fall of 1955. According to the union president, committees representing the company and the engineers had agreed upon the changes incorporated in the new policy as stated in the letter. The union alleged that the unilateral announcement by the company represented a "doublecross." The company's denial notwithstanding, the union's view that it could claim credit for the change was plausible. The announcement read:

> If you have been on your present assignment for an appreciable length of time and believe that neither you nor your company is benefiting from the fullest utilization of your capabilities it may be well for you to investigate the

> possibilities of a transfer. If you decide that you desire to do this, you should contact your immediate supervisor or . . . Engineering Personnel. You may be assured that a full, sympathetic, and open-minded evaluation will be made of your transfer request.

The important aspect of this letter was the new alternative means of entering a request for a transfer—through Engineering Personnel.

The union president believed that the bypassing feature had resulted in more liberal transfer decisions. However, the bypassing feature proved to be of little value in some cases. An editorial of the union's newspaper reported, "the day after the Personnel Department was contacted, the employee was called into the supervisor's office and interrogated on his 'confidential' negotiations of the previous day." The editorial went on to suggest a truly confidential system for handling transfers, whereby an employee might request a transfer via the union office, and then through the personnel department. All transactions would be handled as "blind ads." The plan was not implemented.

Other courses of action have been proposed by the union to alleviate its various objections to the company's transfer policies.

> . . . More adequate internal dissemination of data about opportunities available could be started. . . . Supervisors should be instructed to periodically discuss each man's career with him. . . . And if [the company] is serious about reducing its turnover, it should adopt a policy of giving salary increases when a man transfers, even if these increases be small.

When asked whether the company's transfer practices had been influenced by the union, a company spokesman offered his opinion that transfers had been made more difficult. If a person is not working well on a job, the supervisors in other departments are not as willing to take a chance with the man in question, because under the union it would be harder to get rid of him if he does not work out.

Summary and Conclusion

Unionized companies are handicapped somewhat in recruiting engineers, particularly the recent graduates, who believe that unionism is not compatible with professionalism, and who take a company's unionized status to be a clear signal that its employment practices are deficient; such disadvantage is manifested in specific refusals, a generally higher rate of refusal, and, in the extreme, boycott by engineering schools. Similarly, some quits can be attributed to the union. These tendencies are reinforced if the union involved negotiates a union shop clause, strikes, or affiliates with an AFL-CIO union. The companies declare that the net effect is in recruiting costs; that their quality and quantity of engineers have not suffered. Selection is only influenced slightly in the special way of avoiding certain union types.

Promotions of engineers to supervisory positions have not been adversely affected by unionization. There is no evidence that companies fill management positions any less either from engineering ranks or from ranks of union members. If anything, the individual who accepted leadership and responsibility in the union at some time in the past may have improved his chances for promotion to management.

Changing engineering requirements result in mandatory transfers. The engineers whose own convenience, professional development, and salary advancement are likely to suffer by these transfers have been able to obtain certain mild guarantees to mitigate against these named hardships. The effect of these guarantees is to encourage management to plan in advance what assurances can be made without cost; to make them replace men "in loan" status more often; and to incur some marginal cost to ensure that an engineer does not get overlooked in merit while in transfer status. At least a few companies have tried to improve their methods for selecting men for transfer.

An individual engineer's desire for more challenging or more suitable work or his dissatisfaction with his present supervisor gives rise to requests for transfer. Here the interests of the engineer are in less conflict with that of the company than with that of the supervisor who may be trying to pad his staff, or to spite the engineer requesting a transfer, or to conceal the disfavor with which he is regarded by his men. These supervisory conditions are seldom in the company's interest and the union performs a service for the company by exposing them, either by enabling the engineer to go to the personnel department or by taking the problem to top management itself, although personnel departments do not always recognize the harmony of interest with the union in this area. The cost of a blocked transfer is often low morale resulting in low quality and quantity output or a resignation.

CHAPTER XI

Discipline and Discharge

FOR MAINTENANCE of the industrial organization, discipline and discharge functions are almost as important to management as are employee recruitment and selection. For the employees affected, disciplinary action and discharge can be of greater importance. Consequently, collective bargaining has typically been accompanied by considerable friction in these areas. In the collective bargaining relationship with engineers, however, discharge grievances rarely occur, a condition which must be explained in terms of the attitudes of the parties and the nature of the engineering work.

The first section of this chapter will analyze the reasons for the professional unions' limited interest in discharge cases. Succeeding sections will treat the ways in which the unions have nevertheless influenced managements' actions in this area. Thus the second section will consider the difficulty of building a case for discharge under engineering unionism. Then the discussion will turn to specific actions on the part of the unions in the discharge area, namely refusals to extend probationary periods, challenges to the practice of forced resignation, and insistence upon the right of the individual to be informed of the reason for his termination. Discharges for security reasons present a unique problem and are treated in the latter part of this chapter. Finally, the matter of discipline will be explored—to the extent that it is a problem in the engineering organization and is affected by collective bargaining.

The Union's Interest in Discharge Cases

There is an amazing lack of unanimity among the various unions on the necessity of so basic a provision as "discharge for just cause only." A few union agreements do not contain a "cause" clause. Yet, without such a clause the company could refuse to consider a grievance arising from discharge, and the union certainly would not be assured recourse to arbitration.

During negotiations several years ago, one union asked that a "just cause" clause be included in the contract. The issue was dropped when the company refused and the union's membership did not evince strong sentiment in favor of the clause. Two years later the union again considered proposing the clause during negotiations. A sampling of membership opinions indicated that about 40% were opposed or indifferent to the clause. In its monthly publication, the union leadership listed the possible disadvantages of the clause.

> 1. Existence of such a clause might give rise to the view that [the union] had become "grievance happy" and was looking for issues to dispute with the Company.
> 2. This clause might serve to cause the Company to retain incompetent engineers. This would not, of course, be our intention. . . .
> 3. There is insufficient need, based on the Company's past practice, to warrant its inclusion.
> 4. The decision by the arbiter, as the Company has pointed out, might not be as likely to be correct as that made by the Company. . . .

Admittedly this list represents the view of a minority of engineers in this particular company (and the view is shared by minorities in other unionized companies); however, the significant fact is that a sizable minority is convinced of the validity of these points. The indifference to the discharge clause may be less a function of the inherent disposition of the organized engineers as reflected by the views presented above than it is of some basic characteristics of engineering employment.

These characteristics are identified by the union president in this company in his analysis of the limited role which the union can play in case of an individual discharged for poor performance. First, it should be understood that discharges at this particular company "have been so rare that most engineers have never heard of a single case." In most of these situations the engineer concerned accepts the supervisor's decision, which he knows has been reviewed by higher levels of supervision. The president wrote in the union's monthly publication:

> All of us are aware of our shortcomings and the engineer who is not doing well usually knows it long before anyone else does. He can usually be persuaded that his own best interests would be served by a fresh start in another environment. The Company goes out of its way to insure that his bad record here does not follow him when he leaves and permits him to resign.

The potential "just cause" cases are those rare cases in which the engineer does not agree with his supervisor's judgment. The union president analyzed the problem in this manner:

> The engineer who does not acknowledge having performed poorly faces a difficult situation. His first reaction is to look for an arbiter before whom he can "prove" that his contentions are right and those of his supervisor are wrong. This is a useless endeavor. Suppose such an arbitration system were to be created. Suppose he successfully proved his point. He could not afford to continue working for that same supervisor. An engineer's whole future, both salary-wise and job assignment-wise, depend almost exclusively on his supervisor's opinion of him. At the first sign that his supervisor rates him below his own evaluation, and this difference is not resolved, an engineer simply must transfer to some other supervisor. Thus, if the engineer should be proven right, he

> must change supervisors; if proven wrong, he must change supervisors. The extremely difficult task of judging who was right is clearly not worth the trouble.

When the supervisor decides he no longer wants the engineer working for him, he usually releases him to the personnel department for reassignment elsewhere. More often than not personnel relocates the man so that there still is no need for an appeal procedure.

But a man released by one supervisor is not always successfully relocated within the company:

> The personnel man must depend on the supervisor's judgment. He must relate those opinions to other supervisors he is consulting concerning a new position. He may even decide that the engineer is not suitable for employment in *any* position.

Thus, a discharge clause would still be of little value to this man if the union agreed he was an incompetent engineer and would not support his grievance. How likely is this? The union president said, "In every discharge case which we have discussed with the company we have concurred with management's action."

It is in the limiting case of the engineer who is unwarrantedly terminated because of an "error" in the company's evaluation that the union would *like* to help. But, in practice, even this case is likely to be hopeless:

> If an engineer stoutly maintains that he is being wronged, and vigorously seeks a reversal of the termination decision, he can generate a reaction which is startling in its complete reversal of ordinary practices. Unfortunately, he cannot defend his position without, by implication, questioning his supervisor's judgment. Thus the supervisor, completely apart from his original intention, finds that he has a personal stake in the termination of the engineer! If the engineer is not ultimately terminated, an "error" is "logged" in the supervisor's "record."

The engineer is likely to be dubbed a "troublemaker," or at least a "difficult placement." In a company which places a high value on conformity and affability, this can be fatal.

The personnel man, meanwhile, is under pressure to perform his regular work. He knows from experience that he can make from 10 to 50 "normal" placements—and thereby serve the Company's interests well—in the length of time required to work out one difficult placement. And even then the difficult placement may not work out. Thus all this work will at most save the Company one engineer, and possibly not even that.

In all the situations given above the engineer is on his own. Even in the last one "there is no use in the engineer trying to prove he is right." An engineer meeting certain very limiting prerequisites may, however, have a case:

> If his performance has been, or can be, satisfactory; If he has been with [the company] a few years; If he has worked for a number of other supervisors; If he has earned a good reputation with these other supervisors and his fellow engineers; If a position can be found with a supervisor who (1) wants this engineer to work for him after hearing any and all derogatory reports which might exist and (2) has an authorized vacancy for an engineer at his salary level; If this supervisor maintains his willingness to have this engineer working for him in the face of any who might seek to dissuade him; and If the engineer has the self-confidence and determination to hold firm, it is possible for him to remain in [the company's] employ. These are a lot of Ifs. They seldom all exist in any one case, but if they do the engineer can protect his position.

The union president whose analysis we have presented here concluded:

> If he is not completely *sure* he can meet all of the conditions in the preceding paragraph, he should accept the invitation to resign and take immediate steps to secure other employment. *Only* if he is completely confident that he has

been seriously misjudged—not just slightly misjudged—and can fulfill *all* of the conditions in the preceding paragraph should he try to fight the termination. In this case, he should not sign a resignation and should call the [union] office *immediately*.

The approach to the discharge question taken by this union leader is extreme in that it represents a minimum role defined by the union for itself. Before turning to other companies for contrasts it should be noted that the union did request one change in this area. It was common for personnel to warn an engineer released by his supervisor that if no position was located within a certain period of time, usually two weeks, he would be asked to resign. The union described the confusion which often ensued, and recommended that management modify its procedure:

> . . . Too often, the engineer is confident that another position will be found and takes no steps to secure a position with another company. He usually receives notification that no other position can be found, when this is the case, only a few hours before the deadline. Then he has no notice period in which to secure other employment.
>
> Actually, the engineer himself is frequently to blame for this state of affairs. It often turns out that he read into the personnel man's statements connotations which were not intended. He is inclined to hear what he wants to hear. A natural desire on the part of the personnel man to soften the blow often aids in this misinterpretation. This is a case where kindness can be very unkind.
>
> * * * * *
>
> . . . We believe that they should establish a definite period during which they will seek another position for an engineer. If they are unsuccessful, we are urging that, at the end of this period, they give the engineer an unequivocal termination notice or the option of resigning with the customary notice period.

The union president cited a case in point. One individual

who was released to personnel and then subsequently received his termination slip thought that he had been guaranteed another job. The union brought the matter to the attention of the director of labor relations who was persuaded that the man had been treated unfairly. The engineer was given an additional notice of two weeks, or pay in lieu thereof.

As implied previously, other unions take a more proprietary interest in discharge actions.

Building a Case for Discharge

Until 1957 and 1958, when substantial reductions in force were required in many of the engineering departments included in this study, there had been exceedingly few discharges for poor performance, primarily because of the tight engineering manpower market. There had always been, however, a *need* for selective terminations. As one engineering administrator in an aircraft company said, "We ought to cut off 15 to 40 engineers every year, there is that much deadwood."

The experience of one company that had not had a discharge based on incompetence between 1952 and 1958 is revealing. In the fall of 1958, while discussing this condition, the engineering supervisors expressed their belief that in order to fire a man for lack of competence the supervisor would have to warn the man on several occasions, by citing to him specific performance failures; and that if these warnings were oral, they must be made in the presence of the section representative. The supervisor must log every warning with the details of the man's assignment and his performance in order to accumulate a complete record that would stand up in arbitration.

In practice, it is difficult to build up such a case against an engineer because though the supervisor has an interest in the longer run competence of his engineering group, he also has pressing project goals. Therefore he will not give an incompetent engineer a job which the man cannot do, but will assign him to a less demanding task. Because of this practice, the supervisor has nothing for which to reprimand the man, nothing to log, and no cause for discharge. As one supervisor observed, "You can't very well discharge a man for not being able to do a task the supervisor wouldn't assign to him." Supervisors find it more expedient to improve their own work group by transferring the man to another supervisor.

One supervisor went further than the others by saying that he thought that to make a discharge stick on any one man, it would be necessary for him to keep logs on *all* of his men for two reasons: first, in order to be able to show the normal rate of mistakes, and second, in order to avoid appearing discriminatory. Needless to say, this would be a huge task.

The spokesman for another company cited similar difficulties. In October 1957 one of the company's divisions found it necessary to cut back the size of the design group. Management could identify the poor performers who should be released. However, these men had job priority under the agreement.

> These men could do a part of a job, and were kept under high demand. If we had documented the cases, the men could have been discharged when they were no longer needed. We could use the Navy incident type of evaluation wherein if a man performs below standard in a given job, it is a matter of record, and the man and his representative would be advised that he doesn't meet standards. With the men we wanted to cut we found that the supervisors had not used our present reviews to record the deficiencies that could have justified discharge. In some cases these deficiencies were not even reflected in the point ratings the men received. In one instance a merit increase of 5% had been given just a few months previously. Now we are going to ask managers to evaluate these people and see whether or not there has been better performance.

The man judged incompetent, who was a candidate for discharge, received a *merit* raise just four months earlier! Personnel staff and upper levels of management normally assume that the incompetent engineers can be induced to initiate termination themselves and that the impetus for such terminations is provided by the merit review. Their assumption regarding the impetus provided by the merit review is not realistic in practice for various reasons: sometimes in practice the merit increases become "almost automatic"; another tendency is for the distribution of merit money to be influenced by non-job-performance factors; finally, general increases are granted with such frequency and in such amounts as to provide an acceptable minimum rate of salary growth for some engineers. Thus, it is very difficult to penalize an engineer effectively for lack of ability in order to induce him to resign.

Just as the professional unions do not have as an objective automatic merit increases, so they do not regard it as their mission to keep the incompetents employed. The companies are inclined to confuse their own laxness in initiating discharge proceedings with union pressure to obstruct discharges. The union representing the engineers of a company where management has felt particularly constrained in this area published this statement recently:

> The [union] has demonstrated that unionism is compatible with statesmanship. It can be compatible with professionalism, with technical competence, with high productivity, and with anything else that its members want it to be. The fact that "only supervisors can get fired" is the result of management policy, not the effect of having a union. [The company's] employees have never asked that their unions protect the donderheads and deadwood.

Many other union leaders have expressed the opinion that the incompetents are a drag on the professional status of the union and its members, as well as a burden to the company.

While the unions' *presence* may have limited managements' discharges on the basis of poor performance, they have *behaved* "understandingly" in those instances where management has initiated discharge action for poor performance. A liberal sampling of the grievance records of these unions leads one to conclude that the union has agreed with the company in a majority of discharge cases where grievances were filed. In a few instances the unions disagreed, frequently on the basis of technical points, such as failure to give adequate notice. An inconsequential number resulted in reinstatements.

One potentially basic source of disagreement regarding discharges based on inadequate performance has not received the attention of managements and unions to date. On the one hand, supervisors do not want men who can merely perform in their present classification, such as Associate Engineer; they want men who can grow into Senior Engineers. On the other hand, under the language of the engineering contracts the man needs only "to perform satisfactorily in his present job," which would be interpreted as quite a different matter from "meeting the supervisor's expectations." In a plentiful manpower market supervisors might be disposed to base discharges on their own standards, not the contracts.

Managements feel more restrained by unionism in dealing with instances of misconduct than they do with cases of low performance, probably with good reason. The representatives of the employees are not as ready to agree with management regarding a definition of behavior that would constitute just cause for discharge. Engineers, and engineering management, are generally more tolerant of unusual behavior than are comparable shop groups and production management. Therefore personnel people encounter difficulty in applying the more generally developed standards of behavior to the engineering organization.

The types of misconduct cases which have arisen in engineering organizations can be illustrated by citing several cases.[1] An aircraft design engineer was caught drafting for another firm on company time. The union obtained reinstatement with three weeks' back pay. A man reported for fighting off duty was summarily terminated "for medical reasons" when he claimed that he had experienced a mental blackout during the dispute leading to the fight. Protesting the discharge and changing the story about the blackout, he received a medical diagnosis and was reinstated. An engineer was discharged when the company discovered that he falsified his employment application as to race. The company discharged another for making book, but could not make this discharge stick. Still other engineers were discharged because of an array of irregularities in sexual behavior.

Probationary Period Extensions

The selection process considered in an earlier chapter actually does not end when a man is employed; management continues a critical appraisal of the man throughout his initial assignments. Typically, the engineering contracts preserve managements' unilateral rights to selection of engineering personnel by specifying a probationary period of six to twelve months during which a new employee "may be discharged with or without cause." In practice the specified period is not always sufficient for the supervisor to decide whether a man will make a good engineer. One manager explained: "Engineers do not like to move hastily in human relations. They do not feel comfortable making decisions based on subjective data. Hence, they procrastinate."

An executive in another company offered further explanations:

> Although the education curriculum and our hiring process usually sort out poorly trained applicants, occasionally an employee's technical incompetence is discovered during the

[1] Discipline, short of discharge, will be considered in the final section of this chapter.

first six months. These cases are infrequent and usually discernible.

However, failure to perform is more often reflected in *undelivered competence.* Poor work habits, or personal problems, or other matters affect an employee's performance. Work which is sporadic, inconsistent, and unpredictable is the result, and presents serious problems to the supervisor. These problems are difficult to analyze in six months, even though poor performance is noted.

In the past there have been instances where a probation discharge was warranted, but where the supervisor believed causes could be remedied. They requested and received an extension, and probationers receiving an extended tryout period almost always succeeded.

Under normal circumstances the unions accommodate a reasonable number of requests from management to extend the period. If the parties tend toward the conflict pattern of union-management relationships, however, the union is likely to take advantage of any device it can to make life difficult for the company. The refusal to extend the probationary period was conceived as such a device by a few unions. One manager asserted:

> As the union more vigorously pursued its institutional objectives, the arrangement whereby probationary periods were extended changed. The union began to refuse agreement to extension of the probationary period. As a result supervision began to discharge doubtful performers during the probationary period, since they could not secure additional time for remedial steps.

One case involved a recently graduated engineer whose performance "was inconsistent, apparently lacking maturity to work steadily and to profit from experience with sequential assignments." The supervisor requested an extension because he believed consistency was achievable. The union refused the request on the stated grounds that extension is unfair to the employee who thereby has "an ungrievable dismissal hanging over his head for another six months." When the company said it would be forced to terminate the engineer, it placed the union in an awkward position; yet, after several discussions the union replied, "go ahead," and the man was terminated.

One union expressed doubts about the real reasons behind the discharge of probationary employees, so in 1957 it informed the company of a new policy to restrict the use of the probationary period to that of determining only the technical competence of new employees. Henceforth attitude and disciplinary matters would be regarded as covered by the "cause" provision. Extensions would be granted only where conditions made it impossible for the company to fully evaluate the new employee's competence. Acceptable conditions might be prolonged illness, unavoidable changes in assignment, or changes in supervision. Accordingly the union's new policy would place the burden of proof of demonstrating why an extension was required more clearly on the company. Although the policy was never actually implemented, it signaled some possibilities for other union-management relationships. Indeed, a year later another union did announce a tightened policy on probationary extensions when it took a new tack of stressing that if a man could not do the work, he could be discharged at any time after the probationary period; it followed that this period should merely be used to determine whether a man could work with others ("this determination could be accomplished in three months"). Henceforth the union would accede to requests for extensions only when special conditions warrant its "overlooking management's failure to evaluate the employee."

Forced Resignations

That there are few instances of discharge, even fewer discharge grievances, is not the whole story. Companies are able to "persuade" many of the men to leave by pointing out the advantages of resigning. This persuasion normally includes forecasts of a generally dark future with the company, especially in terms of merit progress, coupled with promises of a smooth, quick, silent termination, without blemish of record and without embarrassment before friends.

Some unions have opposed the practice of securing voluntary terminations on the grounds that it is a means for management to deprive the engineer of his right under the contract to appeal the termination. Accordingly, one union admonished:

> Members should be careful about signing away the rights they have in exchange for a "quiet resignation." The contract guarantees each member the right to call in a representative during any conference involving disciplinary action.

One agreement contains a provision that seems to be designed to give the employee who resigns an opportunity to see whether the company executes its part of the bargain, by allowing the engineer to ascertain that there are no "black marks" on the terminating employee's record: "When an employee voluntarily terminates he may at his request, and at that time, see the Termination of Employment Form which has been executed by the Employer."

Discharges for Security Reasons

The companies studied are heavily engaged in weapons systems engineering and development for the military. Although the engineering union leaders are fully cognizant of the importance of security precautions in the engineering departments they represent, and of the companies' obligations to the government in this respect, this knowledge has not prevented many of them from championing the rights of individuals affected or who may be affected by the companies' security measures. Many of the engineering contracts spell out with varying degrees of detail the respective rights and obligations of the companies and individuals concerned.

The unions have probably participated in hundreds of security cases in the companies studied, processing some of them as grievances and consulting on others with management.

Denials vs. Delays of Security Clearances

The denial of a security clearance by an authorized government agency is explicitly stated under most engineering union agreements as "just cause" for discharge, a notion which the union would not challenge as a general rule. In fact, the agreement in one company provides specifically that such discharges are not subject to the grievance machinery.

An early version of the union agreements above which precluded arbitration of this type of grievance also described just cause in security matters as "failure to receive" a clearance by the security agencies. A question about the meaning of "failure to receive" was raised in 1951 by a discharge case that ended in the federal courts. The engineer involved had been employed by the company in June 1949 to work on a classified missile project. A personnel security questionnaire for the employee was promptly sent to the proper governmental agencies for clearance. When no decision concerning the employee's status had been made by these agencies by March 1951, the company suspended him, and three months later terminated his employment. The company refused to arbitrate the grievance which the union filed, rejecting the union's contract interpretation to the effect that discharge is nonarbitrable only if an employee has failed to receive a favorable *determination* on clearance. Arbitration was finally stayed by the Appelate District Court when the Department of Defense notified the company that access by this employee to work classified as confidential would be "inimical to the best interests of the U. S. for security reasons."

The basic question of the meaning of "failure to receive" was still unanswered. Accordingly, later in 1951 the company announced a new policy that would result in the discharge of all employees whose clearances had not come through by the end of the probationary period. The union called this a "perversion of the probationary concept." The union also charged the company with usurping a governmental function.

The issue was stated by the union in its publication in January 1952:

> The purpose . . . is merely to relieve the Company of any onus in the employment of a person whose clearance may subsequently be denied. It is also intended to circumvent in the future any such costly litigation as is now pending in an actual case of [a union] member who was suspended before a decision on his clearance was received. The result of this policy may be the discomfiture and embarrassment of many individuals of unquestioned loyalty, and may even entail permanent damage to the careers of these men because of the stigma attached to a "security" discharge. An individual so affected does not even have the usual right to an appeal. There can be no appeal where there has not been issued a denial of clearance.

The contract provision worked out in 1954 and preserved in the 1956 and 1958 agreements strikes a balance between the interests of the parties and between the concepts of denial and delay. The denial is just cause for discharge, but a man cleared within one year of discharge shall be fully reinstated with back pay. If there is a delay of one year in clearance ruling, the company may place the employee on leave of absence wtihout pay for one year. If a security clearance is not granted during the leave of absence, the employee is terminated automatically. If he is cleared within the year of absence, the company must compensate him for lost salary.

Company vs. Agency Determination of Security Clearance

Can the company discharge a man for its own reasons based on security considerations? Management in one company decided that the clause applied to its own determination of a man's security status. The contract was clear with respect to delays, and it also referred to denials:

> Delay in obtaining clearance for access to . . . information classified by the U. S. Government shall not constitute grounds for dismissal under this section. Denial of clearance by the cognizant government agency shall be cause for the granting of a leave of absence without pay for one year. . . .

However, the agreement neither stated explicitly that denial by an agency constituted just cause for discharge (although it may be assumed that unless the man was cleared at the end of one year's leave of absence he would be terminated), nor did it make specific reference to any company action based upon the company's own determination of security risk.

Interpreting the agreement's silence on the last issue as a sign of consent, the company, in 1954, decided that a certain employee was a security risk, denied him "clearance," and placed him on leave of absence. The union appealed the case to arbitration. The arbitrator recognized the arguments which the company used to support its action:

> The company has emphasized the unusual character of its operations and the strict provisions of its obligations to the Government. It points out that it is almost exclusively engaged in activities that require its engineering staff to have access to information that is classified as top secret, secret, or confidential by the Department of Defense or AEC. Our attention is directed to the fact that the company's contracts with the government make it directly responsible for safeguarding all classified matter. It is impracticable, if not impossible, the company says, to segregate its engineers who have been granted clearances from those who have not since the close proximity within which such groups would be required to work would, within itself, involve a serious risk.

Nevertheless he ruled in the union's favor. The language of the agreement clearly supported the union's objection. Furthermore, he could not bring himself to believe that:

> . . . it was the intention of the parties to create a situation whereby the Company could deny an employee access to classified security with all the attendant consequences that would flow from such action without affording the employee an opportunity for a hearing or review.

The case received national attention and set a precedent in this area.

In other companies the issue is not whether the company has the right to discharge for its own security reasons but whether the company's reasons constitute just cause. Disagreements occur in a variety of situations of which a couple of cases are illustrative. One management sought to terminate an engineer who was considered to be a possible security risk. The plant security officer had learned that the employee had a police record, and had informed the supervisor that for this reason the engineer's security clearance request would not be forwarded to Washington. The union investigated the case and learned that the police record consisted of one disorderly conduct complaint against the engineer, signed by one person, with no witnesses, which had never been followed up in court. According to the union, the police authorities felt that the man should initiate proceedings to have the case stricken from the records. The results of this grievance were not available for this study.

In another instance, management discharged a man with five years' satisfactory service when his security clearance was revoked by the government for medical reasons. The union supported the engineer's request for a transfer from military into nonsensitive commercial engineering located in a separate establishment. The company refused the request because it preferred to maintain flexibility in its work force. A grievance on the case was appealed to arbitration; the decision rendered in 1959 was in the employee's favor.

Hands Off Policy

The interest exhibited by the unions in companies' actions

on security clearances as described above is not shared by all engineering union leaders. They do not say so publicly but a few personally have a "hands off" policy applied to security cases. One stated:

> When the company decides to get rid of a man about whom they believe they have reason to wonder, I do not stick my neck out in an effort to support the employee's attempts to get the company to state why he is being discharged. Sure, you might say that the union is expected to see to it that an employee receives "due process," but it's different with security questions.

In another company where the union leader has a hands off policy, an executive discussed the problem of termination of "suspected security risks."

> It would be difficult, or impossible, for the company to document their doubts about many of the men they get rid of for this reason. The union does not give us any trouble in this area.

In these companies either the personal inclination on the part of the union leaders or the character of the union-management relationship gives management in these companies a flexibility in the area of security that apparently is not enjoyed in other companies. This flexibility, it should be noted, might be at the expense of the employees' rights under contract clauses which expressly provide that the employees shall be given in writing the reasons (presumably the real reasons) for termination.

Discipline

Discipline in the sense of punishment applied to deportment problems—such as, drinking and fighting on the job, pilferage, or carelessness resulting in damage to company property—is not an important area of engineering management. It was stated earlier that discharge action has sometimes been initiated for reasons of misconduct. Minor instances of these types of misconduct have also been the basis of lesser disciplinary action—invariably reprimands. Occasionally an engineer who received a letter of reprimand which he felt was in error or unfair would file a grievance for an attempt to have the letter rescinded. At least two cases were reported in which the company agreed to remove the letter from the grievant's personnel file, or to modify the letter and permit the grievant to insert into the file his description of the condition leading to the reprimand. More often, however, the union did not become involved in such cases.

The one area of discipline in which engineering has been confronted with difficult problems is that of controlling the amount of time off for personal reasons, frequently referred to as "PR time." Contracts generally provide that engineers may be absent during the regular work week for very short periods without any reduction in salary. A typical provision placed a maximum of 10 days per year on PR time. Various specific problems have arisen in administering the PR allowances. Is each employee *entitled* to the maximum? Is prior notice or approval required? What reasons are acceptable?

One union takes the position that the question "What reasons are acceptable?" is irrelevant since "personal reasons" are private reasons which the professional should not be asked to lay out before his supervisor. He should be trusted to use good judgment. In this union's view, if prior supervisory approval is to be required, the supervisor's decision should be made on the basis of whether the man's work would be unreasonably hindered by his absence. The company's reply is that the supervisor has to evaluate the reason for the absence to see if the work hindrance would be justified by the reason. This is just one example of the types of issues which arise. Irrespective of whether they are actually resolved in the union's favor, they do tend to enlarge the PR privilege granted to employees.

A related problem is that of tardiness and departure before

the end of the day. Almost all the engineers in the companies studied are no longer required to punch a time clock, which in many instances is the result of union actions. The companies agree to the removal of time clocks in an attempt to meet the engineers' legitimate needs for being treated as professionals, but in doing so, make it impossible for supervisors to enforce strict hours. In one sense, managers are willing to concede that strict hours should not be imposed upon professionals, but their actions belie their words. They have tried to substitute various techniques for the function performed by the time clock—private pencil records, late cards issued by guards at the gate, docking for lateness, posting monitors in the halls, cracking down on extended breaks and lunch periods, and so on. One company changed its policy to forbid engineers' use of public telephones during working hours without a supervisor's permission. The unions have protested not only the existence of these controls but also the techniques applied by supervision to enforce them.

From time to time these protestations are effective in causing management to refrain from exercising stricter controls. Two instances illustrate the difficulty encountered by engineering supervision in cracking down on lost time without generating more ill feeling among the engineers than the action is worth. Both instances, occurring in 1958, followed on the heels of criticism from the companies' respective military customers regarding the laxness evidenced in the control of time lost.

The first instance occurred in an aircraft firm. A manager, in an effort to eliminate what he thought was a costly practice among employees—sleeping in the restrooms—had the doors removed from all the toilet facilities for the men employed in his division. The engineers were outraged. The union called management's action "completely intolerable, disgusting, and revolting." Similar feelings were communicated to the company by letter. When this letter and other measures through normal channels failed to produce a reversal of the manager's action, the union threatened to publicize the instance throughout the nation, including every engineering college on its mailing list. Management's decision to replace the doors to the toilet facilities may have been no more than coincidentally related to the union's final threat, but it is likely that management will be more cautious in future disciplinary actions if engineers are involved.

The second instance occurred in an instruments firm which had become concerned with substantial costs incurred by employees coming late, leaving early, and taking long breaks. Deciding to set up a mechanism for continued vigil of such practices, an executive assigned supervisors to man certain stations at given periods during the day to take down the names of individuals not at their work place without reason. The monitors then reported violators to their immediate supervisors who took corrective action. Reflecting the engineers' disgust and dismay, the union reacted intemperately to this practice, charging the company with employing "police state" methods.

Summary and Conclusion

We have gained some insight into why discharge policies and practices are seldom issues in collective bargaining with professional engineers. We have also suggested that the unions may nevertheless have some impact on managements' decisions in this area.

For "professional reasons" engineering unions shy away from the discharge question, especially if technical performance is involved. Some unions make it difficult to have a discharge case qualify as a union matter; then they are apt to agree with management's action. Other unions, however, with specific organizational needs, are happy to get the cases. Even so, the engineers themselves are reluctant to protest a termination since their continued progress in their present job is so dependent upon their relationship with their supervisors, and since their future engineering employment is so dependent upon their current employment record. These factors actually enable the companies to avoid discharges by forcing the resignation of engineers, a practice which many of the unions have opposed.

To a great extent the above considerations were academic because companies have not been inclined to much discharge action. First, the "warm body" hiring policy prior to 1957 could not logically be accompanied by any tighter standard for continued employment. Second, the supervisors claim that they have been hindered in making discharges because of the difficulty of building a case, one that could be used to document the action in arbitration.

The issue over probationary extensions is not one based on disagreement in principle. The difficulty derives from the fact that the company has to ask the union for dispensation. For an organization with little of the power normally possessed by a labor organization, any opportunity to withhold something from the company must be considered a candidate for tactical assignments.

Regarding security discharge, there is divergence in the views between two groups of engineering unions. Some take the role of the individual's advocate, ensuring that the company does not substitute its own stricter security clearance standards for those of the government, and thereby deprive an employee of loss of employment and reputation without due process; they probably complicate managements' job in this area. A few unionists do not choose to become involved; they do not feel they are responsible for employees' interests in matters so sensitive.

Although other areas of discipline have not presented any significant problems for engineering management, some difficulty has arisen in controlling lost time—lateness, long breaks, and so on. Every technique management develops to do the job of the time clock rankles the engineers and becomes an issue for the union.

PART IV

Impact on the Engineering Organization

CHAPTER XII

Jurisdictional Issues and Organizational Flexibility

THIS CHAPTER will treat a miscellany of topics including interunion jurisdictional disputes, supervisors performing bargaining unit work, nonsupervisory specialist classifications outside the bargaining unit, distinctions between supervisory and nonsupervisory engineering personnel, assigning subprofessional work to engineers, placing nonengineers in engineering classifications, job content, and use of contract engineers. These jurisdictional topics will be approached from the point of view of the ways in which they relate to management's flexibility in accomplishing the engineering task. The importance of flexibility was underlined by engineering managers who estimated that personnel costs accounted for as much as 80% of the total engineering cost.

INTERUNION JURISDICTIONAL DISPUTES

Jurisdictional problems between the engineers' union and other unions are rare, although not nonexistent. At that, contested interunion jurisdictional claims are almost never initiated by the engineers' union; they are invariably directed against the engineers. Draftsmen who are organized into a separate unit will often complain that engineers are doing drafting work. Whether a sketch is actually drafting is often the issue, since personnel represented by both unions may make sketches but only draftsmen have the right to do drafting; and since it is the nature of some development engineers to want to refine the sketch until it actually can be called a drafting. In this jurisdictional problem over drawings the fact that the engineers are organized operates to the advantage of both the company and the engineers. It happens that the flexibility which the engineers enjoy is one which the company also wants to maintain.

Disputed jurisdictional claims have arisen between the production and quality control engineers who are located in the plant and represented by the shop local, and the engineers in the engineering department who are represented by the professional local. Normally after a project has been put into production, the test and control engineering functions are performed by production department personnel. On some projects, however, engineering management has technical reasons for continuing to perform these functions. Unresolved differences between the two groups result in duplication of effort.

Jurisdictional problems between the engineers and technicians do not arise where the two groups are in the same bargaining unit. Any contested jurisdictional claims which involve these heterogeneous units arise in the technicians' section of the unit and conflict with the shop unit. These conflicts are common but since they do not directly involve the engineers, they are outside the scope of this study.

Jurisdictional claims by the engineers' union over nonrepresented employees not considered by the company to be within the scope of the bargaining unit do occur occasionally. One such case at an electronics firm involved the Programming and Analysis section of an electronic computer department. When the P & A section was formed, half of its staff was drawn from sections represented by the union. Later, the company attached the P & A section to the marketing department and declared that the union no longer represented any of the section's personnel. This declaration was contested by the union and in 1958 the issue was still unresolved. Another unresolved jurisdictional problem involved the union's claim that it represented two "human engineers," two experimental psychologists who had become engaged in panel layout, work normally performed by engineers.

Supervisors Performing Bargaining Unit Work

Many engineering agreements make specific provision allowing the supervisor to do work normally performed by members of the bargaining unit. Whether the agreements allow for it or not, supervisors in every company studied do engage in engineering work. Indeed by the very nature of the engineering task it would be difficult, if not impossible, for them to do otherwise. Though the unions recognize the necessity of this practice, many would limit it.

One agreement reads:

> It is agreed that in the course of performing their duty as supervisors, it may from time to time be necessary for supervisors to take a direct hand in engineering work, and at times this work may fall directly within the job classifications covered by this agreement. It is further agreed that supervisors will work with engineers toward the engineers' professional and technical advancement.

The union interprets this to mean, "If the supervisor pitches in on a hot job which the employee can't do or can't finish on time, that's O.K.; but if the supervisor performs engineering work day in and day out, that's clearly not 'from time to time'." According to a union source a few grievances which were filed on supervisors regularly doing bargaining unit work were resolved to the satisfaction of the union, the remedy being for the supervisor to cease and desist.

Under the contract in another company the supervisors were allowed to perform bargaining unit work provided the work so performed does not exceed an average of 50% of their time during a three-month period. In the 1958 negotiations the union proposed that supervisors should not be allowed to spend more than 20% of their time on bargaining unit work. The union argued for the change primarily because of the effect it would have on the quality of the engineers' supervision—"It would force supervisors to devote more time to *effective* supervision"—rather than on grounds of "selfish" jurisdictional claims.

Nonsupervisory Classifications Outside the Bargaining Unit

Almost every one of the companies that bargain with engineering unions desire to create positions that are neither supervisory-management nor nonsupervisory-union, and to make these positions available to the best technical brains of the engineering force. These positions, which would be nonsupervisory but management in character, would be given designations such as Design Specialist, Engineering Staff Specialist, Research Associate, Technical Consultant, to mention only a few. Some companies already have such positions. Others have found the union a bar to the establishment of this type of classification outside the bargaining unit where, in the opinion of management, "it belongs."

Let us examine the experiences of some companies around this classification issue. One company created a number of technical positions with salary ranges paralleling those of the administrative positions in its research department in an effort to provide recognition for the top flight research man. A manager in the company stated:

> These positions are definitely considered a part of management, and we must be able to keep them outside the bargaining unit. If the scientists occupying these positions could not be treated specially, the very purpose of establishing the ladder would be defeated.

Another company has two nonsupervisory engineering classifications containing a total of 80 engineers outside the bargaining unit. According to a manager:

> The fact that these classifications are outside the bargaining unit gives the job a certain element of prestige, and it is a greater incentive. We can place greater trust in a man's

loyalty to the company; for example, we have these men attend supervisory conferences. Finally, it is an advantage in recruiting.

Another company in the aircraft industry was considering hiring research scientists into classifications outside of the bargaining unit. An executive stated:

> These people are independent in nature and might be more difficult to recruit if they were to be represented by the union. Also, management would want to extend privileges to these men that are different from those enjoyed by our engineers generally.

The experiences of one company which tried to hire technical consultants tend to lend some support to the companies' fears described above. In 1956 the company created the Staff Engineer classification outside the bargaining unit, and hired about 10 men to fill these positions. The union claimed that each of these men was actually a Senior Engineer, the top classification in the bargaining unit, since that classification had no maximum salary limit. The matter was taken to an arbitrator who ruled in the union's favor despite the company's argument that these men operated across departmental lines and influenced company policy and therefore could not appropriately be placed in the bargaining unit.

After receiving the arbitrator's ruling the company still felt compelled to remove these men from the bargaining unit. It decided to give them supervisory designations, but to make the promotions one by one over a period of time in order to minimize the reaction on the part of the union. As a result of the delay one of the men resigned rather than be placed, even temporarily, in the bargaining unit and thereby "limit his future." Two years later five of the men had been placed in supervisory positions. Management has attempted to give them light supervisory assignments because if they are burdened with administrative responsibilities and supervisory tasks their superior technical qualities are not being fully utilized, and they are not happy.

Some idea that these particular men are highly influential people in management can be gathered from a magazine article on the company. The article included a photograph of the company president and these researchers, designating the group as the Technical Advisory Committee and giving it credit for evolving much of one of the country's successful missile guidance systems. This group passes on the soundness of suggested programs for the company's future and assists in guiding the search for new contracts.

The unions are not opposed to the concept of a parallel ladder by which those who are placed in technical classifications on a level with the supervisory positions also receive comparable treatment. They have, in fact, proposed the creation of such classifications, but within the scope of the bargaining unit.

Supervisory–Nonsupervisory Distinction

The discussions in the two previous sections about supervisors doing bargaining unit work and nonsupervisory personnel being placed in supervisory classifications are based on an assumption that there are recognizable distinctions between supervisory and nonsupervisory engineering work. This assumption is only partially valid, according to several managers interviewed.

The experiences of three companies testify to the absence of a clear distinction existing between supervisory and nonsupervisory engineering employees before the union entered, and to the changes which were required at the time of unionization. Merely to arrive at a meaningful demarcation for the bargaining unit in one company where management had not emphasized the difference between supervisors and nonsupervisors, it was necessary for management to eliminate one entire engineering classification by placing some of the engineers in a supervisory category and by including the remainder in a bargaining unit classification. At the time of the formation of the union in another company many people expressed doubt about whether they were supervisors or not. Soon after the election the company reorganized its system of management in the engineering department, creating a new supervisory position. During NLRB hearings in the third company, management tried to exclude many employees from the bargaining unit as group leaders. In these hearings the chief engineer testified, "The company never made it a practice of telling men they were working group leaders."

The administrative engineer in a division which had not yet felt the impact of the engineers' union stated:

> Engineers must be members of management because they are key to management programs, and because their work is nonroutine. If there were to be a demarcation between the engineers and management, this would be a tragic development. There are many aspects of flexibility that are necessary in engineering and in the labs. For example, an individual who creates should be able to break into the leadership role at any time, spontaneously and informally. There is over time a transition from a student to a teacher; since this is normally a gradual evolution, as little formal distinction as possible is desirable.

In another company an executive indicated that unionization had resulted in sharper distinctions between supervisors and nonsupervisors in his company's research organization:

> Compared with the shop there is much less real difference between the functions of supervisors and nonsupervisors. In the shop to have some directing the work and some doing the work is an appropriate arrangement; not so in research—those who are primarily responsible for directing the work should help do it, and those primarily responsible for the work should assist in directing it.
>
> Growing out of the distinctions of the Taft-Hartley Act—which includes some and excludes others from the union—is a social distinction that prevents the excluded group leader from working with his men and that prevents them from accepting his assistance. For example, when a man is promoted

to a supervisory position, management must write him to the effect that he is now eligible to hear grievances. He is no longer one of the boys. Titles become more important. Group leaders are no longer located in the lab; they have offices.

The executive felt strongly that this last condition (separate offices) "shouldn't be." "The group leaders are good research men and should be working right along with their men." He also said, "If we didn't have the union, we wouldn't need two different policies for our professionals." He also cited the disadvantage recognized by the administrative engineer quoted earlier: management felt it could not experiment with a temporary leader arrangement whereby for each new project the man most suitable to lead in that project would be given the job of group leader.

Several managements felt obliged to treat their engineers differently because of their unionized status. Management was hesitant to ask unionized engineers to sit in on department policy meetings; to inform them of confidential company matters; to grant them full responsibility for dealing with customers; to give them supervisory responsibility; and so on. In a word, management tended to "clip the engineers' wings."

One company which was sponsoring a supervisory training program thought of including certain individuals from the bargaining units who by virtue of their work assignments had many supervisory tasks. But then management decided against the idea because of the risk of a charge that it was attempting to dominate the union. Besides, if engineers who were members of the bargaining unit were to participate, the program's discussions would be somewhat inhibited by the social distinctions that were based on bargaining unit status and firmly implanted in the minds of the participants.

Another company, which reported that it was prevented from giving its engineers an occasional extra supervisory task, indicated that such a practice not only could fill a particular need for the company but could also provide an opportunity for recognition and growth for the individual. Thus, extra supervisory duties could be administered in part as an incentive, a reward for good work. A manager felt that because of the union such opportunities, if extended at all, must be applied rather uniformly among the engineers.

Notwithstanding the sentiments of management reflected above, the enthusiasm of one of the company's systems engineers suggests that there is no lack of responsibility and opportunity for certain engineers.

> I consider this a good company to work for. You would have to burn down the building to get me out. This company gives more responsibility to its engineers than any other company I know. Under normal circumstances as a top rated systems engineer I'll be given a project to supervise technically; that is, to set up, to decide how to go about the project. If it is necessary to make a trip, I just let the leader know where I am going. I make my own arrangements for the time I'll be away. . . . Our decisions are high level and far reaching. In systems, decisions have more impact on the company than 50% of management's decisions.

Assigning Subprofessional Work to Engineers

We saw in the last section that the company may contend that the level of work assigned to engineers is lower than it would be if they were not unionized. The engineers also talk of being used below capacity but approach the problem from a different point of view. Their unions, particularly those representing the engineers employed by aircraft companies, disparage the "malutilization" of engineering talent.[1]

[1] The engineering unions are, of course, not the only group to attack the underutilization of engineering and scientific talent. Spokesmen from the professional societies, educational institutions, governmental agencies, and industry have called attention to the same practices in industry. See, for example:

George S. Odiorne, "Today's Shortage of Engineers: Fact or Fancy," *Advanced Management,* October 1954, pp. 23–25.

National Society of Professional Engineers, *How to Improve the Utilization of Engineering Manpower,* Washington, 1952.

National Manpower Council, *Proceedings of a Conference on The Utilization of Scientific and Professional Manpower,* New York: Columbia University Press, 1954, p. 197.

Though managements agree in principle with the unions' aim of strictly professional duties, they cannot always accommodate this aim. For example, an aircraft engineer must spend a considerable period of time drafting in order to learn how to "lay out and fit." According to an aircraft company executive, the real problem is that the newly graduated engineer who expects professional work during his first year in industry "has too high an opinion of his own abilities."

A proposal for more effective use of professionals submitted by a union committee included the following illustrative recommendations:

1. Use of more clerical help and engineering assistants in data gathering, logging, and analysis, as well as preparing progress reports, and so on.
2. Greater use of draftsmen for detailing design work.
3. Delegation of more work to technicians.

The proposal was taken under consideration by the company. When asked about the proposal in an interview, an executive stated that the company already had a policy of using nonprofessionals whenever it could. This was a standard response from management on the subject.

It is not our task here to decide whether it was possible for management to make greater use of engineering support personnel. Rather we are interested in determining whether they have changed their policies in this area as a result of unionization or of union pressure. A few unions make modest claims that they are responsible for some changes in the utilization of engineers. We have only the statements of the union representatives, one of whom said:

> When we organized there were no engineering aides, but the union kept trying to get rid of menial tasks. The engineer on his own doesn't stop to think whether what he is doing is engineering work or not. When an organization makes a point of this, he thinks of it and brings pressure.

Finally, in 1951 the company increased the number of draftsmen and started using engineering aides.

I think we can say we have contributed to the thinking that led to the changes.

One may not be willing to attribute any part of the change that has taken place over the past dozen years to the persuasion or pressure of the unions. Still, one cannot take the opposite position, which is that the unions have tended to prevent the use of more support personnel. That they have not opposed "better utilization" practices is in one sense a remarkable phenomenon indeed, because these practices tend to reduce the market for professional engineers. Wc have the benefit of the thinking of at least one professional union on this problem:

> During the past few years [the company] has created a sizable staff of draftsmen and aides. The use of these technical assistants began in the Engineering Department and was later extended to the Manufacturing Department. The use of the engineering aide classifications has only recently begun in manufacturing.
>
> Some engineers have expressed concern about the implications of this trend. Will these technicians gradually take over the work now performed by engineers? . . .
>
> The ideal situation, from the engineer's point of view, is well known. The engineer wants to be assigned work which continually challenges his capacity and wants to have the less technical work assigned to less experienced engineers or to technicians. The uneasiness arises when we consider how to effect the transition from the present situation to that ideal situation.
>
> Fortunately, there are some ameliorating circumstances. There is no large pool of draftsmen and aides from which the company may draw as many such employees as it requires, and whenever it requires them. Also the company is maintaining a steady expansion of its engineering staff. Thus it seems likely that these two factors, the company's needs

and the supply of technicians, are in such a balance that the company can proceed toward an increased staff of technical assistants without there being any likelihood of any layoff of engineers. Indeed, this seems to be an ideal time to introduce a substantial staff of assistants since it can be done with negligible dislocation of the engineers.

One might speculate that if the unions had taken a strict "jurisdictional" approach attempting to retain for the engineers all the work performed by engineers during the late 1940's when unionization occurred, they might well have slowed the rate of the change that has taken place in the use of support personnel during the 1950's.

Placing Nonengineers in Engineering Classifications

Unless a company has either minimum objective standards which must be met by employees before they can be placed in engineering classifications or a policy of systematically reviewing each employee placed in these classifications, the lower engineering classifications may become populated with a variety of nonengineers. In some companies supervisors occasionally place an employee in an engineering classification to remove him from the jurisdiction of the shop union, or to give him more money. In other companies the engineering titles which are associated with the classifications are sometimes used as a form of reward and recognition for competent mechanics and technicians.

The practice of placing nonengineers in engineering classifications is closely related to the "malutilization" issue since the position many unions take on both issues is largely based upon the engineers' desire for professional status and recognition. The positions of the unions on these issues are similar in another respect—they both appear to the casual observer to be contrary to the organizational interest of the unions, tending to decrease the membership of their organizations.

After considerable protest on the part of the union in one

company which had a loose policy governing the engineering classifications, management gradually tightened up its practices, adopting the policy that if a man does not have a B.S. degree he cannot be placed in a bargaining unit classification without the approval of the labor relations office.

In another collective bargaining relationship, which was not researched directly for this study, the question of which employees could be placed in the bargaining unit has been of utmost importance. In the agreement between the parties in effect in 1955, the company made certain guarantees that would operate to preserve the professional character of the unit:

> Article [on] Professional Standards
>
> 1. It is recognized that the occupational classifications listed in Appendix A require various degrees of professional qualifications. In the selection of individuals to be hired or transferred into such occupational classifications the company will use its judgment in determining on an individual basis the qualifications for the job to be filled; in the exercise of such judgment, the company shall give consideration to Section 2(12) of the Labor Management Relations Act, 1947 (Taft-Hartley Act). It is agreed that the company will not reduce the minimum qualifications for the occupational classifications involved below those used for the employees in the unit at the time of certification. . . .
>
> 2. The desirability of professional homogenity in the unit represented by the . . . [union] is recognized. To this end the company will not hire or transfer into the unit individuals who are not qualified in accordance with paragraph 1 above for the job or jobs involved through previous experience and/or education.

For several years the union and management differed continually about how the Professional Standards Article should be administered. The union charged the company with diluting the unit by placing nonprofessionals in classifications within the bargaining unit jurisdiction. For its part, the company resented the union's attempts to prevent it from exercising its own discretion in the assignment of classifications or personnel. Accordingly, during negotiations in 1955 the company requested the top union official to sign a "letter of understanding" clarifying the Article of Professional Standards, the effect of which would be to give the company unilateral authority to place employees in bargaining unit classifications. The union refused to sign the letter. The parties remained deadlocked on this issue of professional standards.

Job Content

It was brought out in the chapter on salary structure that engineers as a rule are not conscious of whether or not their work is strictly within their job description. One reason for this attitude is that the engineer welcomes variety in his professional assignments. Another reason relates to the adequacy of the job description itself: engineering type work simply does not lend itself to precise description; therefore it is difficult to ascertain whether a man is working within his description. For these reasons an engineer almost never resists a given assignment merely because it is "someone else's work," or because it seems to be outside his job description or classification.

Contract Engineers

In the dynamic business of research and development for the military, the manpower requirement of employers is subject to sharp changes—upward as well as downward—almost overnight. Success in bidding on a new contract or the discovery of a new dimension to an existing contract commitment will create unforeseen engineering demands. How can these demands be met? Members of the company's technical staff who have the requisite experience may already be heavily engaged. Overtime can be stepped up but soon it reaches the point of diminishing returns. The company can multiply its recruitment efforts, but even then considerable time is required to build a staff. Hiring new people, moreover, is not advisable whenever the demand for the extra engineers is expected to be of a relatively short duration. Nor is subcontracting the work, another alternative, always the answer since small companies may not have the facilities or technically skilled personnel necessary, and since large companies might soon become competitors. Besides, if a company subcontracts too much work, it will lose its status as a prime contractor.

Still another alternative normally available to the employer faced with unfulfilled engineering manpower requirements is the renting or contracting of engineers from a rental agency. The employer contracts with the agency for a specific quantity and quality of engineers for a limited period of time. Contract engineers are subject to the company's technical supervision and discipline, but remain on the payroll of the agency.

Engineering unions generally take a dim view of the practice of using contract engineers. The reasoning of one union leader who was confronted with the company's action of hiring contract engineers can be paraphrased as follows:

> If there are vacancies, it is logical and equitable to promote people within the organization and to fill gaps by hiring at the levels of lesser experience, and by supplementing with overtime. The company is unduly pessimistic about future growth. As to costs, there is no question that the contract engineers are more costly with higher salaries, per diem, travel, etc. If close liaison with engineering is required, this can be accomplished by sending engineers to the subcontractor. Finally, the use of contract engineers inside the plant is demoralizing to the entire department.

Hiring contract engineers is also viewed by the unions as a way of hiring help at higher wages at a time of peak demand and limited supply without having to give the same increases to permanent help. If the companies were to recruit additional employees to handle the peak load, they would be forced to raise starting rates somewhat, providing the company with a compelling reason to raise other rates in the salary structure. Besides, whenever the company encounters difficulty in meeting its manpower needs, the individual and collective bargaining powers of the engineer (with respect to merit and general increases respectively) are enhanced accordingly.

At least one other union apprehension about the practice of using contract engineers has been voiced:

> . . . it is a mechanism whereby the company, if it sees fit, could do all of its technical hiring through those agencies and eventually replace all . . . members with nonunion "contract" employees, thereby destroying . . . [the union].

A variety of measures have been adopted or proposed by the unions to limit the companies' flexibility in the use of contract engineers. At one extreme an agreement contained an unqualified commitment by the employer "not to 'rent' employees from a subcontractor or 'Labor Rental Agency.' "

The recognition clause of the agreement in another company was assumed by both parties to preclude the use of contract engineers without the union's approval. Beginning in 1952, the firm periodically sought, and sometimes received, permission from the union to use contract engineers. A persuasive point was made by management in recounting how by taking on more projects than it could handle during a period in 1945 and 1946, relying upon outside help when it became necessary, the company had begun a long line of projects important to the course of the company's history. The precedent of using contract engineers under unionization was set in 1952 when the company obtained the union's permission to employ ten engineers for a period of three to four months. The company approached the union again in 1954 with a need for four or five engineers. Later when the estimate was revised upward, the union decided to oppose the use of contract engineers, basing its decision "on principle." In January 1956 one division of the company was engaged in design work on a large missile project, looking toward production and test work. The division's employment of 250 engineers would be increased to 450 if the production contract was acquired. The overtime, hiring, and subcontracting alternatives were not enough. The company also wanted to be able to use contract engineers whenever it became necessary. In refusing the company's repeated requests, the union advocated "better utilization of engineers" and greater reliance upon promotion from within.

The agreement in another company contains a statement of policy on the matter that requires management to fully inform the union regarding the company's specific use of contract engineers but does not require the union's approval:

> The management of the company believes that as a general rule it is not desirable to obtain the services of contract engineers who are not employees of the company for the purpose of using such engineers in the plants of the company on work equivalent to that performed in various job classifications covered by this agreement. However, to meet certain emergencies or special conditions, it may be in the best interests of the company to obtain and use such services. In this event, the company shall evaluate the factors involved, make its decision, and notify the association of such decision, the basis for the need, the approximate number of engineers required, and estimated period of utilization. The term contract engineers, as used in this article, does not include consultants or their employees, or employees of subcontractors or vendors.

In a company where the contract did not contain a specific provision covering the use of contract engineers, the union contested the practice as an "unprofessional, shortsighted expedient." The company made use of such outside assistance from time to time throughout its collective bargaining history, but not without receiving bitter criticism from the engineers' representatives. In the spring of 1957 when the company brought contract engineers into the plant in an effort to meet commitments on a particular missile program, the union came forth with its own plan for such a situation:

> If the company decides it has need for more manpower, on certain projects, the following steps should be taken before contract employees could be admitted to the plant:
>
> The positions shall be posted on all [union] and company bulletin boards for a period of two weeks. The job requirements, field of experience, approximate duration, and location of the job will be included in the notice.
>
> The company will submit to [the union]:
>
> A list of those people who have applied for these jobs and have been accepted for or have been refused the position. Once each year, jobs that have not been filled by Bargaining Unit Members, but instead by subcontractors, shall again be posted.

The company was not persuaded, because as a matter of regular practice it makes certain that the possibilities of using existing personnel have been exhausted to its own satisfaction before contracting outside engineers.

The contract engineering issue has not been raised forcefully in all companies. Some managers using contract engineers have experienced difficulties which are not caused by the union. They complain that questions are likely to arise regarding the assignment of responsibility for work, double standards for rules and discipline, and overtime payment. Some feel that the effect on the morale of the permanent engineering staff makes it "too costly an expedient."

On the other hand, one company not deterred by its union in the use of contract engineers reported how significant this option was to its operations. Ten per cent of the force were contract engineers during a 15-month period in 1951 and 1952, about 5% during one period in 1953, and 8% for an 11-month period in 1955. An executive stated:

> This practice enabled the company to bid with confidence on new contracts, which amounted to about $100 million worth of business. We were able to bring in the mediocre kind of engineer to thin out our own trained engineers who could thereby be used much more advantageously. On the other hand, a few of these contract guys were exceptional and because of their breadth of experience were able to infuse new ideas into the sections with which they worked.

The discussion above neither applies to consulting engineers who have special talents and work only part time for the companies studied, nor does it refer to liaison engineers employed by other aircraft or electronics companies, who are working within the unionized companies' plants. The unions normally do not object to these arrangements, although they generally would like to be informed of them by the company.

A related practice against which one union did raise effective objections was the use of student engineers on a part-time basis. The company employed the students attending a local university who were in their fifth year of engineering and had Tuesdays, Thursdays, and Saturdays clear of classes. The company was willing to let the students work Saturday and longer than eight hours on Tuesday and Thursday, all at straight time rates. In fact, unless they could work more than two days at straight time rates the arrangement did not appear to be a practical one for the company. The students were willing to work under the company's conditions. The union, however, would not relieve the company of its obligation under the contract to pay nonexempt employees time and a half for any work over eight hours in one day, and for Saturday work. Thus, for a time the company was not able to hire part-time students, and thereby enter into an employment arrangement which would have been to the company's advantage in terms of quality-cost considerations, university relations, and recruitment (of the better part-time student employees after graduation). The company told the students that the union contract blocked their way. The situation generated some internal conflict, and eventually the union conceded to the company's proposal.

Summary and Conclusion

There is a notable absence of interunion jurisdictional disputes initiated by the engineering unions. Whenever the engineering unions do become involved in such disputes, their interests generally coincide with those of management. The jurisdictional issue, however, takes a variety of other forms. Through limiting contract clauses and periodic pressure, unions probably have placed some restrictions on supervisors doing bargaining unit work, but the more effective means for preventing the supervisors from doing bargaining unit work is the social distinction created between the supervisory position and the nonsupervisory job; that is, in an engineering department without a union the engineer who held supervisory positions would be freer to strike his own balance between technical and supervisory work so long as he met minimum supervisory responsibilities. One consequence of unionization is that the man in a nonbargaining unit classification thinks of himself as a supervisor; he becomes more conscious of distinctions and of his supervisory duties. Whether these distinctions are functional or dysfunctional for the engineering organization is a question which cannot be answered definitely. Certain ways were cited in which it was believed to be dysfunctional; namely, it eliminates spontaneous, temporary leadership in engineering and research groups, and tends to cut down communication between the engineer and his supervisor.

In the case of the technical staff specialist or consultant, the union forces another clarification of status which is embarrassing for management. The company is comfortable with a category of individuals who are nonsupervisory but management. This classification accommodates highly rated technical employees who are frequently consulted by higher levels of management. Some companies have been able to preserve this particular category, but the unions have tried to absorb it. Where these efforts of the unions have met with success, the result is to detract from the prestige associated with the position. This in turn has implications for recruiting and for internal incentive programs. These considerations have operated to deter managements that do not have such positions from establishing them within the bargaining unit. This may mean that they are not created at all.

Many of the professional engineering unions place pressure on management to remove the nonprofessional tasks from the engineering assignments and to prevent the engineering classifications, particularly the lower ones, from being filled with nonprofessionals. While the unions have not developed any reliable techniques for governing these practices, their protestations and other forms of persuasion have probably influenced management to respect their desires.

Finally some companies may have been materially handicapped because of their inability to use contract engineers. They have been forced to rely more upon overtime and recruitment because the contract engineering alternative was not open to them, or because it was a source of friction in their union relations.

Only in this last mentioned effect regarding contract engineers has the engineering union's influence on jurisdictional matters been the same as its counterpart in the shop. While some of the other influences summarized above are similar to those in the shop, such as clauses limiting supervisors' performance of bargaining unit work, they are much more moderate in their effect when they occur in the engineering department. The influence of still other engineering union policies are just the opposite from those normally encountered in the shop; an example is the pressure for an exclusive rather than inclusive bargaining unit.

CHAPTER XIII

Management Organization and Responsibility

IN THE preceding chapters we have been concerned with the substantive changes which have occurred in the policies and practices in many areas or functions of management. We have had a further interest in learning of the ways in which management shares effective authority for these functions with the employees' bargaining agent. In this chapter we shall be concerned with certain changes which have occurred *within management:* (a) changes in the attitudes and activities of management groups, and (b) shifts in the location of authority and responsibility for certain management functions. Naturally, we shall also be inquiring as to how these changes relate to the presence of the union.

We shall attempt to determine what changes have occurred by asking several specific questions: Who in management handles individual grievances? Who represents the company in daily union contacts? Who participates in contract negotiations? How is responsibility for other personnel functions shared by various management groups? Each of these questions will be the subject of a separate section of this chapter. A final section will be devoted to supervisory training.

GRIEVANCE HANDLING

The grievance procedures provided by engineering union contracts vary widely in terms of the participants for the company, and in terms of the number of review steps before arbitration. An agreement in one company on one end of the spectrum provides two steps within line engineering management, two additional steps within the labor relations department, and an appeal step to arbitration. Another engineering contract features three steps of appeal to line managers—immediate supervisor, department head, and division manager—and then arbitration. A more common procedure contained in most of the engineering agreements involves the supervisor in the first step, the labor relations staff in the second step, and arbitration in a third step.

One unique agreement allows the employee to bypass his immediate supervisor and have his grievance considered first by the department head during the latter official's weekly meeting with the senior union representative of the department; second, by the industrial relations office in consultation with representatives of the union; and third, by an "Employment Relations Committee" consisting of not more than six members representing the company and not more than six representing the union. The decisions of the committee on grievances is considered final if a majority of the union representatives and a majority of the company representatives concur. Otherwise, the grievance may be appealed to arbitration.

It should be borne in mind that while the appeals in later steps are made to labor relations officials, line engineering managers may continue to participate in the grievance sessions. This statement, however, and the description of the contractual procedures in the preceding paragraph tend to overstate the amount that line managers actually participate in the handling of employee grievances in the unionized companies studied. There has been a trend that began with the first years of collective bargaining and has continued until recently—a trend for the handling of grievances to be shifted from engineering management to the industrial relations staff. This shift was reflected in the change in the second step in one agreement whereby the union could no longer appeal a grievance to the vice president of engineering, but must confine such appeals to the personnel manager. Moreover, the person who must actually consider the grievance is not always specified in the language of the agreement; the contract may only require that a given line manager must "answer" the grievance.

The line manager may not even answer the grievance himself, since under many agreements he may designate a representative to do this for him. In practice, where this alternative exists grievances are almost invariably handled by his designee, who is frequently from the labor relations or personnel staff, not from among his line subordinates or administrative assistants.

The role of the line manager is further diminished by the practice of waiving his particular step in the procedure at the request of management. The contractual procedures in some companies have been dispensed with almost entirely, with all grievances being handled between one top official in the union and a company representative from the labor relations staff. Under this arrangement the individual will call the union president or whoever has assumed the grievance job, who will, in turn, telephone his counterpart in the company's labor relations office. They either "thrash the thing out then and there" or they go back to their principals for more information and meet with each other on the grievance at a later date.

Some companies deliberately "insulate" engineering management, particularly the engineering supervisor, from all contact with the union, so that relationships within engineering will not be affected. Applied to grievance adjustment this means "discouraging the union from taking up an employee's grievance initially with supervision," despite this option under the agreement. The managers who reported this policy did not specify how it is implemented, but testified that it was effective.

In one company where the union was extremely weak the personnel manager of the engineering department, who was described by the chief engineer as the "key link" between the industrial relations department and the engineering department, reported that he had actually spent "negligible time" on strictly union problems. He was designated as the one whom the area representative of the union should contact, yet in four years he had not been contacted. He did not even know the union area representatives or their names. Grievances arising in the engineering department were presented directly to the assistant director of industrial relations by the union president.

The president of the union in one aircraft company resented the labor relation staff's efforts to have him confine his contacts to their office. Since, in his opinion, the crucial power resides in the engineering department in an aircraft company, he believed that he could do much better by contacting engineering management directly on matters of contract administration. But then, he considered, this might be precisely why labor relations would be embarrassed if the union did contact engineering. Moreover, labor relations does not want to risk having bargains struck by the engineers' union with engineering management which will complicate their dealings with shop unions. How does labor relations prevent the engineers' union from approaching engineering management directly? The president commented, "The labor relations department could make life miserable for me, by refusing to send the company directory, refusing information, etc., etc.,—a thousand different ways."

Whatever procedures are specified in the agreement or are followed in practice, the amount of time spent in the grievance process by any of the participants for the company depends upon the amount of grievance activity. A wide range of experiences was represented by the engineering unions studied. One unit with 500 engineers had over 50 grievances in a single year. Another unit with about 1,500 engineers had a dozen or so per year until recent years when the number exceeded 100. Still another unit with over 3,000 engineers had less than 20 grievances per year. The first experience mentioned was not typical of those of other companies, but the second two were. One must conclude that by and large grievances are filed by engineers in relatively small numbers. Therefore in most companies no substantial amount of time of anyone in management was devoted strictly to this activity. Regarding engineering managers, they appear to have been only minimally involved.

The tendency for employee grievances to be processed through a minimum number of informal steps with responsibility for resolving the grievances centering in the labor relations department has been reversed in recent years in a few companies. These companies have adopted policies of forcing the supervisor and, subsequently, his superior to deal with the grievances of their employees. At the same time, they have shown more favor for formalized and written grievances. This new tendency in these companies has been accompanied by an increase in the number of grievances filed.

One interpretation offered by the writer of first the one tendency and then its reversal is as follows: when the early engineering union agreements were drawn up, the parties borrowed from shop agreements to arrive at elaborate contractual grievance procedures involving line management above the immediate supervisor. The size of the bargaining unit was relatively small and the rate of grievances very low, allowing any employee's problem which was not resolved between the engineer and his immediate supervisor to be handled informally. Neither the engineer with the grievance nor engineering management above the immediate supervisor, however, had any desire to become involved in grievance processing. The engineer did not want to jeopardize his relationship with his immediate superiors, or to draw attention to himself by going personally to the personnel department. At the same time, engineering managers, who are even less "people oriented" than production managers, naturally shied away from individual complaints whether they involved personalities or administrative problems. Hence, the task of resolving grievances fell upon the engineers' representative and the labor relations officials, both of whom were willing, sometimes eager, to perform these functions for their principals. At some point, however, the growing size of the bargaining unit and the increased willingness of engineers to file grievances resulted in more grievances than could be handled personally by a single union official and his contact in the labor relations department. Consequently, officials in both organizations began to stress the need to follow the formal procedure, and to settle the grievances at the lowest possible level. As this trend continues, line engineering management becomes increasingly involved in employee grievance matters.

Daily Union Contacts

Institutional grievances that are submitted by the union and meetings that are held with the union on general matters of interest are even more clearly within the province of the labor relations staff. Exceptions occur in a few companies where regular weekly, biweekly, or monthly meetings are held with representatives of the engineering department to consider matters of mutual interest. Members of engineering management sometimes participate in these meetings, although the man on the labor relations staff who has been designated as the company's principal contact with the union usually assumes a leadership role at these regular meetings. It usually works out that the company's contact man spends much of his time on engineering union matters.

A variety of arrangements providing for the principal contacts is found in the companies studied. The representative in one company is one of three assistant industrial relations managers, each of whom is responsible for one of three local unions representing respectively, the engineering, clerical, and shop employees. In a second company the representative is an employee relations supervisor, who also has responsibility for nonunion salaried personnel and some nonunion hourly personnel. The principal contact in a third company is in the central personnel office but has the title of Administrator of Engineering Personnel Relations. Because his interests comprehend a functional area, training, he also has responsibility in this area outside engineering. In a company with several divisions, one division personnel manager also served as that company's chief representative in all matters relating to the engineers' union, coordinating the efforts of the other three divisional personnel managers located in the same geographical area. These are only a few of the dozen arrangements studied, no two of which are alike.

Sometimes the unions try to bypass the contact man and the labor relations department and request a hearing with the company president or the top operating official in the organization with which the union bargains. Bids of this kind have been successful on rare occasions, when the top company official has invited the union committee to his office to present its problems.

Contract Negotiations

What roles are played by engineering management and labor relations respectively in negotiations with the engineers' union? By and large, in 1958 the labor relations staff groups assumed the task of conducting negotiations—determining strategies and tactics—and exercised preponderate influence over the size of the maximum package, while engineering management played a supporting role, an arrangement which has not always been considered satisfactory by all concerned. The unions generally would prefer to negotiate with engineering management. Likewise engineering management has from time to time had a taste for handling negotiations, manifesting the proprietary feeling that engineering managers have about engineering matters.

Some companies have tried assigning primary responsibility for negotiations to engineering management for a period of time, but not without encountering certain problems, as illustrated by the experiences of Company A. After labor relations had negotiated the first annual contract in this company, engineering management asked to be given responsibility for bargaining with the union, basing its request on the often repeated contention that "only engineers understand engineers." Engineering management got the job of negotiating the second agreement. The vice president of engineering chaired the negotiating committee, with labor relations in attendance only to keep the engineering managers out of trouble legally—"It was engineering's show." After two or three annual contract negotiations, however, the negotiating job was shifted back to labor relations.

Why were negotiations returned to the staff group? Inasmuch as negotiations were exceedingly time consuming, the president of the company decided that he could not justify the engineering vice president's time. The engineering official himself became somewhat disillusioned with the task because "punk kids" representing the union were getting rough with him, "in a way discomforting to one of the ten best engineers in the field," as one manager expressed it. Anyway, as the union committee members began to repeat themselves, the curiosity of engineering management wore thin. Still another problem had arisen: engineering management could not avoid sympathizing with the union's proposals, especially those concerning salary increases or improvements in physical surroundings; but for business reasons it could not make concessions. The union would exploit this ambivalance by saying in effect: "You, Mr. X, as head of the engineering department are a traitor because you believe in these ideas but you won't agree with them here." Finally, engineering management found bargaining was a highly specialized activity and required a distinct type of temperament. As a labor relations executive said:

> We in labor relations now assume the conflict role and take the pressure away from the top man in engineering who

has to go out and fire up 40 or 50 engineers on a new project. It was hard for one man to perform both functions. In effect what you have [in your labor relations official] is a paid hatchet man.

Engineering management in this company continues to be directly represented at the negotiation table, but by persons from progressively lower levels of the engineering hierarchy. In 1958 the assistant to the vice president of engineering administration and a member of supervision were present from the engineering department. The remainder of the negotiating team consisted of the director of labor relations, the employment officer, and three other persons from labor relations.

The president of the union said about the relatively little participation by engineering management in negotiations, "We don't like this but there is nothing we can do about it." The fact that they were not even afforded an opportunity to negotiate with the top man in labor relations, the corporate vice president of labor relations, was of further annoyance to the union committeemen.[1]

A picture of the role engineering management does play in current negotiations should be developed. A spokesman for Company B, which had a similarly constituted bargaining committee, explained how joint consultation between staff and line management was conducted outside negotiations. The actual methods for obtaining the viewpoints of engineering managers varied with the type of item up for negotiation and whether it was one the company chose to consider. Although from time to time supervisory representatives entered negotiating sessions, this occurred only when a subject of primary concern to line management was being discussed *seriously*. On the majority of issues, even those potentially

[1] The makeup of company negotiating teams has been publicly denounced as a stratagem of "Calculated Incompetence" by an engineering union leader, Everett Taft, in a paper entitled "Unions Among Engineers" published in the *Ninth Annual Proceedings of the Industrial Relations Research Association*. IRRA, Madison: 1957, p. 246.

of great importance to engineering operations, line management made its position known to company negotiators and thereby *precluded serious discussion* from the company's side on the issue. Thus, it was clear that by virtue of the superior bargaining power it possessed the company did not feel compelled to discuss or seriously consider many of the subjects that the union "gets worked up over." On negotiation issues which would affect operations, the chief engineers individually made their views known to the industrial relations people. If labor relations believed, however, that there was need for a company counter proposal embodying a positive plan, the chief engineers might be assembled to consider this matter. One chief engineer stated that he and other chief engineers definitely regarded "as a nuisance" having to present a plan on a subject raised by the union.

By 1958 the type of arrangement which had evolved in this firm, and similarly in many others, between the labor relations staff and engineering management was "an accepted way of life," not expected by management to change. In at least one firm, Company C, however, the respective roles of engineering management and the labor relations staff were being given close scrutiny in 1958. Labor relations was currently responsible for bargaining with the professional engineers' union, but engineering management was not certain that it was satisfied with this arrangement.

Going back in history, a review of the reports on negotiation sessions leading up to the first agreement shows that engineering management in Company C did not participate in any active way in the writing of this agreement although both the union and the labor relations staff participants expected them to do so. The engineering managers either would fail to attend scheduled sessions or would arrive without having read any of the material to be discussed. When apparent indifference on the part of engineering management turned to active interest several years later, the chief engineer made a bid to take over the engineering union relations. The chief engineer began scheduling meetings with the union executive board. As a result of these meetings engineering management and the union decided to get together among themselves and decide upon a contract with which they could live and then take it to labor relations, according to one union leader who was active at that time. Labor relations depreciated the idea of engineering management getting together with the engineers on contract terms, and discouraged the chief engineer from carrying it out.

The same general question was raised again in 1958 when the relationship between the engineers' union and Company C deteriorated to its lowest point in their collective bargaining history. Negotiations were being conducted unproductively. Disagreement between engineering management and labor relations developed, apparently over what position the company should take with respect to certain items at issue. Labor relations was reported to be resentful of the attempts of engineering management to intervene in negotiations. Engineering management, for its part, tended to blame labor relations for the state of affairs which existed between the company and the union. At the same time, those from engineering management who sat in on negotiations regarded the sessions as "tremendous time wasters." Therefore, it was not clear just how those from engineering management wanted negotiations to be conducted, but they did want more influence over the bargaining process and its results.

One observer, who was close to the scene but not directly involved in the conflict, placed friction over the handling of negotiations in a more general pattern of conflict between engineering management and top management, including corporate labor relations.

> Top management does not allow engineering management to play an important part in broad planning or policy decisions. Rather, it hands to engineering rigidly conceived assignments and expects performance. Among the consequences of this practice are less status for engineering man-

agement and a lack of motivation on their part toward company goals.

According to this view, the union's presence as it is felt through the negotiation process may not necessarily be the cause of friction between engineering management and labor relations (or the vehicle of accommodation) but may sometimes merely provide a means for this friction to manifest itself for better or for worse.

Almost everyone who argued strongly in favor of union-management matters being handled by labor relations cited the telling experience of one instruments firm, Company D. Inexperienced engineering management negotiated the company's first agreement with the union in 1951, at which time they conceded numerous provisions that continued to handicap the company in 1958—such as a union shop, a guaranteed merit kitty, and strict seniority rights.

Regardless of the manner in which negotiation sessions are conducted, the labor relations staff makes extensive preparations. The practices of other companies must be analyzed and compared with those of the subject company. Counter arguments for items which might be proposed by the union must be developed and sounded to ensure that they are convincing and are not subject to misinterpretation that is damaging to the company. The recommendations of supervisors regarding contract changes to the company's advantage must be polled and then evaluated.

Sharing Responsibility

We have examined the matter of which groups in the company have been involved in the processes required under collective bargaining: grievance settlement, periodic conferences, and contract negotiations. Of what significance is the participation of the various management groups in terms of (a) shift in authority within the company between staff groups, (b) shift in authority from line to staff, and (c) upward communication?

Shift in Authority Between Staff Groups

The personnel staff is one of the first to feel the impact of unionization. Without an engineering union this staff plays an important role in the formulation of personnel policies and of policing, inspecting, and controlling the application of these policies as they are implemented by line officials. To the personnel staff the union may appear as an expression of criticism since the very presence of the union seems to call into question the adequacy of personnel policies and/or the effectiveness with which they have been policed. This is especially true because unionization has occurred only among a small minority of engineers throughout the country. To add injury to insult, the policy formulation function of the personnel department must now be shared with the union. The personnel department must also contend with the union as a competitor in the policing of personnel policies.

In firms where the plant employees are unionized and the large engineering staff is not unionized, personnel policies are usually administered by separate staffs, one designated as "labor relations" and the other as "personnel." When the company enters into a collective bargaining arrangement with its engineers, the skills of labor negotiation become as important to success in engineering employee relations as the skills in personnel. The staff in the personnel office must develop the new skills, or some engineering personnel functions previously performed by personnel may be transferred to labor relations, such as aspects of merit review, transfers, discharge, discipline, promotion, layoff, and fringe programs.

The question about which staff group should assist in the performance of these functions, coordinating supervisors' decisions, often takes the form of whether this responsibility should be located in a personnel section of the engineering department or in the central industrial relations department. Some of the unionized companies have experimented with having a separate personnel section report to engineering management, only to abandon the arrangement later in favor of placing responsibility with the centralized staff group. Where special engineering personnel staffs do exist, they perform only limited functions.

The union's presence, in a paradoxical way, seems to tip the scales in favor of the centralized labor relations approach. On the one hand, the engineering union generally favors having more responsibility deposited in a special personnel section in engineering, although this is not one of the union's bargaining objectives. On the other hand, utilizing a centralized staff becomes more important for management when engineers are organized. There are two reasons: First, differences in the company's policies and practices toward different unions can be exploited by those unions through the well-known whipsaw; centralization of the personnel and labor relations functions is a better arrangement for preventing differences in policies from developing. Second, centralized personnel and labor relations operate to diminish the risk that engineering management might treat the unionized engineers too liberally.[2]

The following report of a shift of responsibility within management appeared in the publication of one union which had in 1957 recently stepped up its union activities:

> We must also note changes in the company's structure as it relates to us. During the year past, the Engineering Division personnel staff, with whom we have many of our dealings, has been expanded. One of the new staff members is a lawyer who is specializing in revisions of our contract. Also, as [the union's] interests have expanded to involve the whole plant, and problems which involved the other unions, we have dealt more frequently with members of the Industrial Relations Department outside of the Engineering Division.

2 There was little empirical data available which would bear on the desirability of a separate personnel section in the engineering department. The issue is an important one, however, and will be explored further in the final chapter on general implications of the study.

Shift in Authority from Line to Staff

Line management is also affected by the penetration of labor relations. The handling of grievances through the labor relations office rather than through supervisory channels is one way in which this occurs. Inasmuch as grievances relate to substantive matters—merit increases or decisions regarding layoff status, to cite two examples—the authority of line management in these matters is shared in some degree with labor relations because this staff is influential (a) in determining what language shall govern those functions, and then (b) in administering that language. Just how far the proprietary interest in management functions of one labor relations official has progressed is reflected in his statement:

> Some of the union's demands lay completely in the labor relations field: recognition, rights, joint committees, detailed provisions covering layoff, transfer, dues, checkoff, upgrading, seniority clause. Others are matters of joint concern with other management groups: wages, a new system of rating, and so on.

Transfer, upgrading, and seniority lay "completely in the labor relations field"!

A labor relations executive in one company invoked "union considerations" to force certain aspects of a manpower control plan upon personnel and line management who were undecided among themselves about what features the plan should include. The plan would be applied to transfers and layoffs. Since the layoff aspect clearly related to a union contract provision, labor relations' responsibility was apparent. What about internal transfers, a subject not covered by the contract language? The executive said:

> Where we have one bargaining unit for all our engineers, scattered in several divisions, we must control labor relations or we will get into a whipsaw position. Transfers are clearly "union relations."

An official in the labor relations and personnel department of another company offered further evidence on the point:

> We would not be as active in engineering if it were not for the union. Collective bargaining has forced engineering management to go to labor relations and personnel for advice; and they don't like it. There is more day-to-day interchange between engineering management and our own people.

Communication

The middle and top managers' lack of knowledge about the employees' thinking and managements' inability to communicate their own needs, plans, and policies to the employees are regarded as a critical problem facing business organization. Few managers in the companies studied would state that supervisors were doing an adequate job of communication. Indeed there may be important blocks to communication *inherent* in the superior-subordinate relationship of the management organization. Perhaps there are more reasons for the subordinate to deny information to his superior than there are reasons to provide such information. Collective bargaining, however—grievances, conferences, and negotiations—bring those who participate for the company into contact with employee representatives. Some of the companies studied have taken deliberate advantage of the opportunity for two-way communication offered; others have minimized (but cannot completely deny) this function of the union organization.

Much of what has been discussed in previous chapters—the unions' demands (as reflecting engineers' needs), their descriptions of weaknesses in company policies and implementation, and the companies' replies—is illustrative of the unions' communication function. Nevertheless it is appropriate to cite a couple of instances where management has made deliberate use of the union's channel to the engineers.

One company began to make use of the union communication channel in recent years. Previously that channel carried only employee and union complaints upward to management. Negotiations were legalistic and highly tense. Beginning with 1956 the information began to flow both ways and the substance of these communications became more constructive. For example, in one of the regular union-management conferences dealing with general matters of interest to the parties, the union representatives explained how the company could get an increase in productivity if it would reduce the number of engineers on given projects. These representatives were simply reflecting the desire of individual engineers for increased responsibility which would enhance their opportunity for growth. Since the supervisors have a hand in overstaffing conditions where they exist, they are not an effective link in any communication chain that could transmit this information to higher levels of management.[3] Thus, the union plays a unique role because it has access to upper management and does not need to fear supervision for its security.

The union can also be an effective channel for downward communication, and an agency for implementing change. This is illustrated in the same company by the implementation of a change in the policy covering time off for personal reasons. PR time off was covered by a letter agreement in which the company agreed that exempt employees would not be docked for time off. It was understood, however, that excessive time off would be the subject of disciplinary action. This time paid for but not worked was charged to a special account, since only job time could be charged directly to a government contract. The government then picked up a portion of the PR time with each contract. Early in 1958 the company was trying to consummate several new contracts with the government when the government came across the

[3] It is true that top management sometimes condones overstaffing, particularly when a larger engineering staff will increase the company's revenue under a military cost-plus contract. In the instance cited here management was interested in tightening up the efficiency of the engineering staff.

account. The government warned that the amount was excessive; it would not pay any such amounts in the future. Top management put the pressure on the labor relations staff, who in turn presented the problem to the union leaders. The most the company hoped for was a promise from the union leaders that they would not resist the discipline necessary to tighten up on PR time; but the union, agreeing that excessive time off was a reflection on professional standards, requested its membership to cooperate in tightening up. The results were dramatic. In a matter of a few months the total weekly PR time dropped to 40% of its previous average and leveled off.

An engineering executive of an aircraft company provided further direct testimony regarding the constructive role the union can play in communications.

> Through the union's questioning we have been able to educate them as to why we do what we do and how it takes their best interests into account; that is, through negotiation the union becomes cognizant of management's problems.
>
> . . . At the same time the union gives management a central organization with which to work in reaching the engineering force. Management's task then is to satisfy a small group which will in turn help sell the 2,000 engineers.

But a labor relations executive in the same company thought, "It would probably be wrong to leave this subject with the impression that the union was *necessary* to get that kind of communication."

Several executives interviewed could not bring themselves to believe that the unions aided communications even when there was strong evidence suggesting that they did.

Supervisory Training

In a collective bargaining situation personnel policies may take on more importance. Management becomes more conscious of the need for "progressive" employee relations programs to maintain harmonious relations. Notwithstanding the tendency for some functions to be shifted from line management and personnel staff to labor relations, personnel may find it possible to expand its activities in other areas. Supervisory training programs offer an important example.

It has been common among the companies studied for line officials to be found wanting in the skills of employee relations and union relations after unionization. An executive stated that collective bargaining "focused attention on poor supervision," because "little problems became tougher ones to solve." Another cited the increased need for consistency in supervisory decisions, for example, in the merit review; and the greater cost in laxness, for example, in documenting deficient performance. Accordingly several companies have instituted supervisory training programs dealing with union contract interpretation, human relations, and effective manpower utilization.

Similarly the weakness of the orientation toward management on the part of the lower levels of supervision may be revealed under union-management stress. For example, during an engineering union strike in one company, supervisory engineers were found to be largely sympathetic with the union; some even looked down upon those engineers who came to work during the stoppage. Management took this condition as evidence that the supervisors did not fully appreciate the broad planning policies or objectives of the company. Personnel developed a training program for engineering supervision designed to remedy this situation.

Summary and Conclusion

Handling grievances, maintaining daily contact with the engineers' union, and negotiating the collective agreement are handled almost wholly by staff groups. Although the original procedures allowed for engineering supervision to play a major role in grievance settlement, supervisors have not in practice played such a role, not only by their own choice, but also by virtue of staff's interest in taking over the responsibility. There are some signs that engineering management may become more involved in the future. The job of negotiating the engineers' agreement has been assigned to engineering management in some companies but such an arrangement has usually been abandoned, to the mutual relief of both engineering managers and labor relations officials.

Through participation in the formal processes of collective bargaining the staff groups take on greater authority and responsibility for many management functions, such as salary adjustment, transfer, layoff, discharge, and so on. Within the two staff groups, personnel and labor relations, where it is possible to distinguish between them, responsibility and authority appear to shift toward labor relations, because of the latter's aptitude for handling these matters in a collective bargaining framework. These shifts in authority are similar to those which typically occur under collective bargaining in the plant.

The management organization is affected in still another way. Top management through labor relations and the union has access to another channel of communication with the engineers, a channel which is for many purposes a manifoldly more effective one than the supervisory channel. Among other information that derives from the new channel, some pertains to the deficiencies of supervision, a factor which has led many companies to institute supervisory training courses.

CHAPTER XIV

Employee Relations

THE EFFECTIVENESS and efficiency of any industrial organization depend largely on the collaborative relationships that exist among its members. This is decidedly true in engineering and research organizations in which the nature of the work often requires team effort—teamwork on the idea level.[1] The cooperative, integrative arrangements within and among such groups are delicately balanced mechanisms; they can easily go haywire. The problem of group collaboration is related to the problem of maintaining good employee relations. Let us examine the effect of the engineering union on certain aspects of employee relations, including the engineers' relationship with supervision, their attitude toward the company and toward their job, employee morale, and supervisory morale.

ENGINEER–SUPERVISOR RELATIONS

Evaluating the effect of the union on the supervisor's relationship with his engineers is a difficult proposition. On the one hand, a chief engineer said that the union had its greatest impact of a detrimental nature on this relationship. He made several points in one brief statement:

> The union creates an artificial barrier in this relationship which tends to become less personal and professional. Individual problems must be resolved by formal channels now;

1 G. P. Bush and L. H. Hattery, editors, *Teamwork in Research* Washington: American University Press, 1953. See especially Chapter 8, "Human Factors in Research Teamwork" by David P. Hertz.

> if these channels did not exist, the engineers and supervisors would be forced to use human relations.

On the other hand, another engineering manager in the same firm spoke of relationships between the engineer and his supervisor as being excellent. Both of these statements are typical of those made by executives in other unionized companies. Although the two observations appear to be contradictory, both contain essential truths. Let us analyze each of the points made by these executives.

First, with regard to "artificial barriers," we have already seen in Chapter XII that under unionization additional distinctions are made between supervisory and nonsupervisory engineers. To quote one manager: "The supervisor is now able to hear grievances. He is no longer one of the boys. Titles become important. Group leaders are no longer in the lab; they have offices." It stands to reason that these divisions and distinctions enlarged the social distance between these groups. To the extent that the duties and responsibilities did not change with these designative changes, the new distinctions were indeed "artificial." Tabbing these distinctions "barriers," however, is probably a little too strong, as will become apparent in the light of later discussions in this section.

The second point made by the first executive was that individual problems must be resolved by formal channels. The study revealed that many individual problems continue to be handled by supervisory channels. Although a few union agreements require a union representative to be present in the first step, most of them encourage the engineer to take up his complaint first with his supervisor orally and on his own. Still, the executive's point contains validity in that individual problems *tend* to be handled more formally. Moreover, the trend is in that direction. In recent years more attention is being given a proposal that would require that a union representative be notified whenever a man is called in for disciplinary action, allowing him to be present for any discussions between the supervisor and the engineer. Relationships between the engineer and the supervisor tend to be formalized also by the requirement that warnings and performance deficiencies be documented. An institutional framework is forced onto discipline cases in at least one other way: under collective bargaining there becomes less room for differences of viewpoint among management people over such cases. One manager learned this by experience. He tried to intervene in behalf of a highly regarded engineer who was to be discharged because he had been caught by the security guards with liquor in his desk. For his trouble the manager found himself embroiled in a union-management dispute, and on the side of the union!

The first executive's final statement that if the formal channels did not exist, the engineers and supervisors would "be forced to use human relations" is much more speculative than his other points. Perhaps those grievances that do enter formal union channels are precisely those that could not be resolved by supervision's channels. A statement made by a union official in a speech to new employees bears on this point:

> . . . If you do a good job for them technically, you can become friendly with them or not, as suits your personalities. . . . When your business with the company is in matters which are covered by the contract . . . you have a right to have a representative there to help you in dealing with your supervisor if you choose; you have the right to deal with him directly if you choose. We've tried to maintain, in setting up this organization, because the members in it want it that way, the benefits of both having an organization there and not having it there when it's not wanted. . . .

One thing the engineering union stresses is the obligation of the individual engineer to do what he can for himself before he approaches his bargaining agent.

Although the above factors indicate that under collective

bargaining the engineer may be partially alienated from his supervisor, actually the more noteworthy condition is the extent to which such alienation has *not* taken place. There is very close identity of the engineering supervisors with their engineers, and vice versa. Engineers and supervisors alike mention the absence of a "boss relationship." In one company the engineers interviewed indicated that the engineer was on a first name basis with first and second line supervisors "immediately," and with third line supervision "soon," with fourth level supervision, "it depends." This informality, reflecting a certain affinity between the supervisor and his men, varied with the type of work group being considered. The flexibility allowed in research and advanced development where the professionals are extremely task oriented and highly motivated permits any kind of relationship that is satisfactory to the men. For example, in these groups continuous evaluation of the work is done jointly by the supervisor and the engineer since the latter may be more competent technically. Such flexibility does not hold for the engineering jobs requiring less technical skill. In the latter jobs the supervisor is capable of performing any of the tasks he assigns to his men; and because he supervises a greater number of men, he has fewer face-to-face contacts with any of them. Among groups falling into the latter category "Mister" is appropriate at one level of supervision lower than mentioned above.

Several factors account for the close identity between a supervisor and his men. First, there is the strong professional tie that exists among engineers. Second, among the lower ranks of engineering management are many former union members who still feel a kinship with the unionized engineers. With the rapid advancement of the past ten years, even second and third levels of management are populated by men only a few years removed from the bargaining unit who, regardless of their former union status, are contemporaries of many engineers in the present unit. The third reason for the close relationship between the engineer and his supervisor is a practical one; the engineers' union is actually viewed as working to the supervisors' benefit in many respects. This point, invariably mentioned by the unionists and sometimes conceded by company spokesmen, was well developed by one union official:

> Union gains in economics or status will be enjoyed by management. When we get more money, they get more money. When we push up the top of our salary structure, we push up the supervisory and management salary structure too. If we get parking space, or go off the clock, management has to grant some other privileges to the supervisors to preserve the distinctions. On working conditions, if it's too hot, too cold, too sunny, too dark the manager has more leverage to have these conditions changed—he can use the union's threat to turn in a grievance.

The union official extended this logic to such things as voluntary overtime, right to select vacation period, and an "objective" merit review system, which actually tend to detract from the authority of the supervisors. For example, he stated:

> If the voluntary overtime policy is recognized, this is a frame of mind that will to some extent be shared up and down the line. If a supervisor can say to his superior, "I couldn't force my men to work," there are two effects: (1) he is a little off the hook himself on that project, and (2) his boss is going to be more inclined to give him more freedom in his assignments.

A manager contributed to this line of thinking when he said:

> Sometimes engineering management will endorse a union position because it might give them more control. Take the merit kitty: management would like to have a budget to work with, so there were some features of this they liked.

Certain changes have taken place in the engineer-supervisor relationship which cannot be described in terms previously used—artificial barriers, formalization and affinity. An executive in one company referred to a "great desire on the part of the union to legislate human relations, including supervisory sentiments and behavior." For example, the union sought contract language to prevent supervisors from asking engineers to postpone a vacation already scheduled and planned. Inasmuch as it was expected by both parties that the engineers would continue to reschedule personal plans voluntarily to accommodate work schedules, this executive could readily see what kind of behavior was appropriate here: "The man has loyalties to his family [vacation plans] and loyalties to the work project that are in conflict. He should approach the supervisor and talk with him on an *interpersonal* basis, not on a *contractual* basis." However, the executive's prescription for behavior missed the point as far as the unionized engineers were concerned. They wanted to place the contract "right" on the engineer's side so that the burden of proof would lie with the supervisor when he wanted an already scheduled vaction cancelled. Then it would be incumbent upon the *supervisor* to deal interpersonally with the engineer.

The effect of the change in wording is to shift slightly the balance of personal bargaining power from the supervisor to the engineer. It is no wonder they both want greater specified rights (ultimate right to demand reschedule vs. ultimate right to refuse), not because they will always or even normally want to exercise a particular right. Rather, if the right can be waived voluntarily by one party, this will tend to build up informal obligations on the part of the other. It enhances their respective personal bargaining power, which can be used in various ways in such an interdependent relationship as that existing between the engineer and his supervisor. The supervisor has considerable discretion in assigning tasks, recommending salary adjustments, processing transfer requests, and so on; but balancing these factors he is completely dependent upon the engineer for thc quality of the output, for meeting deadlines, for "looking good" generally before his superiors—and often without being able to measure whether the engineer is actually exerting himself in these respects. The importance to the supervisor of the attitudes and feelings of his engineers toward himself in this context is signaled by the way the supervisor often distributes merit: in such a way as to "minimize discomfort" in daily work relationships.

Another change in the relationship being examined here is the lessening dependence of the engineer upon his supervisor for information. We have seen that through his union the engineer now has access to salary data and to statements of the policies, rules, and regulations governing work assignments, merit review, transfers, and so on. Before unionization the engineer generally would have to rely upon his supervisor who would parcel the information out as he saw fit. Today, the dependency relationship may have reversed itself. The salary data published by the union are often "news" even to the supervisor and is of use to him. On occasion supervisors will approach union representatives for insight into the prospects for a salary increase. Naturally this, too, has tended to favor the personal bargaining power of the engineer *vis á vis* his supervisor.

The unions are inclined to agree that the supervisors have little authority but attribute this condition, not to an erosion of authority through collective bargaining, but rather to the fact that the company *withholds* authority from the supervisors. Below we shall see how this contention of the union may be used to alienate the supervisors from the rest of management. By regarding the supervisors as without real authority the unions can absolve them from responsibility for the conditions under attack by the union. Note, for example, the statement appearing in one union publication a year or so after the union was organized:

> In spite of the *best of intentions of supervisors and department heads* the company will ride rough-shod over their

recommendation which in the past have always been respected. [Italics added]

Sometimes the whole of engineering management is absolved from blame. A typical statement taken from one union publication reads:

> . . . our Personnel Department still does not understand [us], and evidently they prevent Engineering Management from implementing whatever understanding *it* has.

Attitude Toward Top Management and the Company

The discussion in the previous section leads to the conclusion that it is with respect to top management or "the company" that the engineers' attitudes are influenced by the union. In a policy statement which offers us direct testimony on the point, one management views this tendency with alarm.

> Professional men have prepared for careers in which they will exercise individual initiative and judgment and take personal responsibility. Their work necessarily involves group effort and cooperation, but its success is dependent upon the productivity and accomplishment of individuals. Very junior men may well initiate and develop ideas of major significance. It is inherent in this type of work, and it is also to the best interests of the company, that such professional men substantially consider themselves members of the management team. . . .
>
> * * * * *
>
> In recent years, there has been a growing tendency with the association to emphasize this difference between management and the nonsupervisory employees. There appear to be some who regard . . . [the association] as an end in itself and who want to promote its expansion beyond [X city] and even beyond the company. In an effort to stimulate support for such a program, these members have adopted an increasingly antagonistic attitude toward the

> company. The tone of many pronouncements in the [association publication] is such as to undermine the loyalty of its readers toward the company. Such an influence can seriously impair morale in an organization of professionals where common purpose and mutual confidence are essential.

Many companies express similar alarm at the anticompany tone of their respective union publications. One manager characterized the pieces of such union propaganda as "never ending drops of water eroding away company loyalty." The effect is for the engineer to have just a little less faith in management's decisions and even in management's motivations.

Orientation to company and management—to achieve this is a major task of engineering management—is inhibited by the engineers' and scientists' tendency to have professional goals that differ from business goals and by their tendency to reject an authority and control hierarchy. The unions add another factor influencing the engineers' orientation. The companies have been particularly vulnerable to the unions' competition for the engineers' loyalty or orientation during the recent period of rapid growth of engineering departments and the high turnover of personnel. As if to encourage this competition, a few companies have granted their unions certain rights regarding introduction to new employees. How the union continues to elaborate its own procedures of introductions were described by one union member, paraphrased here:

> The contract requires that whenever a man joins or is transferred within the bargaining unit, the company must send an Introduction Card to the union office. A copy of this card is turned over by the man's supervisor to the departmental representative when the new man is formally introduced. The introduction card supplies the representative with enough background on the new employee to enable him to talk intelligently to the prospective member. Most prospective members are reluctant to commit themselves

to the representative because of the uncertainty of their new environment. Therefore when a new employee is hired into the jurisdiction of a specific department, the representative arranges a schedule that is designed to systematically have each member talk to the new employee. If conducted on a casual basis, the new employee is gradually indoctrinated in the views of his fellow workers and this makes him more susceptible to the union representatives' advances.

The union's competition for the orientation of the engineers led an executive in one company to state what also bothered other managers: "In a tough financial or employment situation the engineer will be inclined to look to the union rather than to the company for leadership." Also, the very fact that the company shares credit with the union for money increases (general or merit) has taken away from "the company" some of its "mystic" importance or "sacredness" to the engineer, according to both union and company officials.

The matter of company loyalty may have implications beyond the company organization. An engineering organization has primarily its reputation to sell when it is bidding on a government contract. Naturally, past performance contributes to reputation but the behavior of the firm's engineers is also important. Doubts about whether the firm has the loyalty of its engineers—doubts which might develop, for example, as a result of a bitter strike or continuing conflict between the parties—give rise to apprehension about letting the contract to that firm.[2]

2 Thus the union probably has an effect on each of three important public relations objectives of the research administrator listed by G. Edward Pendray of Pendray & Co., New York, in an address entitled, "Public Relations and Industrial Research" before the 5th Annual Conference of the Administration of Research at the University of Michigan, September 24–26, 1951, and published in the *Proceedings*. He stated:

"The first of these [public-relations objectives], it seems to me, is to retain and increase loyalty and efficiency of staff and department employees. The second may be to aid recruitment of a good new staff and to reduce turnover, both of which are especially important now. The third is to add the values of good research reputation to the company's public and customer relations program. The fourth is. . . ."

Attitude Toward the Job and Professional Ethics

A related concern of management is how the engineer's attitude toward his work has been affected by unionization. Evidently the engineer takes a stricter view of the hours he is willing to put in on the job. The administrative problems associated with this tendency were discussed in Chapter IV; here we are interested in the significance of the attitude itself. One executive testified:

> There was a decrease in the amount of casual overtime. Before the union a man was oriented to his work, not to the clock, but after the men were conditioned to think otherwise one could walk in the engineering area at 5:05 and not see a soul. The actual loss of time on the job was not as important as the "hired hand" attitude indicated by this pattern.

Another manager said:

> We find that even the very professional and competent engineer is more hour conscious. He has lost his sense of when it is appropriate to "give" time and when it is appropriate to "sell" it.

The unions cite the same tendency to put in fewer uncompensated overtime hours, but for them it has a different meaning. One union leader who as an old timer was familiar with preunion conditions stated:

> The contract has eliminated a great deal of the unpaid overtime expected from engineers. Before, the union engineers thought that in order to ingratiate themselves with management it was necessary to work some voluntary overtime. Men would put in overtime hours doing nothing, sometimes.

Recall that some managers believe that the unions' salary studies focus the engineers' attention on dollars and cents to an unhealthy degree. One executive thought the engineers and scientists must decide whether they mean (a) what they say in response to attitude surveys, namely, that "the work's the thing," or (b) what they say through their union, namely, that their services are for sale to the highest bidder. According to this executive: "The professional should be more concerned with his job, serving his employer, and making a contribution to mankind, and less concerned with how he is rated and other matters of collective bargaining."

Many managers expressed a belief that unionism presents a challenge to professional ethics, particularly as it could affect the engineer's obligation to his client. These managers had not yet experienced any significant problems in this area, but their *apprehensions* appeared to be real. The published statement of an executive of a company which was at that time organized by a professional union sets forth the ethical aspects of the relationship between engineers and management which seem to be vulnerable to forces operating under collective bargaining.[3]

> The engineer in modern industry works in areas that are close to the very core of management decision. The engineer is responsible for the technical development of the products, processes, and customer applications on which the success of the business depends. His ability to create, test, control, and improve the product, and the soundness and practicality of his professional judgments are important elements in determining the fortunes of the organization. Because the organization is dependent upon him, and because he is entrusted with a responsibility that others in it cannot do or often cannot even check, it is essential that the engineer be clearly aware of the ethical requirements of his profession.
>
> While questions of ethics may arise in any interpersonal relationship where one puts himself or his fortunes in the hands of another, they tend to be most serious when professional service is involved. Two basic elements in the professional relationship are responsible. First, a profession is distinguished from a skill or a craft, no matter of how high an order the latter may be, by the degree of subjectivity involved. The professional goes beyond a routine, a formula, or an established habit pattern. . . . Ethically, he has the

[3] Gerry E. Morse, "Engineering Ethics—From the Viewpoint of Industry," *Journal of Engineering Education*. November 1954, p. 214.

responsibility to advise his client or employer if other help is required. . . .

Second, the professional is characterized by the specialization of his aptitude, education, and experience. He knows and can do what the nonprofessional does not know and cannot do. In professional matters the nonprofessional is almost completely and blindly dependent on him. Ethically, therefore, he has the responsibility to protect his client or employer and the client's or employer's interest. . . .

Both of these aspects of the ethics of engineering, or of any profession, may be summarized in the concept that no intentional, and insofar as possible no unintentional, unfair advantage is to be taken of the client, employer, or user. Or, to say it another way the true professional does not trade dishonestly upon the ignorance of others.

Ethics is largely an individual matter. The ethics of an organization or of a group tends to be simply an integration of the ethics of its members. It is from this point of view that we approach the question of ethical practice in the engineering profession as it relates to collective bargaining. It is not reasonable to say that membership in a collective bargaining organization in itself alone constitutes a breach of ethics for the individual engineer. Nor is it sound to make a charge of unethical practice on the part of engineering unions except in specific cases where such lack of integrity on their part has actually taken place. Experience to date seems to support the hope that we can have enough faith in engineers as individuals to expect that unethical practice will be found to be one of the least important faults of engineering unions. There are aspects of the problem, nevertheless, which do warrant our study and concern.

Employee Morale

Most of the managers interviewed are inclined to attribute to the union an adverse effect on morale. At worst the union is charged with "deliberate demoralization of the engineering force, through teachings of hate and fear." More often the union is described as a "mobilizer of discontent"; that is, matters that might otherwise cause some people consternation are publicized by the union and used to "stir up" other professionals. Even in its mildest form the union is sometimes the center of discussions and undercurrents on the floor during breaks. Such discussions or arguments, usually related to negotiations or some other current activity of the union, are viewed by management as undesirable, not only because they often carry over onto company time, but also because they are a source of further discontent and preoccupation on the part of the engineers. One of the more common sources of friction is the techniques used to increase union membership. A review of some of these techniques will suggest why this is so.

The direct forms of recruitment are "bad enough." The informal solicitation made by fellow workers who belong to the union and the follow-up by the official union representative can have their disruptive influences on the participants. The plant-wide or department-wide rallies sometimes held during the lunch periods can be even more trouble.

Other recruiting efforts by the union, labeled by one company official as "more insidious," can be more disconcerting to employee morale. The experiences of one union will illustrate this "insidious" type of effort. This union decided upon a strategy of distinguishing between union members and nonmembers by every means available. Its policy was

> to point out to the nonmember that he is anti-[union] if he does not join. Demonstrate to him that he is not retaining a much-cherished ideal by not joining. In this battle he cannot sit on the fence. If he is a nonmember, he is working against us and assisting the management in maintaining substandard conditions. . . .

Previously, the union leaders thought it was best to win the nonmembers over to support of the union by letting them taste the benefits, such as the salary surveys and the union publication. Then the leaders decided that it would take pressure to get these "free riders" to join: They made the single issue of the monthly publication which details the company's contract offer available to nonmembers only at the prohibitive price of $40. All of the publications now carried an overlay stating "For . . . Members Only" on the front page. The union attempted to limit the distribution of salary surveys to members only. In addition, union representatives began to discriminate between members and nonmembers in the dissemination of salary data about individuals.

Other devices to set off union members from nonmembers in the same company have run into the opposition of management because of their disruptive influence. First, the union was requested by the company to instruct its members not to place union stickers on individual name plates. When the members placed union prisms on their desks, the company ordered individuals to remove these as well; these prisms were reported as having the function of providing the representatives with a rapid means of member indentification to expedite distribution of literature to members only; nevertheless the union compiled. Some members ran into static from their supervisors on another "badge": One member wrote, "My supervisor has stated that it is unprofessional for me to wear a pocket protector [bearing the Association's insignia] —can I file a grievance?"

The union recruitment drives also extended to nonmembers' homes. The 1955 drive (which involved 75 teams calling at nonmembers' homes) is described in a union newspaper:

> Home visits to nonmembers by [union] recruiting teams are being stepped up now that winter exams are over and weather has improved. Potential members who have not yet been visited should be patient. Nonmembers are demonstrating so much interest in [the union] during the home conferences that individual visits are taking much more time than was planned for.

Hundreds of letters have been sent to potential members inviting them to join. . . . These effective letters, signed by groups of [union] members, made a direct appeal to friends and acquaintances. Members are continuing this direct approach by sending postcards to friends throughout the bargaining unit.

The Recruitment Committee has distributed many aids to bring the record of [union] accomplishments and future goals to the nonmember. The big gun of the campaign, however, is the man-to-man approach of members to potential members. . . .

The following "question" sent to the union publication by a nonmember offers evidence of the existence of pressure to join the union:

QUESTION: I am not a [union] member; my group leader is. He is always after me to join. . . . I do not belong . . . because I believe that unions are morally wrong. Can I file a grievance?

Even more persuasive testimony is contained in this letter:

Dear . . . [union official]:

To say that I feel that the tenor of the latest [union] membership drive, in which I and others are accused of being "free-riders," is insulting to my character and intelligence is putting the situation mildly. I am absolutely astonished at the nonfree-rider pledge placed on my desk yesterday.

. . . the accompanying flyer incorrectly implies that the recipient must either join the [union] or sign the nonfree-rider pledge. . . .

Strike action when it has occurred has been the source of the most dramatic type of discontent and friction among the engineers. We can refer to the strike experiences of three companies. During the strike and its aftermath in Company A the loyal unionists administered social isolation to those who did not support the union. They conducted an around-the-clock telephone campaign threatening and harassing those who refused to walk the picketline. When they returned to work they gave them the silent treatment. Also, in a variety of subtle ways, they tried to undercut the contribution of the "noncooperating" individuals on the engineering teams.

One way this undercutting operation could be performed was cited by a manager at Company B. "After the strike some members were withholding technical information from non-members and feeding it to fellow members, who would then solve the problem." The union president offered his description:

> In one department where there was only one scab; in entirely legal and courteous fashion, the fellows in that department just couldn't see him as a social equal any longer. He was pretty damn miserable. I'm neither advocating it nor condemning it. But those fellows who stood in the rain while he was back in the plant had a core of opinion which somehow or another gave them something—they've got a solid, self-sustaining group. It was the rare department that behaved that way. We've got many more departments where we have an appeasing attitude toward the fellows that scabbed, and the fellows that didn't support us, and the fellows that won't join.

A third strike had slightly different results. It was conducted by the union at Company C with the overwhelming support from its members, but still conducted in a very gentlemanly manner. The company and the union spokesmen both mentioned that there were only a few incidents, and that there was no general antagonism between those who supported the strike and those who did not. Actually, some ex-union supervisors were more disapproving of the strike breakers than the current members. However, at least a few engineers were quite upset: those individuals who had been elected to offices in the association but had never approved of the idea of unionism, much less economic sanctions. They felt that they were put in an awkward position by the strike. One letter from a councilman to a local newspaper described the dilemma he had faced. He wanted to quit the union in the interest of his professional ideals; but he did not want to appear to be a deserter, nor did he want to alienate his fellow workers; what could he do? It was signed, "Frustrated Engineer."

An advanced development engineer in the same company who was not a union officer expressed his sentiments. He criticized the company on its actions on three important issues: the layoff, merit review monies, and the company's strategy during the strike. The company's actions in all three instances had an adverse effect on the engineer's morale. Some of his comments on the strike are particularly interesting:

> The company was equally foolish on their strategy during the strike of instructing the supervisors to call their engineers and tell them to return to work. The supervisors were embarrassed and disgusted that they should be given such an assignment. Joe, our supervisor, called as instructed but just chatted without once mentioning the strike. When the engineers saw what management was trying to do, they really closed ranks.

We have reviewed several incidents and activities that were believed to have an adverse effect on morale. The next question is, "Did this tension and resultant preoccupation reduce the productivity of the creative mind?" In this study the researcher had to rely largely upon the testimony of the managers involved.[4] An executive in one company said:

> In the very complex and creative job, the individual will be soured by conflict and also by thinking in terms of mini-

[4] The problem of reliably determining what impact the professional union has on output of the R & D organization, if any, is extraordinarily difficult. A basic difficulty is that output itself seems to deny measurement or meaningful evaluation. See J. B. Quinn, *Yardsticks for Industrial Research,* New York: Ronald Press Co., 1959.

mum performance. We have no direct evidence to support what we believe to be true. We did find that during the period of militancy of the [union] the tremendous advantage gained by our [XYZ] Division during World War II and in 1949 was being sacrificed.

The spokesman for another company said:

> It is very important in this type of work not to have social pressures. There is no doubt that union-generated discontent does influence work enthusiasm and work relationships. However, when work is affected there is no conscious conspiracy to slow down; rather a spontaneous relaxing of effort and enthusiasm.

Another executive thought that the deterioration of union-management relations that started one year and led to a strike the following year in his company did affect morale adversely. "With so much conflict, there just can't be as much productivity and creativity; when there is digression there can't be concentration."

There were managers who did not wholly accept this view. Referring to the several pockets of union members located throughout the company's engineering department one manager stated, "These groups produce just as well; it's just a flavor of attitudes that management doesn't like."[5] In another company an executive indicated that the majority, or at least a substantial percentage, probably have their morale improved by the union. Why? Because their dues and support for the union are regarded as "insurance premiums for security." The engineers feel more secure because of the union.

Finally, the union officers or ex-officers interviewed seemed to be saying that the significance of the unions to the engi-

[5] This point, like so many touched upon by this study, should be the object of specific research employing the appropriate methodology of work level observation and interview. What *is* the importance of union membership and nonmembership patterns to the engineering work group: its informal structure and related indices of morale, cooperation, and productivity?

neers was to be found in the fact that it was "an organization *of* engineers, *for* engineers, and *by* engineers." The effect of this factor on morale is undoubtedly positive.

Supervisory Morale

The unions' effect on morale also reached into managements' ranks in a few companies. According to one executive a favorite theme of the union concerned the supervisors: "Pity your supervisor, after all, many are from our own ranks." The supervisor was characterized as inept—a confused, ineffective guy—but not really at fault. The "fault" lies with an impersonal "They," somewhere above the supervisory ranks.

A sample of this theme is offered by a letter to the editor in a union publication. It shows the supervisor to be a kindred victim of the impersonal "They." In this letter the engineer-correspondent raised the question of job security, asking "Do supervisors need unions more than we do?" He reported the demotion of a supervisor who had worked for the company since 1932. The supervisor was regarded as quite capable and well liked. One day the employees who formerly worked for the supervisor came to work to find a new name on the office door, and the ex-supervisor's desk outside, alongside the other employees. The letter concluded, "There may be a satisfactory explanation for this maneuver, but they'll have to be much clearer than the fuzzy memo ["They" issued] on the subject, the only information available to date on the 'why' of this shocking move." The engineer's letter was signed, "Puzzled Engineer."

This illustration emphasizes the union's sympathetic interest in the supervisor. Sympathy demonstrated by the union in this way, however, also serves to highlight the supervisor's helplessness. In this and similar ways in other companies the unions undercut the prestige of the supervisors, thereby presenting a very serious challenge to management. The supervisors' morale is affected because they feel that they have lost the respect of the men; moreover, they do not know whether the company or the union is responsible for their status.

Summary and Conclusion

Collective bargaining tends to institutionalize some aspects of the engineer-supervisor relationship such as grievance settlement, reprimands, and discipline. Still, affinity between the engineer and his supervisor continues to a remarkable degree based on their common professional status and their nearness in age; moreover, the supervisor often identifies with the engineers because he shares the gains negotiated by their union. The personal bargaining power equation that underlies this relationship, however, has shifted in favor of the engineer. The union has obtained for the engineer contractual rights that bear on that relationship and has severed the engineer's dependency upon his supervisor for information.

The engineers' attitude toward higher levels of management has been influenced by the anti-management tone of many union publications, according to management, weakening its own leadership position and compromising the engineers' loyalty to the company. The latter effect may operate against the company competitively, for example, in bidding on a government contract. Further, for tactical purposes, a few unions endeavored to alienate the supervisors from the rest of management, and with a degree of success.

The union may intentionally affect morale for its own organizational purposes, or it may do so incidentally by its very presence and activity. A frequent source of friction at the work level is the recruitment activity conducted continually and aggressively by the engineering unions which must often struggle to claim a majority of the unit as members. During a strike even greater dissention is manifested between the union and nonunion groups in the engineering force—social isolation, technical noncooperation. Management generally believes, but cannot prove, that productivity has suffered along with morale. A minority wondered if the union did not in some ways improve morale.

PART V

Conclusion

CHAPTER XV

Conclusion on Impact

THE PURPOSE of this chapter is to give the findings of the preceding chapters additional significance. We shall be interested in conclusions regarding several questions. How do the actions and objectives of the professional union contrast with the more familiar forms of unionism? How do the findings differ from those expected or predicted by the employers interviewed who had had no experience with a professional union? What significance does management attach to the changes caused by the union? The last question is one of especial interest here and will provide the basis for organizing the chapter.

Just how severely do the changes affect management's interests? These interests are at least twofold. As an agent of the stockholders, management is seen as interested in getting the job done as effectively and as efficiently as possible. As a participant in an organization, with authority and status in the company hierarchy, management is viewed as interested in preserving or enhancing its own influence, its own leadership status. We do not assume at this point that the two types of interests are in conflict, or that they are parallel, only that they are not synonymous. Therefore this dichotomy of interests gives us a basis for distinguishing between two types of impact.

Impacts of the first type are those impinging upon company goals. These impacts we shall examine in the section headed Impact on Management's Operational Standards. The second type includes impacts upon one of management's own institutional objectives. These are considered in the succeeding section entitled Impact on Management's Leadership Status.

Impact on Management's Operational Standards

Management would appear to be oriented to the following company goals: profit, growth, and product leadership. Therefore, we wonder how the union has affected certain operational standards within the engineering department which are requisite to the realization of these goals, such standards being: (a) high quality and quantity of output, (b) minimum costs, (c) effective and efficient personnel management, (d) high reputation of the engineering department.

High Quality and Quantity of Output

The union can affect the quality or quantity of output by directly subtracting from hours worked. Or it can have such effects by operating to lessen the intensity with which the engineer applies himself to his assignments during working time: through the removal of incentives; through the development of an "unhealthy" work climate; and through "feather-bedding" tactics resulting in poor utilization of manpower.

Lost Time. This study reveals that on the first count, subtracting from hours worked, there has been little impact, especially when compared with the experiences of collective bargaining in the shop. There have been few work stoppages or demonstrations that took the engineers from their work. Union activity and grievance processing on company time have on occasion disturbed many managements, but the total amount of time involved has been small, except in one or two companies. Still, controlling time lost through lateness, absences, and early departures has become somewhat more of a problem under conditions negotiated by the professional unions. Whereas the entrance of the shop union frequently led management to devise more formal controls over working time, collective bargaining with the engineers has resulted in management's agreeing to remove some formal controls—the time clock, procedures for docking latecomers, monitoring systems, and so on.

Removal of Incentives. How does the union influence the engineer's incentive to apply himself in his work? Many of the managers interviewed from companies where the engineers were not organized expressed fear that unionization of their engineering force would lead to pinpoint salary rates, accompanied by an abandonment of the merit principle in promotions, which they are aware has happened typically under collective bargaining in the shop. This has decidedly not occurred in the unionized companies studied. To the contrary, the engineering unions' efforts appear to be in the interest of preserving the merit principle by improving the merit system. Furthermore, the union has endorsed other incentive techniques such as patent bonuses, profit sharing, stock option plans, and recognition for technical papers. In other ways, however, the union tends to diminish the importance of certain financial, status, and security factors which perform an incentive function.[1] By negotiating general increases, the union confines the operation of the merit principle in salary adjustment to a smaller area. By including the highest technical engineering positions in the bargaining unit, the unions subtract from the prestige of these positions. By enhancing the importance of fixed factors in the determination of layoff sequences, the union depreciates the relative importance of demonstrated skill and ability. However, no company actually lays off engineers strictly by seniority, a practice which obtains in the shop and a practice which many nonunion employers believed would be extended to

[1] We are ignoring here, as elsewhere in this concluding chapter on impact, the persuasive arguments the unions make for their positions on each of the issues.

the engineering department. In fact, a few unions have the opposite influence, ensuring that the layoff decisions are made on the basis of ability factors.

Effect on Work Climate. How does the union affect the work climate in the engineering department? Actually we are not certain what climate best nourishes or least impedes output, and particularly creativity, among engineering and research groups. For purposes of this analysis, however, it is assumed that those factors which create distractions, antagonisms, and conflict within the engineering force also have a harmful effect on productivity.

The union has aroused the engineers by focusing attention upon (a) inconsistencies between merit and layoff decisions, (b) management's use of the merit system for nonmerit purposes, (c) "inadequate" overtime payment practices—to cite only a few of the instances mentioned in the study. The ability of the union to affect morale adversely is often a factor persuading management to give more serious consideration to union proposals. For example, the more persuasive the union is in presenting its case for general increases, the more hesitant the company is about refusing the demand.

Even where discontent is not "mobilized" by the union deliberately for organizational purposes, the union in and of itself is an element of controversy in the engineering department. To consider an extreme form of union activity, an engineering strike certainly has more implications for the company than the delay in certain projects. Are these engineers as creative as in another company not troubled by union-management conflict? The situation is not comparable with that of the production union where the specifications of the product must be met and can be checked, and where the only worry in such a circumstance is sabotage. In the case of the professional engineer, the research and development work is often assigned on an open-ended basis; that is, the limits of what is possible are not even known. There are no ready standards with which to check such an engineering product. Another type of activity illustrated by the instances of social isolation and technical noncooperation cited in this study is viewed by management with the greatest apprehension. To cite a third activity, the recruiting efforts of the engineering union were shown to give management similar concern, but in somewhat lesser degree.

Certain procedures providing avenues for grievances which are often viewed by management as adding irritants to employee relations may also be viewed as having the opposite impact, improving morale. Examples of these procedures are (a) merit notification and interview requirements, (b) specification of merit factors, (c) dissemination of salary data. In still other circumstances, the effect of the union on morale in some circumstances is more certainly salutary. For instance, both managers and union officials believe that more regular and more conscientious employee appraisals boost morale. Similarly, by enabling the engineers to bring into the open personal antagonisms which have entered into the merit and transfer decisions of supervisors, the union helps improve morale. Morale is also enhanced by the improvements in working conditions which result from union efforts.

Underutilization. The final way in which it was suggested for purposes of analysis that the union might affect output was through feather-bedding practices, practices which are sometimes found among other forms of unionism. Significantly, the engineering union has the opposite effect. The engineers want to be fully utilized, because their future professional careers and salary growth, as well as their day-to-day satisfaction from their work, depend upon it. Thus, the union provides a mechanism used by engineers to rectify supervisory "empire building" or padding practices which are not in the company's interests; and to eliminate the use of engineers on menial tasks which are below their intellectual capacity.

Minimum Costs

The union can have a direct effect on costs by raising the levels of salaries and fringe benefits, by obtaining premium pay, by placing a minimum on the merit budget, and by removing management's discretion in extending minor privileges. Generally the gains of the engineering union in these areas have been small and fall far short of the corresponding achievements of the shop union. The union, however, has added more significantly to the company's recruitment costs.

Effective and Efficient Personnel Management

On the one hand, the presence of a union can impose serious limitations on effectiveness and efficiency in personnel management—promotion, transfer, discipline, discharge, work assignment, salary administration, and complaint adjustment. The limitations imposed take two direct forms. First, the basic decisions in these areas may be affected by contract provisions. Second, the union may add encumbrances to the administrative process, and yet not affect the decisions which are produced by that process. A third restriction is not directly imposed by the union; it results when the company compromises its practices because of the difficulty of administering a given function under collective bargaining. On the other hand, many changes made as a result of engineering unionism represent more effective and efficient personnel management.

Contractual Procedures. Considering one limitation of the first form, contract provisions governing layoff sequence do place such emphasis on seniority and other fixed factors that management is prevented from following its own judgment. One contract also specifically prevents certain interdivisional transfers during a layoff period. Another requires management to exhaust certain alternatives to layoff which represent a deviation from management's normal course of action. A few other clauses directly alter the course of management's actions; for example, the clause which prohibits the use of contract engineers, and other clauses which prevent management from creating a staff position outside the bargaining unit.

Encumbrances to the Administrative Process. Often the significance of engineering union contract provisions is chiefly in the way in which they add to and complicate the administrative job of management. Examples of these provisions are those covering grievance adjustment, union-management conferences, various notification requirements, merit reporting and employee appraisal procedures, job posting procedures, man-to-man comparisons, transfer procedures, and periodic ratings for layoff.

Compromise for Expediency. Usually the limitations take the third form, where for reasons of expediency management alters its practices under collective bargaining in ways not specifically required by contract. Let us review some of the examples from the study. Companies are partially prevented from using the individual increase system for nonmerit purposes, and from adjusting the total level of merit to conform with general economic circumstances. Management has been inhibited from taking discharge action which it felt was justified because of the presence of the union although, by and large, the union has not intended to limit management's flexibility in that way. In sharp contrast with industrial unionism, the engineering union often openly concurs with management's discharge actions. In fact certain union policies, namely those regarding layoffs, have encouraged the company to terminate marginal engineers, rather than to place them on layoff status. In so doing, however, management sacrifices some ability to recover its full force if that becomes necessary. There were no cases reported where management has promoted less able individuals because of the agreement or direct union pressure, as is often the case with the shop union. Use of job descriptions, however, has given rise to claims for more rapid advancement, and may be responsible for some modifications in promotion practices. Companies experience other limitations under collective bargaining in the areas of: supervisors doing bargaining unit work; temporary leadership and supervisory assignments to bargaining unit personnel; assignment of nonprofessionals to engineering classifications; and so on.

Assistance to Personnel Management. There are many ways in which the union may contribute to the efficiency and effectiveness of management functions. First, the union is often used by management as the reason for insisting upon the performance of certain supervisory tasks, such as employee appraisals and interviewing. Second, the union frequently causes management to think through and revise its practices; examples of this influence are provided by the war gaming and the skill inventory which arose out of the contractual requirement to make man-to-man comparisons in event of a layoff. Then too, merit plans incorporating point systems and growth curves contain opportunities for management to improve its policies and practices. Third, the union often assists management even more directly in the administrative processes. The union helps police company policies by reporting to top management violations which occur at the supervisory level—empire building, for example. And it can assist management in implementing change by providing an effective channel for downward communication, such as it did in the case of the management which wanted to tighten up on lost time.

Another generally positive influence from the point of view of improved operational standards is the tendency for management decisions to become more consistent and more objective. For example, by making data available to engineers and supervisors the union may contribute to more uniform salary treatment. By bringing into the open personal antagonisms affecting supervisors' merit and transfer decisions it is possible to improve the objective quality of these decisions. Formalizing the merit, transfer, and layoff policies has resulted in more consistent and uniform treatment.

It is interesting to observe, however, that this last influence has not always worked out to a company's advantage, primarily because of management's own weakness. On the one hand, the union urges management to find more rigorous means for defining, measuring, and then utilizing *ability* factors—in layoffs and individual salary adjustment. Thus, the objectives of the two are not in great conflict. The union appears to be forcing management into patterns that management would have taken, or that are at least consistent with management's operational standards. On the other hand, under collective bargaining supervisors often tend to shrink from exercising judgment based on these specified subjective factors, and to give more weight to objective factors such as education and length of engineering experience. Often it is management, of its own doing, that backs away from discretionary decisions when these decisions can be the subject of further scrutiny.

Finally, and this is in part by way of summary of the previous points, collective bargaining has encouraged the development of management by policy which results in considerable mutual gain for both parties. Recall especially the development of the salary administration system.

High Reputation of the Engineering Department

An engineering department's most important asset is its reputation. First, reputation is a critical factor in landing government contracts because more direct measurement of the department's capacity and efficiency itself is nearly impossible. Second, the department's reputation is equally important to it in its efforts to recruit first-rate talent. This is especially true because the engineers know that their own professional development and standing will be inextricably bound to the engineering organization with which they associate themselves. The unions have occasionally had harmful effects on reputation, through their strikes and demonstrations and through their publications, with consequences in the two areas mentioned above. This type of impact is probably unique to engineering unionism.

Impact on Management's Leadership Status

Management as an institution has as a fundamental objective the maintenance and preservation of the existing authority and status structure. In a word, management wants to preserve its leadership status. Two conditions that relate importantly to the attainment of this institutional objective of management are (a) the engineers' orientation toward management, and (b) the unilateral authority system of management in the engineering department.

Engineers' Orientation Toward Management

The union can undermine orientation toward management in many ways: by affecting the way engineers associate themselves with company goals; by stressing the conflicts of interest between engineers and the company; by questioning management's motives; by assuming credit for improvements in conditions of employment; by reducing the engineers' reliance upon management for information; and by competing for the sympathy of certain management groups.

Orientation to Company Goals. Basic to a management orientation, the engineers must accept the company's goals as they are translated by management. If the engineer does not acknowledge these particular company goals as paramount, he cannot be expected to share management's values; and he cannot be expected to orient himself naturally to management's guidance. Because of the nature of their intellectual training many engineers and scientists do not share management's emphasis on the marketable utility of their efforts and on time and cost considerations; they have more concern for ideas. The engineering union does not deliberately interfere with management's attempts to indoctrinate the engineers to these aspects of the company's program objectives; however, the very distinctions which the union produces between supervision (management) and engineers (nonmanagement) tends to free the engineers so that they may question the specific goals and program objectives of the company. Then, when the engineering union succeeds in subordinating "attitude" as a factor in merit distribution, it eliminates one avenue management has to influence the engineers' orientation to the company's purposes.

Conflicts of Interests. The engineering union does not merely tend to release the engineer from strict adherence to company goals; it goes on to discover and elaborate the conflicts of interest between the engineer and the company. These conflicts center on many issues, such as, in the area of transferring personnel, the company's project requirements versus the engineer's professional needs. Similarly, in the layoff area the company's need to maintain maximum ability to perform current and future engineering assignments is partially in conflict with the engineer's need for job security based on length of service and predictable standards of ability. Another important issue is created by the fact that the company's flexibility necessary for accomplishing changing objectives in salary administration often runs counter to the engineer's notion of merit as a pure concept.

In these illustrative conflicts the union quite naturally champions the interests of the engineers. Since management is charged with the company's interests the conflict can be described as one between management and the engineer, in this way alienating the engineer from management. It must be borne in mind that the matter of the engineer's management orientation or his alienation from management is a relative concept. It must be emphasized here—as it has been suggested in the discussions of the engineer's approaches to merit, layoff, and discharge—that the professional employee has a high degree of management orientation, far greater than that of the shop employee, for example. The conclusion here is that by emphasizing certain conflicts of interest collective bargaining *tends* to alienate the engineer from management.

Beliefs About Management's Motives. Furthermore management is sometimes depicted as an *untrustworthy* agent of the company. This has been especially true in the few companies when the relationship has neared or entered the conflict stages. Where the union's existence is being challenged, the dedicated union officials, sensing their own personal insecurity, are likely to go beyond the sentiments of the majority of the engineers in the extent to which they manifest militancy. Largely as a result of the anti-management tone of their writings, management becomes the object of the engineer's distrust. Even in companies in an accommodative pattern the union leaders whose business it is to scrutinize management's actions discover the vulnerabilities in these actions and call them to the attention of the engineers. Management's motives have been challenged in many areas: in layoff and merit; in the control of lost time by "police state methods"; in the use of contract engineers to avoid making "warranted" salary increases; "circumventing the contract" to use engineers for overtime work without pay; and so forth.

Competition for Credit. The engineering union also competes for the engineers' allegiance by accepting credit for itself for improvements in the terms of employment: general increases, overtime and fringe benefits, merit monies, transfer policies, to mention a few. This is an important point which has been discussed frequently throughout the study and requires no further elaboration here.

Extent of Dependence Upon Supervision. Another element of management's leadership is "encroached" upon when the union eliminates the engineers' reliance upon management for information, such as salary data, explanations of the merit review system, and statements of company policy. By eliminating the supervisor as a source of information, the union diminishes the supervisor's status and authority. The right of the employee to these types of information from other sources symbolizes and fosters a greater degree of employee independence from management, especially from the supervisor; in fact, the supervisor may become partially dependent upon the engineers and their bargaining agent for certain information.

Division Within Management. Finally, the engineering union has a divisive influence within management, further jeopardizing the leadership status of management. In the engineering supervisor's mind the engineers' union may symbolize a professional counterweight to the business interests of management. Moreover, engineering supervision may think of the engineers' union as bargaining for improvements for engineering as a whole, as negotiating gains they will share. The union has divided the orientation of another group which is marginal to management, the consultant and staff type of engineers and scientists. By including this group the union tends to strengthen its own position with respect to both the other engineers it represents and the engineering managers it wishes to influence, since both of these groups have the highest regard for the staff and consultant engineers.

The union divides management in another way. With respect to most of the concessions negotiated by the engineering union, one can find either engineering management or the personnel staff sharing an interest with the engineers. If the engineers' proposals would improve the salaries or conditions in engineering, engineering management may privately side with the engineers. If the proposals embody sound personnel principles, as they often do, the personnel staff may be inclined to sympathize with the engineers. In the company's relationship with the engineering union, to a much greater degree than with other unions, the several management groups do not stand united.

Unilateral Authority of Management in the Engineering Department

The ways in which management is limited in performing many functions have been detailed and then discussed at length throughout the study. The limitations were summarized earlier in this chapter under the subsection Effective and Efficient Personnel Management. That subsection stressed the loss of *efficiency,* when there was any, in arrangements resulting from collective bargaining. Here, without citing those arrangements again, we are interested primarily in the loss of management authority inherent in the restrictions placed on flexibility. The point here is that this loss of authority is important to management in and of itself (whether or not it also results in any loss of efficiency and hence impinges upon company goals).

The important point that authority is shared will stand generally without further elaboration here. Only three aspects of this phenomenon require special mention.

First, management has lost unilateral control of incentives. For example, supervision has lost the right of extending many minor privileges now covered by contract provisions or company policies. To illustrate, management regards sponsoring a man to a technical meeting as an incentive; when it becomes an engineer's right or the subject of union-management deliberations, management has lost control of an incentive. Supervision and management have lost the right to distribute all salary increases; part of the increases are negotiated generally. They have lost unilateral control of the merit system by providing for union participation in an appeal machinery.

Second, there has been a subtle shift in bargaining power from first-line supervision to the individual engineer. Underlying many comments and observations in this study is a concept of a face-to-face bargaining relationship between the engineer and his supervisor wherein certain factors cited have enhanced the engineer at the expense of the supervisor. For example, the mandatory appraisal interview under some contracts operates in this direction. Whereas previously an engineer had to ask for the interview as a favor to himself and thereby indebted himself in some degree to his supervisor, now the engineer has a right to the interview. The interview itself continues to strengthen the position of the engineer, because the prospects of that interview are an additional reminder to the supervisor of the need to maintain good relationships with his men. Other factors tend to enhance the individual engineer's bargaining power, such as the right to refuse overtime and access to individual salary data.

Third, management has been forced to specify its decision criteria. Moreover, the specified criteria for salary adjustments and layoffs usually do not include attitude, a factor which supervision otherwise takes into account in order to develop and preserve the loyalty of the subordinate engineers.

Further Points of Contrast

Perhaps it is also important to summarize the ways in which the engineering union has *not* been important to management. The foregoing discussion in this chapter contains several contrasts with the impacts of industrial unionism. We have also noted some contrasts with the predictions made by nonunionized engineering employers about engineering unionism, but let us add other points of contrast here.

The nonunionized engineering employers interviewed thought that among other consequences the unions would "breed mediocrity" and "sanction minimum performance," "control thinking and creativity as shop unions control productive effort," prevent the company from differentiating between the abilities of individuals, cut off the engineering force as a source of future managers, and "limit full professional viewpoint." These views of engineer managers, expressed early in the study, were probably based on their prior knowledge of, or beliefs about the effects of the production union. This study concludes that these fears are thus far largely unfounded.

Final Comment on Impact

It has been shown that the engineering union has an impact upon efficiency and other operational standards in the engineering department. With one or two specific unions as exceptions, however, this impact is neither large when compared with the impact of shop unions upon manufacturing management, nor substantial when measured in terms of the net impact upon the company's competitive standing. The union affects a company's output, its costs, and its ability to recruit, select, motivate, and utilize talent, but the union is not the controlling factor in these areas. Moreover, just as it has proven to be a limitation on management efficiency in certain respects, it has also assisted management in doing a better job in other respects. In fact, although the positive effects on managements' operational standards could be summarized concisely, and were dealt with only briefly, this does not mean that they were not significant. If anything, we have understated the mutual gains of collective bargaining.

Let us turn to a second conclusion. Too often students of industrial relations are preoccupied with the impact of the union upon efficiency. An equally important consequence of the professional engineering union is the way it impinges upon the authority and status structure of management. Apart from the analysis presented in this and other chapters on the point, this conclusion was indicated in the research by the items the managers wanted to talk about and the way they talked about them. Managers viewed the engineers as having been "split off from management." Unionization of professionals was regarded as a slap in the face—as one manager said, "It doesn't hurt, it stings!" The conditions underlying this second conclusion undoubtedly account for the fact that management's reaction to the engineering union is largely an emotional one, a reaction of an entirely different order from that which managers would exhibit if they were talking about a factor that merely encroached upon the ability of their companies to produce, or to sell, or to stay in business. They were talking about something that affected them personally, individually and collectively, as managers.

CHAPTER XVI

Implications for Analysis and Administration

THE FORMAL and primary purposes for which the study was undertaken now being completed, we have an opportunity to reflect upon the findings of the study and explore some of their broader implications. In the first section of this chapter we shall analyze the conditions creating a need for collective action. In the second, we shall consider the implications of the uniqueness of engineering unionism for management. A final plea will be made for an innovative approach on the part of both parties to the problems dealt with in this study.

CONDITIONS CREATING A NEED FOR COLLECTIVE EMPLOYEE ACTION

A Relative Decline in the Rewards of Engineering Employment

Chapter II listed the manifest reasons why engineers resorted to unionization: narrowed wage differentials, insecurity of employment, threatening shop unions. Also noted were the factors which continue to foster unionization: lack of identification with management, inadequate channels of communication, lack of professional recognition, dissatisfaction with merit system, etc. These reasons, which were those offered by management, unions, and outside observers alike, were mentioned as a part of the historical treatment of the phenomenon. Cited in this way it would appear that the problem is largely that of lax or faulty management and further that each factor suggests its own remedy: namely, enhance the management status of engineers, improve communication, enlarge professional privileges, rationalize and explain the merit review system, etc. There is some validity to these conclusions. Such an explanation of the problem tells only part of the story, however; such solutions offer only partial remedies. For one thing, management is limited in what it can do to redress the above cited grievances; the numbers and nature of the jobs in the large engineering department militate against identification, communication, recognition, etc. Moreover, these "reasons" and "factors" are probably symptomatic of more fundamental difficulties; if one eliminated these particular problem areas, other problem areas would appear. Therefore, we need to look deeper, at the basic changes in the conditions and context of engineering employment which have created the need for collective action.

A Decline in the Engineers' Influence Over the Job

In an earlier day professional engineers and scientists in industry performed individual duties, were individually recognized, and exercised individual bargaining power. Growth and rationalization of the engineering function have deprived the individual professional of most of his influence over the many aspects of the employment relationship. He lost a share in the control of the job: the nature of the work assignment, the methods and pace of the specific task assignment, working conditions, pay, and status.[1]

Three basic changes associated with increased size and rationalization have operated to reduce the professional's control of the job: (1) greater formality in engineering organization and work assignment; (2) increased separation

[1] Thus, "control of the job" as used here is intended to mean more than control of job opportunities.

between the engineers and the decision-making levels of management; (3) diminished individual bargaining power.

Formality. When the methods of accomplishing the engineering task are themselves engineered and principles of division of labor and specialization are applied to research and development, the area of discretion of the engineer is reduced correspondingly. The specifications of the larger project of which his assignment is but one part strictly define his objectives for him, largely determine the methods he must use to attack the problem, and indicate the pace at which he must complete the task. The large area of judgment the engineer once exercised in these matters is being sacrificed to the logics of technical organization, just as worker discretion in the methods of performing tasks in manufacturing plants has long been eliminated by the imperatives of advanced production technology.

While it is necessary to recognize this change as reducing the individual engineer's authority on the job, it is apparent that collective action offers the engineers little promise of restoring that authority or otherwise offsetting the effect of the change. Still, the change, including the loss of individuality which results, contributes to a frame of mind on the part of the engineer which makes him more amenable to collective action for other purposes.

Separation. When the engineering organization grows, there is an inevitable separation between those who occupy the engineering jobs and those who determine working conditions, salary levels and salary structure, other personnel policies, and formal job status. This insularity eliminates direct and mutual influence between those who make decisions and those who are vitally affected by the decisions. Many observers are inclined to view the frustrations which occur with separation of employees and decisionmakers simply as a problem of "communication" between these individuals or groups. The study suggests that the difficulties arise because *negotiation*—a more potent process than mere communication—has been eliminated. This latter view is seldom advanced because we are generally unaware of the extent to which negotiation takes place in our daily face-to-face relationships even in the absence of formal bargaining arrangements. Thus, in the small laboratory the engineer worked directly with the director whom he thereby had the opportunity to influence; but when levels of intermediate supervision developed, the negotiation process became considerably more difficult.

An individual employee in the large nonunionized engineering department might theoretically have the right to bargain about the policies which determine the conditions and context of his employment. Moreover he probably still possesses some bargaining power. To exercise these rights and this power, however, he requires new forms for action. Collective bargaining, of course, is one such form. It enables the engineer through his own elected representatives to bypass intermediate levels of supervision who merely implement policies, and deal directly with those who have authority to make decisions affecting all the elements of the engineers' job.

In practice, the engineering unions do not completely replace individual bargaining with collective bargaining. Supervisors still retain some discretion in implementing personnel policies, especially in administering the merit system. Here the engineer still exercises such individual bargaining power as he may possess.

Diminished Bargaining Power. As the individual contributes a smaller and smaller proportion of the total output in a growing organization, he personally becomes less critical to the continued operation of the business and his individual bargaining power declines accordingly. His bargaining power is diminished still further whenever the level of utilization falls and in effect brings the job occupied by the engineer within the reach of a greater segment of the work force. If the individual acts in concert with other employees performing the same function, however, the employees together regain sufficient power to share in decisions affecting their jobs. Moreover, this study noted that collective bargaining as practiced by engineering unions operated to enhance, as well, the individual's bargaining power.

The Case for Collective Action—A Twofold Need

The foregoing analysis leads to the conclusion that unionization represents a basic organizational reaction to some important organizational changes which are occurring in the engineering departments throughout this country and which affect professionals in several fundamental ways. Thus, while managements' attempts to discourage engineering unionism by deploring it as a social ill may be successful in avoiding unionism, such efforts do not meet the needs for which the engineers are considering collective bargaining. This point is supported by the following analysis of the needs of the engineer in industry.

Like the manager's interest outlined in Chapter XV, the engineer's needs are twofold: First, as an employee-consumer he wants more of many more-or-less substantive rewards of employment: money, security, recognition of differential ability, opportunity for maximum technical development, etc. Second, as a member of a formalized work community, he wishes to share authority and influence over his working environment. (Admittedly, for the typical professional this second ambition is far from being an all-consuming one, but it is operative in some degree.)

How can these needs be met? The first type of need has been documented by many observers; moreover, managements have on their own or under the threat of unionization taken some steps to meet the engineers' specific desires. The large majority of managers, however, have not taken appropriate measures because they confuse what "ought to be" with what *is*. For managers to say that an engineer "should not" be concerned with his specific status relative to a potential layoff because this represents an "unproductive preoccupation" is to miss the point entirely. The same criticism applies to managers' expressions of "for shame" about the engineers' concern for their salaries and overtime pay. The reasons for the engineers' preoccupations are fundamental to the organizational and employment context in which they find themselves today. The unions may express these preoccupations but the manager who believes that the unions are responsible for creating them is deluding himself. If the engineer is preoccupied, this preoccupation is a reality the manager must work with. Since in practice most managers have not perceived the full array of needs of the first type, these needs continue to represent one important reason for collective action.

The second type of need of the engineer—that of influence over his environment—by definition cannot be fulfilled by management unilaterally. This need of the engineering employee to share authority, which probably is equally as important as the first, is not fulfilled except by more direct participation. Nor do there appear to be any means short of some form of collective action of restoring to the members of this employee group a real influence over their employment environment.

Unionization—A Less Than Satisfactory Solution to Date

Is unionization of engineers the answer? Quite apart from our consideration of the negative and positive impacts of the unions upon managements, most of the engineers in unionized companies themselves have mixed feelings about unions. Some of these engineers are union members, others are not; some participate in union activities, others do not. But they all share the feeling that unionism is an uncomfortable solution at best. This middle-of-the-road majority remain unconvinced despite the efforts of the vocal minority who support not only the specific employee organization but also the idea of unionism and the efforts of the other minority who adamantly oppose unionism. The chief source of the discomfort of this majority is the lack of compatibility between the engineers' concept of unionism and their concept of professionalism. As long as this incompatibility exists in the minds of engineers, unionization, whatever form it actually takes, will represent not only a problem for management, but a less than satisfactory solution for the engineers.

Moreover, the study reveals that collective bargaining contains many other paradoxes for engineers. To cite a few: First, the existence of the collective bargaining relationship increases management's reluctance to experiment with personnel programs, often the very ones advocated by the engineers through their union. Second, the engineers demand to be treated separately and differently from other employee groups, but the very fact that they, too, have become unionized increases management's tendency to treat the groups similarly. Third, the engineers prefer a separate engineering personnel department but the effect of unionization is to strengthen central personnel and labor relations departments. Fourth, the engineers wish that their immediate supervisors had more authority; however, unionization has contributed to the centralization of authority up the line. Fifth, an important objective of unionization is to enhance the engineer's status; in certain respects unionization has had the opposite effect.

It is a conclusion of this study that engineering unionism is a unique phenomenon, differing in important respects from other forms of unionism, particularly the production union. Thus, the system of industrial relations which develops in the engineering departments differs radically from the system which occurs in the production departments of the same industries. This characteristic, together with the conditions creating a felt need for collective action, affect considerably the implications of professional unionism for management.

Administrative Implications

The preceding section emphasized the basic changes that have underlain the resort to collective action. To what extent have managements affected by professional unionism recognized these factors and acted accordingly? Not adequately, in most cases.

Let us consider the consequences of the failure of many managements to distinguish between professional engineering unionism and other forms of unionism. Four topic headings correspond to management's response to the engineering union along four different dimensions. The first—Public Pronouncements—signals in the most direct terms management's basic sentiments about engineering unionism. The second—Other Personnel Policies—deals with management's hesitancy to distinguish in substantive policy areas between employee groups. The third—Management Organization—treats the procedural or organizational pattern of management's relation to the engineers and their representatives. The fourth—Pattern of Relationships—relates to the overall type of relationship which management helps structure.

Public Pronouncements

Labor relations officials of unionized companies have failed to make appropriate distinctions between engineering unions and other types of unionism, both in word and in deed. Here we are interested in their words—memos, papers, and speeches, often written only for consumption by their engineering staff, but at other times developed primarily for external purposes. These labor relations officials deplored engineering unionism by citing issues, objectives, and behavior of professional unions which were usually typical of production unions but which at best described or characterized the engineering union of only one company included in this study.

These utterances seem to have been unfortunate for several reasons. First, the single really "bad" example of engineering unionism referred to could be explained, and only in terms of the very unusual situation in which it had appeared, certainly not in terms of any inherent tendency of "unionism." Second, the portrait of professional unionism painted by these management officials did not in the least resemble the organization which represented their own engineers and with which they bargained. Third, the result was to antagonize their own union leaders, and perhaps to insult the intelligence of other engineers. The apparent purpose—to slander the union and alarm the engineer—was probably not sufficiently realized to justify management's action.

Other Personnel Policies

Managements say that they cannot give the engineering union separate consideration because it *is* a union, and because such consideration would therefore complicate the company's dealing with other unions, making the company vulnerable to whipsaw tactics. Management often denies the separate consideration requested by the engineers, however, partly for punitive reasons—"the engineers made their bed, let them sleep in it." Management wants to teach them a lesson. Actually, management can, if it seriously desires, accord the engineers' bargaining organization different treatment. This would mean, of course, acknowledging that the engineers' brand of unionism is something different. It would also imply more recognition of the engineering union as an effective bargaining agent. Finally, it might complicate other union-management relationships somewhat, but only slightly, since, in the author's opinion, this particular objection has generally been overstated; moreover, by the very act of acknowledging the essential uniqueness of engineering unionism management will have gone a long way in separating the contractual relationships it has with the engineering union from those with other unions.

The chief advantages that accrue to the company under a frank policy of separate treatment are as follows:

1. It can make more intelligent settlements, based on (a) the specific needs of the company's professional engineers, and (b) the supply and demand conditions of the national engineering manpower market.
2. One grievance of the engineer—namely, that they are not treated differently—will be eliminated.
3. The company will be taking a step toward structuring a more accommodative or cooperative union-management relationship.

Management Organization

Organizational Location. Should the staff group which assists in administering merit review, transfers, discharge, discipline, promotion, layoff, and fringe program be located within the engineering department or in the regular personnel and labor relations department? What about the group which deals with the engineering union?

The two reasons associated with keeping these functions within the central staff department were cited earlier in the study: this arrangement operates to diminish the risk that engineering management might treat the unionized engineers too liberally; it also prevents differences from developing between the policies affecting the company's several unions where they later could exploit the differences to their own advantage. In the author's opinion, these advantages associated with the central staff are more than offset by several reasons favoring the alternative arrangement, especially since, as has been stated previously, the second consideration cited above is generally overestimated or at least overstated. The advantages that would seem to be inherent in an arrangement placing major responsibility for engineering personnel and union relations with a separate staff group located within the large engineering department are as follows:

1. Specialization by type of employee. Engineers have special requirements in the areas of professional status, compensation, and placement. Also because of their relative inexperience in their supervisory jobs, engineering supervision requires considerable assistance from personnel officials.
2. Recognition for engineers. Regardless of whether the engineers' beliefs that they are "different" are fully shared by management, the engineers' beliefs are real. Therefore a separate personnel staff is regarded as a form of recognition by the engineers.
3. Familiarity. The personnel and union relations staff becomes better acquainted with individuals in the engineering department. Sharing sentiments of the engineering groups, the personnel staff is better able to recognize their needs; and it is more important to these staff members personally to service these needs. Moreover, in negotiating and administrating the collective agreement they are able to assess more accurately the relative importance of the many expressed needs.
4. Acceptance by operating management. Familiarity works both ways. Engineering management probably is more apt to accept progressive personnel practices regarding appraisals, merit ratings, testing, training, and so on, if these are developed or negotiated by a staff within the engineering department.
5. Latitude. The separate personnel staff for engineering is in a better position to experiment with personnel practices; they are better able to advance or accept in negotiations policies that differ from those of the rest of the company than is a central personnel department.

Another recommendation in keeping with the other suggestions regarding differentiating the engineers and their type of collective bargaining is that management should refer to its staff department or section dealing with the engineering union as "Professional Relations" or "Engineering Relations," rather than "Labor Relations."

Staff. Irrespective of where staff responsibility for dealing with the engineers is located, management should exercise great care in selecting the personnel for representing the company in its daily relations with the union and in annual contract negotiations. On the one hand, there has been a tendency to use labor relations officials who had previously earned their spurs in dealing with other unions and who sometimes have continuing responsibility in representing the company in other union-management relationships. This prior experience is both an asset and a liability. It is an asset because the individual has gained knowledge and experience in the procedures and legal framework of collective bargaining; he has also learned to think in terms of objectives, strategies, and tactics, a mental set essential to acting effectively in the collective bargaining process. The experience also constitutes a liability because too often it has taught him to expect from the union *certain kinds* of behavior—certain strategies and tactics—and to attribute to the union *given* objectives. Moreover, he may have learned that *certain types* of company strategies and tactics are appropriate in dealing with unions. These lessons gained from service in bargaining with other unions often prevent the labor relations official from dealing with engineering unionism for what it is or can be, rather than for what it "surely must be."

On the other hand, line engineering managers have often experienced difficulty when they have assumed responsibility for dealing with the union. In part at least, this is because they lack the specific qualities listed above as the assets of the experienced labor relations official.

Accordingly, the choice should not be one of a "labor relations type" or an "engineering management type." It is a matter of selecting a person who falls somewhere between the two types; as logical as this prescription might sound here it does not seem to have been applied to any great extent in the companies studies. Several companies, however, have eminently competent men in these spots doing an excellent job; in other companies the men who have responsibility for dealing with the engineering union seem to have no particular aptitudes which qualify them for the job. If there is any occasion where management could profit from raiding union leadership (not necessarily from within its own force) for its union relations staff, unionized engineering departments probably qualify. Such an engineer often possesses about the right mix of technical and social aptitudes for the job of professional relations manager for the company. And if this company appointment coincided with a change in attitude on its part toward the professional union, the engineer who joins the company's professional relations staff need not feel he has abandoned a cause. Indeed, he could probably see an opportunity to contribute significantly to constructive engineering-management relations.

Pattern of Relationships

The foregoing discussions have indicated the uniqueness of engineering unionism. A more accurate statement about this phenomenon is: Engineering unionism, *especially when it is regarded by management as a unique phenomenon,* tends to be quite different from other forms of unionism. It is necessary to make this qualification in a discussion of the various possible patterns of union-management relationships because of the following empirical relationships observed during this study:

1. The fundamental assumption management had about the nature of engineering unionism shaped its own actions and its attitude toward the engineers' organiza-

tion. One such assumption, for instance, was that "unionism is unionism wherever it is found—in the shop, in the office, or in the laboratory."

2. The resultant actions and attitude of management toward the union largely influenced the development of a particular union-management relationship pattern.
3. The type of relationship pattern that existed then tended to determine the types of objectives the engineering unions stressed and the types of means they employed.

Thus, an engineering union whose legitimacy was questioned and whose security was challenged because management attributed to it essentially the same characteristics as those of the production union would in fact be likely to become more interested in traditional union objectives. The threatened engineering union would also be more likely to consider joining forces with production and maintenance bargaining units in order to bring more pressure to bear on management. We see that in the conflict and containment-aggression patterns, the engineering union's behavior more closely approaches that of what management thinks of as typical "trade unionism." Management's hypothesis is a self-fulfilling one.

Similarly, an alternate assumption about the nature of engineering unionism, when consistently applied in practice, has led to quite different results. A few managements have recognized the essential uniqueness of the engineering union, have ceased challenging the security of the union and its leadership, and have even been willing to accord to the union some recognition as an effective bargaining agent. These managements have found that the union, for its part, becomes more anxious to place greatest emphasis on the basic substantive needs of the engineers, approaching these needs in a problem-solving manner, with due regard for the companies' operating requirements. It is in the accommodative and cooperative patterns that the engineering unions least resemble other unions, and that they have the least interest in associating with the other unions of the same company.

A Final Word—A Plea for Innovation

The professionals in industry have a basic urge to influence their working environment. The chain of command which links the managers and the engineers in the large engineering department probably cannot accommodate this urge.[2] That linkage system is primarily designed to handle the downward flow of authority. Engineers in these organizations need an independent mechanism for being heard that is influential at the level where decisions are made affecting the multifarious terms of engineering employment. Collective bargaining as we know it, even as it was being practiced in the companies studied, does not fit this need perfectly. Some readers will regard it as an improvement over the nonunionized engineering department, others will not. Hopefully all readers will agree that innovative thinking about engineer-management relations is urgent. What is required is research into, innovation of, and experimentation with a variety of employee organizational forms. These should include, but not necessarily be confined to, collective bargaining.

Let us have one final say about collective bargaining, however, the institution which related the parties in the companies studied in this research project. The same point is valid here—innovation is essential. To cite a particular need, the engineering groups involved should consider new ways of implementing their collective bargaining objectives.

2 A somewhat different view is advanced by Louis B. Barnes in his provocative study, *Organizational Systems and Engineering Groups,* Boston: Division of Research, Graduate School of Business Administration, Harvard University, 1960. Professor Barnes seems to suggest that by reconceiving this chain of command management can provide for mutual influence between management and engineers. His reconceived linkage system is referred to as an "open organizational system" and allows for autonomy, interaction among engineers, and mutual influence up and down the line.

The strike, for example, which many engineering union leaders still cite as their best weapon, is probably much more destructive to the morale of the engineering force, including their own members, than it is effective in supporting bargaining proposals. The particular need noted here is for bargaining tactics which are effective but still compatible with the self-concepts of engineers, self-concepts which are also functional for the engineering department. The point can now be stated more broadly: collective bargaining is a label for a general idea; it must not be regarded by either engineers or management as a prescription for goals, policies, and behavior. If the institution of collective bargaining is to be applied to the engineer-management relationship, it must undergo still further modification and adaptation.

APPENDICES

APPENDIX A

COMPILATION OF UNIONS REPRESENTING ENGINEERING AND TECHNICAL EMPLOYEES

Compiled by National Society of Professional Engineers
2029 K Street, N. W., Washington 6, D. C.

Employer	*Name of Union*	*Total Represented*	*Number Members*	*Unit Representation*	
				Professional Employees	*Nonprofessional Employees*
American Bosch Arma Brooklyn, N. Y.	Engineers' Association of Arma, International Union of Electrical, Radio and Machine Workers, AFL–CIO	1,260	1,260 (union shop)	860	400
Boeing Airplane Co. Continental Can Co. Seattle, Washington	Seattle Professional Engineering Employees' Association, ESA*	7,950[1]	2,643[1]	7,400	550
Boeing Airplane Co. Wichita, Kansas	Wichita Engineering Association, ESA	1,127[2]	367[2]	1,127	—

* Engineers and Scientists of America (ESA) is an independent federation of engineering/scientific unions.
1 "Northwest Professional Engineer," Seattle Professional Engineering Employees' Association, February–March 1959, p. 2.
2 "The Wichita Engineer," May–June 1958, p. 9.

Employer	Name of Union	Total Represented	Number Members	Unit Representation: Professional Employees	Unit Representation: Nonprofessional Employees
Douglas Aircraft Corp. Santa Monica, Calif.	Southern California Professional Engineers Association, ESA	6,448[3]	3,990	5,000	1,448
Douglas Aircraft Corp. Tulsa, Oklahoma	(Southern California Professional Engineers Association, ESA)	280[4]	n.a.	280	—
General Dynamics Convair Division Pomona, Calif.	Engineers and Architects Association, Pomona Valley Chapter, ESG**	1,300	550	910	390
General Dynamics Convair Division San Diego, Calif.	Engineers and Architects Association, San Diego Chapter, ESG	5,400[5]	2,500	3,300	2,100
General Electric Co. Philadelphia Works Drexel Hill, Penna.	Association of Engineers and Engineering Assistants	245[6]	141	178	67

** Engineers and Scientists Guild (ESG) is a federation of engineering/technician unions provisionally organized in 1958. Final organization is pending subject to ratification by proposed member units.

[3] "Southern California Professional Engineer," November–December 1958, p. 16.

[4] Bureau of National Affairs, "White Collar Report," No. 81, September 22, 1958, p. A–9.

[5] "Monthly Labor Review," January 1958, p. 38.

[6] AEEA "Switchgear Engineer," January–February 1959.

Employer	Name of Union	Total Represented	Number Members	Unit Representation: Professional Employees	Unit Representation: Nonprofessional Employees
Great Northern; Chicago Northwest; Chicago, St. Paul, Minn. and Omaha	Railway Technical Engineers, ESG	350[7]	250	230	120
Greer Hydraulics, Inc. International Airport New York	United Auto Workers, AFL–CIO Local 365	50[8]	50 (union shop)	n.a.	n.a.
ITT Laboratories[9] Nutley, New Jersey	Local 400, Professional Technical and Salaried Div. IUE, AFL–CIO	856	n.a.	556	300
Lionel Corporation Irvington, New Jersey	Professional Technical Workers Union, Local 1	66[10]	n.a.	n.a.	n.a.

7 "Exponent," Association of Professional Engineering Personnel, September 1957, p. 5.

8 Bureau of National Affairs, "White Collar Report," No. 88, November 10, 1958, p. X–1. (The bargaining unit includes design engineers (A, B, C), junior design engineers, engineering trainees, test engineers (A & B), laboratory technicians, senior design engineer, draftsmen trainee, junior draftsmen, draftsmen, layout draftsmen, and designer. Excluded are chief engineer, assistant chief engineer, project and assistant project engineers, administrative engineers, consulting engineers, and sales engineers.)

9 Formerly Federal Telecommunications Laboratory.

10 Bureau of National Affairs, "White Collar Report," No. 75, August 11, 1958, p. A–1.

Employer	Name of Union	Total Represented	Number Members	Unit Representation: Professional Employees	Unit Representation: Nonprofessional Employees
Lockheed Aircraft Corp.	Engineers & Scientists Guild—Lockheed Section	2,320[11]	1,044[12]	2,027	293[13]
Lockheed Aircraft Service International, Inc. New York International Airport	Lockheed International Engineers Association	50	n.a.	30	20
Los Angeles, City and County	Engineers and Architects Association, Metropolitan Chapter, ESG	1,100	500	700	400
Los Angeles Dept. of Water and Power, and City and County of Los Angeles	Engineers and Architects Association, Civic Center Chapter ESG	1,600	950	1,300	300
Multi-employer	American Federation of Technical Engineers, AFL–CIO	15,000[14]	15,000	1,000	14,000

11 Engineers and Scientists Guild, Lockheed Section, Salary Survey, Part 2, February 4, 1959.

12 Bureau of National Affairs, "White Collar Report," No. 98, January 19, 1959. (According to the union, present membership consists of 45% of the eligible jurisdiction.)

13 Engineers and Scientists Guild, Lockheed Section, Salary Survey, Part 2, February 4, 1959. (The union declares that 293 personnel out of the Guild's total jurisdiction of 2,320 are hourly paid.)

14 AFTE "Engineers' Outlook," September 1958, p. 3. (Membership figure based on union claim.)

Employer	Name of Union	Total Represented	Number Members	Unit Representation: Professional Employees	Unit Representation: Nonprofessional Employees
Multi-employer Milwaukee, Wisc. Watertown, Wisc.	Technical Engineers Association	n.a.	722[15]	—	n.a.
Otis Elevator Co. New York	District 1, IUE, AFL–CIO	40	n.a.	30	10
Radio Corporation of America, Camden Plant Camden, New Jersey	Association of Professional Engineering Personnel, ESA	1,800[16]	1,450[17]	1,800	—
Rheem Mfg. Co. Downey, California	Engineers and Architects Association, Southeast Chapter, ESG	80	80	—	80
Shell Development Co. Emeryville, California	Association of Industrial Scientists	390	330	390	—
Southern California Gas Company	Southern California Professional Engineers Association, ESA	140	n.a.	n.a.	n.a.

15 "Directory of National and International Labor Unions in the United States, 1957," U. S. Department of Labor, Bulletin No. 1222.

16 Bureau of National Affairs, "White Collar Report," No. 103, February 23, 1959, p. X–1.

17 APEP "Exponent," March–April 1959. (The union claims a membership ratio of 80.6%.)

Employer	Name of Union	Total Represented	Number Members	Unit Representation: Professional Employees	Unit Representation: Nonprofessional Employees
Sperry Gyroscope Corp. Great Neck, N. Y.	Engineers' Association, ESG	3,400	1,800[18]	2,670	730
Sperry Rand Corp. Ford Instrument Div. New York City	Local 471, IUE, AFL–CIO	300[19]	n.a.	n.a.	n.a.
Standard Oil Co. (Ind.) Whiting, Indiana	Research and Engineering Professional Employees Association	550[20]	n.a.	550	—
Chicago, Illinois		28[21]	n.a.	28	—
Tennessee Valley Authority (17 locations)	TVA Engineers Association	2,300[22]	1,955[22]	1,917	383
Ward Leonard Electric Co. Mount Vernon, N. Y.	Technical Association of Ward Leonard, Dist. 4, IUE, AFL–CIO	75[23]	55	50	25

18 "The Sperry Engineer," October 1958, p. 2. (The union claims as members slightly more than one-half of those represented.)

19 Bureau of National Affairs, "White Collar Report," No. 95, December 29, 1958, p. A–1.

20 "Chemical & Engineering News," January 19, 1959, p. 13.

21 Bureau of National Affairs, "White Collar Report," November 10, 1958, p. A–1. (Vote for union was 18 to 9—unit includes some architects.)

22 TVAEA "Volts and Jolts," November, 1958, p. 2. (The Association claims that its membership equals about 85% of the potential.)

23 "Exponent," Association of Professional Engineering Personnel, September 1957, p. 5.

Employer	Name of Union	Total Represented	Number Members	Unit Representation: Professional Employees	Unit Representation: Nonprofessional Employees
Western Ass'n of Engineers, Architects and Surveyors—Pacific Gas and Electric Co.—Four Bay Area Soil and Foundation Engineering Firms Sacramento, California	Engineers and Scientists of California, ESG	1,800	1,000	900	900
Western Electric Co. (Nationwide)	Council of Western Electric Professional Employees—National, ESA	[24]	—	—	—
Westinghouse Electric Corporation	Federation of Westinghouse Independent Salaried Unions	1,700[25]	1,500	1,445	255

24 The union has filed a petition for a new certification election, which is now pending before the NLRB. Accordingly, the union does not presently represent any employees. The parties have stipulated that between 5,500 and 6,000 engineer-employees are "professionals." The professional status of approximately 450 to 500 engineer-employees remains in dispute.

25 FWISU represents salaried, white collar employees at several Westinghouse plants. Included in this figure are 500 professional employees at the company's South Philadelphia Works plant. (See *Westinghouse Electric Corp.*, 98 NLRB 463.)

Employer	Name of Union	Total Represented	Number Members	Unit Representation: Professional Employees	Unit Representation: Nonprofessional Employees
Westinghouse Electric Corp.	Westinghouse Engineers Association— National, ESA				
Bloomfield, N. J.		160[26]	152	160	—
Buffalo, N. Y.		295[27]	224[28]	295	—
Jersey City, N. J.		300	n.a.	300	—
Mansfield, Ohio		75[29]	n.a.	75	—
Newark, N. J.		40[30]	n.a.	40	—

26 "WEA Newsletter," Buffalo Section, September 26, 1958, p. 2.
27 Bureau of National Affairs, "White Collar Report," No. 110, April 13, 1959, p. A–10.
28 "WEA Newsletter," Buffalo Section, April, 1959. (According to the union, 76% of all eligible engineers are members of the Buffalo Section.)
29 "WEA Newsletter," Buffalo Section, September 26, 1958, p. 2.
30 Bureau of National Affairs, "White Collar Report," No. 77, August 25, 1958, p. A–5.

APPENDIX B

Rating Form

THE PROPOSED rating form is submitted for examination. The weightings for the several performance characteristics are chosen to make the maximum attainable score equal to 1,000. It is stated in the proposed contract that the average engineer at any salary level shall receive a score of 500 on each performance review. The formula for computing the amount of increase to be granted is devised so that an average score of 500 for the two reviews completed during an eligibility period will result in an engineer receiving the average amount of increase. (This average amount of increase must be negotiated.) It should further be noted that the weightings for the several performance characteristics are proposed for the purpose of illustration only, and are also subject to modification during the processes of negotiations.

How it Works

The procedure to be used by a supervisor for rating an engineer will include the following steps:

(1) The supervisor will consider the assignments the engineer has had since his last performance review, and compare the requirements of these assignments with each of the performance characteristics on the review form. For each characteristic, he will: (a) circle the number in the V.I. column, indicating that he considers that the characteristic was very important in the engineer's assignments; or (b) circle the number in the M.I. column, indicating that it was moderately important; or (c) circle neither number, indicating that it was not important. No more than one number will be circled for a characteristic.

(2) The supervisor will rate the man's performance for each characteristic where the number in the V.I. or M.I. column was

encircled. The rating will be in comparison to the performance to be expected from the average engineer making the same salary as the man being rated. The rating will be 0, 1, 2, 3, or 4, where (0) is the poorest, (2) is average, and (4) is the best. These numbers will be written in the Rating column opposite the characteristic in question.

(3) The supervisor will now multiply the numbers he has just written in the Rating column by the encircled number in the V.I. or M.I. column for the particular characteristic. The product of the two numbers will be inserted in the Weighted Rating column.

(4) The supervisor will now perform the following process for each characteristic:

(a) If the number in the V.I. column was encircled, he will do nothing.

(b) If the number in the M.I. column was encircled, he will multiply this number by 4, and write the resulting product in the Residue column.

(c) If no number was encircled, he will multiply the number in the V.I. column by 4, and write the resulting product in the Residue column.

The number in the Residue column, in each case, will now be the number of points for the particular characteristic which were unavailable to the engineer being rated.

(5) The supervisor will now total the numbers in the Weighted Rating column and the numbers in the Residue column.

(6) The supervisor will now subtract the total in the Residue column from 1,000, multiply the result by 10^{-3}, and divide the resulting decimal fraction into the total of the Weighted Rating column. This process normalizes the score of the performance review to a constant 1,000 points.

Example

Total of Weighted Rating column = 460
Total of Residue column = 65

$$1000 - 65 = 935$$

$$\text{Normalized point score} = \frac{460}{.935} = 492$$

	Weights V.I.	Weights M.I.	Rating	Weighted Rating	Residue
I. *Communication*					
a. Transmits instructions clearly to subordinates	8	4			
b. Apprises management of progress and unusual problems in a timely fashion	8	4			
c. Offers constructive suggestions and opinions	8	4			
d. Communicates technical information clearly and understandably	8	4			
II. *Organization, Scheduling, Planning*					
a. Effectively plans project work sequence	8	4			
b. Has ability to break down large projects into manageable portions	4	2			
c. Schedules own work effectively	6	3			
d. Schedules work of subordinates effectively	8	4			
e. Maintains effective control over the efforts of subordinates	8	4			
III. *Producing Results*					
a. Meets project objectives	12	6			
b. Has consistent and dependable performance	10	5			
c. Has ability to operate effectively within the company organizational structure	6	3			
d. Gets results from subordinates	8	4			
e. Follows through despite obstacles	4	2			
f. Works well under pressure	4	2			
IV. *Technical Competence*					
a. Has adequate technical knowledge and ability	20	10			
b. Can acquire and apply technical knowledge in new fields	14	7			
c. Can evaluate technical results	10	5			
d. Demonstrates imagination and creativity	14	7			
Subtotals					

	Weights V.I.	Weights M.I.	Rating	Weighted Rating	Residue
V. *Judgment, Understanding, Manner of Approach to Assignments*					
a. Has ability to make sound decisions on available data	10	5			
b. Has a systematic approach to technical problems	8	4			
c. Has ability to grasp the scope of assignments	6	3			
d. Assumes responsibility with a minimum of instruction	4	2			
e. Is willing to accept counsel from others	4	2			
VI. *Work with Others*					
a. Is willing to delegate authority	6	3			
b. Can obtain cooperation from others	6	3			
c. Provides cooperation to others	8	4			
d. Has good work habits	2	1			
VII. *Professional, Personal, and General Characteristics*					
a. Is personally dependable	6	3			
b. Has high estimated potential for growth	6	3			
c. Has good attitude toward responsibility to the company	4	2			
d. Participates in Professional Societies	2	1			
e. Holds a Professional Engineering License	2	1			
f. Holds advanced degrees	4	2			
g. Has taken or is taking advanced courses	2	1			
h. Participates in community projects and activities	2	1			
Subtotal					
Previous Subtotal					
Total					
Adjusted Total					

BIBLIOGRAPHY

An explanation of the following bibliography is in order. Only some of the bibliographical items have entered into the presentation of the study—they have been footnoted or otherwise cited at the appropriate points. Unfortunately, the other important sources used directly in the study—interviews, intra-management communications, union publications, and so on—cannot be listed here just as they could not be cited in the text of the study because of the obligation of the author to preserve the anonymity of the participants in the study.

The source materials, however, which contributed most to the background information required to undertake and then analyze the research are presented below. The sources that were especially efficient in providing background on professional unionization have been annotated and are designated with an asterisk. Also, bibliographies available on other aspects of industrial research employment and administration are listed for those readers who would like to gain a better idea of the broader context within which professional unionism functions.

American Society of Chemical Engineers, "Collective Bargaining—A Historical Review," *Civil Engineering,* July 1944, p. 311 ff.

American Society of Civil Engineers, *Collective Bargaining for Professional Engineers.* New York: Engineers Joint Council, 1947.

Bambrick, J. J., "Professional Status—Goal of Engineering Unions," *Management Record,* July 1955, pp, 279–281.

Barnes, L. B., *Organizational Systems and Engineering Groups.* Boston: Division of Research, Graduate School of Business Administration, Harvard University, 1960.

Benge, E. J., "Promotional Practices for Technical Men," *Advanced Management,* March 1956, pp. 10–12.

Blank, M., and Stigler, J., *The Demand and Supply of Scientific Personnel.* New York: National Bureau of Economic Research, 1957.

Bush, G. P., and Hattery, L. H., editors, *Teamwork in Research.* Washington: American University Press, 1953.

Carey, W. N., "Engineering Profession in Transition: Report on Economic Status," *Civil Engineering,* August 1947, pp. 441–443.

Chamberlain, N. W., *The Union Challenge to Management Control.* New York: Harper and Brothers, 1948.

Chamberlain, N. W., Pierson, F. C., and Wolfson, T., editors, *A*

Decade of Industrial Relations Research. New York: Harper and Brothers, 1958.

*Chandler, E. L., "Union and the Engineer," *Mechanical Engineering*, October 1949, pp. 826–830.
Articulates professional societies' view on unionism among engineers.

Clague, E., "The Shifting Industrial and Occupational Composition of the Work Force During the Next Ten Years," an address to AFL-CIO Conference on Changing Character of American Industry, Washington, D. C., January 16, 1958.

Coleman, J. R., "Research on Union Challenge and Management Response," *Proceedings of the Ninth Annual Meeting*, Madison: Industrial Relations Research Association, 1957, pp. 306–317.

Council of Western Electric Technical Employees, *Council Compass*. Newark: Council of Western Electric Technical Employees, January 1953.

Dalton, M., "Unofficial Union-Management Relations," *American Sociological Review*, October 1950, pp. 611–619.

Davis, R. C., "Factors Related to Scientific Research Performance," *Interpersonal Factors in Research*, Part I. Ann Arbor: Institute for Social Research, University of Michigan, 1954.

"Depression Grads: Still Trying to Catch Up," *Chemical Engineering*, November 1954, p. 264.

Deutsch, Z. C., "Collective Bargaining: Does it Conflict with Engineering Ethics?" *Chemical and Metallurgical Engineering*, August 1944, p. 264.

Deutsch and Shea, Inc., New York. "The Supply and Demand of Engineers: 1950–1960," *Industrial Relations News*, 1957.

*Drucker, P., "Management and the Professional Employee." *Harvard Business Review*, May–June 1952, pp. 84–90.

Points to several ways in which the basic attitudes of engineers differ from those of management and from those of other employees. The writer cites points of friction between engineers and management which can for the most part be remedied, he believes, by designing new personnel policies for professionals.

Dunlop, J. T., *Industrial Relations Systems*. New York: Holt-Dryden, 1958.

"Engineering Unions Grow," *Steel*, August 13, 1956, pp. 53–54.

Engineers and Scientists of America, *Constitution and By-Laws*. Washington, 1957.

Engineers and Scientists of America, "Minimum Starting Salaries," Special Report, Washington, 1957.

Engineers and Scientists Guild, *E. S. G. Outlook*. New Hyde Park, New York, July, 1957.

"Engineers Hoist Banner: Walkout at Minneapolis-Honeywell," *Business Week,* May 28, 1955, pp. 168–169.

Engineers Joint Council, *Manual of Collective Bargaining for Professional Employees.* New York, 1947.

Engineers Joint Council, *Professional Standards and Employment Conditions,* Report 101, New York, 1956.

"Engineers Need Unionism," *The American Federationist,* May 1955, pp. 19–20.

"Engineers' Stand on 'Right to Work,'" *Business Week,* October 25, 1958, p. 139.

Engstrom, E. W., "What Industry Requires of the Research Worker." Paper delivered at Third Annual Conference on Industrial Research, June 1952, pp. 121–141, published in B. Hertz and A. N. Rubenstein, *Research Operations in Industry.* New York: King's Crown Press, Columbia University, 1953.

Fair Labor Standards Act of June 25, 1938, as amended by Public Law 393, January 25, 1950.

Fernelius, W. C., "Why Professional Employees Should Not be Unionized," *Chemical and Engineering News,* November 8, 1954, p. 4457 ff.

Fisher, E., "Why Engineers Join Labor Organizations," *Engineering and Science Monthly,* June 1946.

Form, W. H., and Dausereau, H. K., "Union Member Orientations and Patterns of Social Integration," *Industrial and Labor Relations Review,* October 1957, pp. 3–12.

Forshay, R. L., "Collective Bargaining for Professional Employees," *Mechanical Engineering,* November 1946.

Furnas, C., editor, *Research in Industry: Its Organization and Management.* New York: D. Van Nostrand, 1948.

*Goldstein, B., "Unionism Among Salaried Professionals in Industry," *American Sociological Review,* April, 1955, pp. 199–205.

Presents the hypothesis that salaried professional unions are significantly different from traditional trade unionism, and that this difference is reflected in four fundamental relationships: first, between the professional employee and management; second, between the professional employee and the professional union; third, between the professional union and management; fourth, between the professional union and the labor movement.

*Goldstein, B., "Unions and the Professional Employee," *Journal of Business,* October 1954, pp. 276–284.

Treats the development of professional unionism, noting the changes which have occurred over the years in the employment of professionals and analyzing the inducements and deterrents to unionization.

Gray, C. E., "Appraising Professional Personnel: One Company's Experience," *Personnel,* March 1957, p. 442.

Griffin, C. W., "Why Oppose Collective Bargaining?" *Civil Engineering,* May 1955, p. 290.

Griffin, C. W., Jr., and Carpenter, J. D., "Does the Large Engineering Office Present Special Challenges to Employer and Employee?" *Civil Engineering,* February 1957, pp. 96–98.

Haber, W., and Levinson, H., *Labor Relations and Productivity in the Building Trades.* Ann Arbor: Bureau of Industrial Relations, University of Michigan, 1956.

Hay, E. N., "Overtime Pay for Engineers," *Personnel Journal,* July–August 1957, pp. 90–91.

Hertz, D. B., and Rubenstein, A. H., "Industrial Research Practices in 41 Companies," *Management Review,* October 1950, pp. 609–610.

Hertz, D. B., and Rubenstein, A. H., "Personnel Practices and Communications in 41 Industrial Research Labs," *Personnel,* November 1951, pp. 247–251.

Hill, S. E., and Harbison, F., *Manpower and Innovation in American Industry.* Princeton: Industrial Relations Section, Princeton University, 1959.

Hirsch, I., and Oakes, W. J., Jr., "Increasing the Productivity of Scientists," *Harvard Business Review,* March-April 1958, pp. 66–76.

Ireson, W. G. and Grant, E. L., editors, *Handbook of Industrial Engineering and Management.* New York: Prentice-Hall, Inc., 1955.

Kaplan, A., "An Informal Discussion of the Subject—Engineers and Collective Bargaining," *Lockheed Engineer,* Burbank, California, September 1956.

Kaplan, N., "Some Organizational Factors Affecting Creativity," *IRE Transactions on Engineering Management,* Institute of Radio Expenses, Inc., March 1960.

Labor Management Relations Act, 1947, as Amended by Public Law, 189, 1951.

Lester, R. A., and Shister, J., editors, *Insights into Labor Issues.* New York: The Macmillan Company, 1948, pp. 163–193.

McGregor, D., *The Human Side of Enterprise.* New York: McGraw-Hill Company, 1960.

McIver, M. E., Wagner, H. A., and McGirr, M. P., *Technologists' Stake in the Wagner Act.* Chicago: American Association of Engineers, 1944.

Marcson, S., *The Scientist in American Industry: Some Organizational Determinants in Manpower Utilization,* Research Report Series No. 99. Princeton: Industrial Relations Section, Princeton University, 1960.

Michigan State University, "Proceedings: Conference on Effective Utilization of Engineering Personnel, March 27 and 30, 1957," Lansing, Michigan, 1957.

Miller, G. W., "Unionization of Engineers—A Re-examination," *Journal of Engineering Education,* June 1955, p. 775 ff.

Mills, J., *The Engineer in Society.* New York: Van Nostrand, 1946.

Moore, D., and Renck, R., "The Professional Employee in Industry," *Journal of Business,* January 1955, p. 66 ff.

*Morse, G., "Engineering Ethics—From the Viewpoint of Industry," *Journal of Engineering Education,* November 1954, p. 214 ff.

Presents a strongly felt point of view on unionism: that the engineer alone possesses answers crucial to the firm and to industry; that the ethics of the professional-client relationship require him to protect his employer's interests; that it is increasingly difficult for the engineer to honor these ethics under unionism.

*National Industrial Conference Board, Inc., *Unionization Among American Engineers.* Studies in Personnel Policy, No. 155. New York: National Industrial Conference Board, 1956.

A very good source for descriptions of the contract provisions in many of the collective agreements of engineering unions.

National Manpower Council, *Proceedings of a Conference on the Utilization of Scientific and Professional Manpower.* New York: Columbia University Press, 1954.

National Science Foundation, "Research and Development Costs in American Industry, 1956," *Reviews of Data on Research and Development,* No. 10, May 1958.

National Science Foundation, "Scientists and Engineers in American Industry—January, 1957," *Scientific Manpower Bulletin,* No. 10, December 1958.

National Science Foundation. "Shortages of Scientists and Engineers in Industrial Research," *Scientific Manpower Bulletin,* No. 6, August 1, 1955.

National Science Foundation, "Trends in the Employment and Training of Scientists and Engineers," Washington, May 1956.

*National Society of Professional Engineers, "A Professional Look at the Engineer in Industry," Washington, 1955.

An excellent single source for various kinds of background information on engineering unionism.

National Society of Professional Engineers, *Collective Bargaining for Professional Employees.* Washington, 1957.

National Society of Professional Engineers, *How to Improve the Utilization of Engineering Manpower.* Washington, 1952.

National Society of Professional Engineers, *Tabulation of Unions Representing Engineers and Technical Employees.* Third Edition, Washington, 1959.

*Northrup, H. R., *Unionization of Professional Engineers and Chemists.* (Monograph No. 12.) New York: Industrial Relations Counselors, Inc., 1946.

Includes treatment of antagonisms of professional engineers toward AFL and CIO during early 1940's.

Ober, H., "Occupational Wage Differentials, 1907–1947," *Monthly Labor Review,* August 1948, pp. 127–134.

Oberg, W., "Age and Achievement—and the Technical Man," *Personnel Psychology,* Autumn 1960, pp. 245–259.

Odiorne, G. S., "Today's Shortage of Engineers: Fact or Fancy," *Advanced Management,* October 1954, pp. 23–25.

Orth, C. D., "More Productivity from Engineers," *Harvard Business Review,* March-April 1957, pp. 54–62.

Quinn, J. B., *Yardsticks for Industrial Research.* New York: Ronald Press Co., 1959.

Randall, C. W., "Problems of R & D Management," *Harvard Business Review,* January-February 1959, pp. 128–136.

Reynolds, L. G., and Taft, C. H., *The Evolution of Wage Structure.* New Haven: Yale University Press, 1956.

Riegel, J. W., *Administration of Salaries for Engineers and Scientists,* Report No. 8. Ann Arbor: Bureau of Industrial Relations, University of Michigan, 1959.

Riegel, J. W., *Collective Bargaining as Viewed by Unorganized Engineers and Scientists,* Report No. 10. Ann Arbor: Bureau of Industrial Relations, University of Michigan, 1959.

Selekman, B. M., Selekman, S. K., and Fuller, S. H. *Problems in Labor Relations.* New York: McGraw-Hill Book Company, 2d edition, 1958.

Shoch, C. T., "The Professional Union—A Contradiction." Washington: National Society of Professional Engineers, 1956.

Slichter, S. H., *Union Policies and Industrial Management.* Washington: The Brookings Institute, 1941.

Slichter, S. H., Livernash, E. R., and Healy, J. J., *The Impact of Collective Bargaining on Management.* Washington: The Brookings Institute, 1960.

Strauss, G., "White Collar Workers are Different," *Harvard Business Review,* September-October 1954, pp. 73–82.

"Survey Shows Engineers Thinking About Collective Bargaining Issue," *Engineering News,* November 12, 1953, p. 28.

Taft, E., "Unions Among Engineers," *Proceedings of the Ninth Annual Proceedings,* Madison: Industrial Relations Research Association, 1957, pp. 244–247.

*Taft, J. E., "Why Engineers Join Unions," *Personnel,* September-October 1957, pp. 66–67.

A good summary of the reasons for unionization offered by many engineering union leaders.

Taylor, G. W., and Pierson, F. C., editors, *New Concepts in Wage Determination.* New York: McGraw-Hill Book Company, 1957.

"The End of an Era?" *Wall Street Journal,* July 31, 1957, p. 1.

"UAW's Quiet Transformation," *Business Week,* April 20, 1957, pp. 153–154.

United States Department of Labor, *Scientific Research and Development in American Industry—A Study in Manpower and Costs,* Bulletin No. 1148. Washington, 1953.

Walsh-Healy, Public Contracts Act, Public Law No. 846.

Wehrstedt, G. G., "Personnel Departments in Research Laboratories," *Personnel Administration,* September 1954, pp. 25–31.

Wood, H., "Manpower and Expenditures in Industrial Research," *Monthly Labor Review,* March 1956, pp. 274–278.

*Yarnall, D. R., "Unionism and Collective Bargaining," *Mechanical Engineering,* January 1947, pp. 80–81.

Reflects the interest professional engineering societies have in doing something about the causes of engineering unionism.

Bibliographies on Industrial Research Employment and Administration

Arlen, E., *Industrial Research and the Professional Employee—A Bibliographic Review.* Chicago: University of Chicago, Industrial Relations Center, 1955.

Bush, G. P., *Bibliography on Research Administration—Annotated.* Washington: University Press of Washington, 1954.

Horowitz, M. S., *Bibliography on Engineering and Scientific Manpower Problem—Annotated.* Boston: Northeastern University, 1957.

Rubenstein, A. H., and Shepard, H. A., *Bibliography on Human Relations in Research Laboratories.* Cambridge: Massachusetts Institute of Technology, February 1956.

Index